PENGUIN BOOKS

One Minute to Ten

Dan Hodges is a political commentator for the *Daily Telegraph* and the *Spectator*. He previously worked for the GMB trade union and as a Labour Party researcher at the House of Commons. He lives in south London with his wife, son, mother and cat.

One Minute to Ten

DAN HODGES

PENGUIN BOOKS

PENGUIN BOOKS

UK | USA | Canada | Ireland | Australia
India | New Zealand | South Africa

Penguin Books is part of the Penguin Random House group of companies
whose addresses can be found at global.penguinrandomhouse.com.

First published by Michael Joseph 2015
Published in Penguin Books 2016
001

Copyright © Dan Hodges, 2015

The moral right of the author has been asserted

Set in 12.96/15.40 pt Garamond MT Std
Typeset by Jouve (UK), Milton Keynes
Printed in Great Britain by Clays Ltd, St Ives plc

A CIP catalogue record for this book is available from the British Library

ISBN: 978-1-405-92440-5

www.greenpenguin.co.uk

*For my Mum and Dad and Jack
and Michelle. For everything.*

If you can dream – and not make dreams your master;
If you can think – and not make thoughts your aim;
If you can meet with Triumph and Disaster
And treat those two impostors just the same

Rudyard Kipling

Contents

Contents

1. Three Boys

There were the tastes and the smells. That delicious acidic bite as the cloud of cigarette smoke drifted lower, gradually invading his nostrils and settling on his tongue. The sounds too. That hypnotic staccato of words drumming out their timeless rhythm. A sudden rise in volume. The rhetorical club. A subtle shift in intonation. The debater's rapier.

And then there was the simple thrill of presence. Of just being there. Of seeing.

Not being seen, of course. He was invisible. His brother, sitting that single proprietorial half-space ahead of him, was invisible too. The men had entered their own, exclusive world.

Exclusive, but not private. From here he could watch. And listen. And smell. And taste.

And learn. Slowly he was learning. Like a foreign language, it was starting to come alive to him. A familiar name here. A recognizable phrase there. One time, oh yes, what a time that was! That magical moment when the names and the phrases and the words all suddenly slotted together. And formed an idea. His first proper political idea!

OK, it wasn't his idea. Much as he wanted to, he knew

he couldn't claim it as his own. Not yet. But he could follow it. From A to B to . . . well . . . wherever. It didn't really matter.

And there was something else. Something else? No. Everything. The whole thing.

The way he looked. His father. Leaning forward, on the edge of his chair, his right hand tightly clasped, as if he was trying to physically squeeze his thoughts into existence. His left hand extending, imploring – or was it ordering – his tiny, enthralled audience to see the world through his eyes.

And that was what Edward wanted. More than anything. To see that world his father saw. To reach out and embrace him. To connect with that slight, frail giant who could reshape entire continents with his mind.

The early morning dew had evaporated by now, and as he stretched out his fingers the pristine green carpet felt smooth and warm to his touch. His chin rested on the back of his hands, and every so often he would raise it slightly, allowing him to watch the progress of the shiny red ball as it scurried away towards the boundary rope.

The straps of his pads felt tight against his calves, but they didn't bother him. To be honest, nothing much bothered him at the moment. A glorious sunny day. A gentle breeze. A nice even wicket. What more could you want?

A crack, a bit like a whip striking against stone, rang across the field. His head lifted in time to see the ball tracing another high, lazy arc towards the trees lining Agar's Plough.

Of course you always could want more. It was important to want more. To keep pushing yourself.

Dad kept pushing. Despite a body that seemed to have been created solely for the purpose of holding him back.

Alex kept pushing. He kept pushing them both in his own way. Your older brother kisses a girl. So you have to kiss a girl. Your older brother starts getting good at football. You have to get good at football. Your older brother can survive those long, lonely nights at Heatherdown, with its paper-thin blankets and icicles clustering on the inside of the dormitory windows. Then you can survive it.

In fact, you could do more than survive. You could grow. Flourish.

He gazed along the line of white-clad figures spread out beside him. Some were short. Some were tall. Some were fat. Some were thin. Some were taut. Some were rangy. But they knew; each of them knew. This was their place. Their time.

People said they were privileged – these Eton Rifles. But it wasn't about privilege. It was just how things were.

If you worked hard. But not too hard. If you played by the rules. Or at least, the rules that mattered. Then you'd get on.

And that was precisely how things were supposed to be. The system, or whatever you wanted to call it, worked. The world worked. Life worked.

A sound like glass breaking, then a muted cheer.

'You're in, David.'

Easing himself up from the grass, he reached down for his bat. It felt strong in his hand. Solid. He could tell. He was going to get some runs today.

Occasionally he could see a light piercing the darkness. A farmhouse, or one of those tiny cafés set back from the road, waiting expectantly for another hardy traveller to surrender to the night.

They wouldn't be surrendering. Well, they might, just for a short while. Now and again the Peugeot's engine would ease down, and he'd sense the car gradually coasting to a standstill. Then he'd hear the creak of doors opening, and a cold breeze would come barrelling in. The sound of feet on gravel, a few muttered words of Dutch or English, and then they'd be off again. Moving. Always moving.

He enjoyed these driving holidays. When they finally got where they were going. Amsterdam to see the cousins was great. Across on the ferry, then a short dash up the coast. France could be OK. But Switzerland was a real drag. Don't get him started on Italy.

It would always be the same. Everyone would be fine, excited and laughing and chatty. And then people would begin to get tired. And then someone would try and steal a bit more space, or someone would accidentally elbow someone else, or the dog would decide it was getting bored. And then it would all go off. The four of them squashed on to that back seat, and hours and hours and hours and hours of road ahead of them. Moving. Always moving.

It was a nomadic family trait. His grandmother Kira had moved from Russia to Estonia, then to London. His grandfather Hemm had moved from the Netherlands to Java. His mother had moved from Java back to the Netherlands and then on to Cambridge. His father had moved from London to New York, then to Connecticut, then back to Britain (the West Country), back to London, then off to the Netherlands, then to Belgium, then back to Britain again (Buckinghamshire).

He should be grateful, he supposed. Being able to tour the world via his family tree. And he was. He loved hearing about his great-aunt Maria, who had been some sort of spy or revolutionary. And Mother's tales of the air raid sirens, and having to put cotton wool in her ears whilst she hid from the Japanese air raids. Though he always sensed there were other things from that time she didn't want to share.

A soft grunt to his right, and Ibby's head was suddenly resting against his shoulder. He could feel his sister's breath tickling his ear. Through the gap between the two headrests the narrow country road sat frozen in the beam of the car's headlights. Only the insects dancing their wild, frantic dance across the windshield gave him any sense of being in motion.

And that was the thing that bothered him. When he thought about it, his relatives hadn't really been moving.

They'd actually been running. His grandmother had run away from the Bolsheviks. His father had run away from Hitler's bombs. His mother had run away from the Japanese, and then run away again from the Indonesian nationalists.

Being on the move was all well and good. But didn't they all just want to stop moving? To settle down for a bit. Get a sense of belonging somewhere. Become a fixture. Feel secure. Feel safe.

Off to the left, the light of another solitary farmhouse cut through the darkness. Nicklaus closed his eyes. Moving. They always seemed to be moving.

2. Twenty-One Fifty-Five

They are men now, those three boys. With families of their own. Children who hang on their every word, who look to them for reassurance that the world around them works. That it's a good world, in which they can feel safe and secure.

Everything has changed. Even their names have changed. Edward has become Ed. A first-name brand, something most politicians crave. Ken. Boris. Maggie. When you become a first-name politician, you've made it. Or that's what they keep telling him. But then again, they've told him a lot of things.

Nicklaus – to his brothers and sisters it was always the Dutch pronunciation 'Nickje' (with the 'je' sounded like 'jay') – is simply Nick. Or he was. 'I agree with Nick.' For a while it became a political catchphrase. For one insane, intoxicating moment back in 2010 everyone, everywhere was agreeing with Nick. But then they stopped agreeing with him. And started hating him. So now he's just 'Clegg'. Or worse.

David is Dave. Though that's primarily to his enemies. A sarcastic form of address. An imposed affectation. 'That Tory toff Dave? Don't make us laugh!' It annoys him. Though he tries to hide it, the Tory toff jibes do rankle. But he still has the last laugh. Because when people aren't calling him David or Dave they're having to call him Prime Minister. Or 'PM'. Whenever you speak to one of his team it's always 'The PM'. With a subconscious emphasis on 'The'. Not just any old PM. *The* PM.

So for now it's David – or Dave – Cameron who holds the office. And the trump card. For now.

Five to ten on the evening of Thursday 7 May, 2015. And the three men are together. In the same place.

Not physically together. Ed Miliband is in his constituency home in Doncaster. It isn't the elegant Victorian townhouse with two kitchens that's caused all the fuss, but a small detached cottage, with white stonework and a red slate roof that makes it look a bit like it's made of Lego. If he's honest, it's not really his and Justine's thing. But they aren't there all that much. And this is Doncaster after all.

Nick Clegg is in his Sheffield flat. On the day of the last election he'd watched the results in his comfy pebble-dashed semi in Ecclesall. But there'd been a bit of a ruckus over expenses. The place had been in a state when they'd first moved in. They'd had to spend £3,000 just on fitting a new kitchen. And another £6,000 on redecorating the rest of the house. But then the press had got wind of it, and anyway, the rules on claiming for second homes had changed. So they'd sold it. And now he was renting the flat. On the move again.

David Cameron is in his house in Oxfordshire. 'The Manor' was how one paper described it recently. That was the sort of stuff that always drove Samantha insane. 'It's a house,' she would fume. 'A bloody house. They make it sound like we live in a mansion.'

It isn't a mansion. Although it does have several bedrooms. And quite a large garden. And a small conservatory. So what can he do? Get someone to ring up and put them right? 'The PM lives in an ordinary house in his constituency.' And then wake up to a picture of some family of eight from Trafford who have just been thrown out of their cramped council flat by Iain Duncan Smith and his damned Bedroom Tax?

So he's sitting there in his ordinary house that isn't a mansion. And Nick Clegg is in his flat. And Ed Miliband is in his tiny Lego cottage.

But really, they're all in the same place. Their mouths feel a little dry. And each has a tight sensation in his chest. And words and voices and sounds suddenly have a distant quality, as if they're being heard under water.

Not that anybody's really saying much. They haven't for the past hour or so. People have still been coming in and out. With a rumour here: 'They say Croydon Central's looking quite good.' Or a straw in the wind there: 'It looks like things are holding up in Finchley.' But no-one really has anything concrete. So slowly the conversation fades. Every now and then someone will try and lighten the mood with a joke. But everyone knows it's forced. So they all laugh a little too hard.

And while it's getting quieter each of the three men feels it. The way the tension is increasing. And the attention is gradually shifting. To them.

Of course, it's always on them. They've got used to being the most scrutinized person in every room they ever walk into. But now people really are watching them. Because this is the moment. The one everyone's going to ask about. 'How was he? You were in there with him. How did he handle it?'

And the standard line will get trotted out in response. 'Oh, he was the coolest man in the room. Not a trace of emotion. Real pro.' But the team aren't just hoovering up dinner party throw-aways this time. They're really looking. And wondering. 'How is he bearing up? Can my guy really take this? He could be running the country tomorrow. Did I make the right choice? I know he's my guy. But is he really THE guy?'

So they have to play the part. Make sure they genuinely are the coolest man in the room. Keep all those emotions bottled up. Be the pro, basically.

That's why Ed Miliband is sitting there working through his speech. The speech he's going to give in a few hours, calling for David Cameron to stand down. The people have spoken. Clear repudiation of five years of Tory-led government. Though they have their differences, he knows his opponent is an honourable man. And he trusts he will do what's in the best interests of the country. Or something like that. The words aren't lying quite straight on the page. They're floating around.

But sitting there calmly working on your speech – it's the sort of thing future prime ministers do.

It's why David Cameron is engaging in a bit of banter with his press spokesman Craig Oliver. What is it with this fucking BBC clock? They've got a countdown clock running on the screen. Second by second. 4.03 . . . 4.02 . . . 4.01 . . . right down to the moment Big Ben strikes ten and they can release the exit poll. It's like a Doomsday clock. What idiot came up with that?

Of course, he knows full well which idiot came up with it. It was Craig, five years ago, when he was still a BBC producer, running the 2010 election night coverage. 'The PM? Oh, he was bantering with the team. Coolest man in the room.' Seriously though, what sort of sadist comes up with a Doomsday clock?

Nick Clegg is just placing a packet of Marlboro Lights on the mantelpiece above the sofa. He's kept promising Miriam he'll give up, and he's been doing pretty well recently. He never was a heavy smoker anyway. He'd go through the entire day without one, then light up a couple in the evening, just to unwind a bit. It's just his crisis packet. Only to be broken open in the event of an emergency.

And here's the strange thing. There are plenty of people around. The spinners, the numbers men, the body men (and women), the speech writers, the party staffers and the close protection guys. Then outside are the TV anchors, the snappers, the scribblers and the onlookers.

But really, they're alone. The wives are there, obviously. And they can understand, probably better than anyone. They've lived with it more or less from the beginning. But even though they understand, they don't *know*.

How can they? How can anyone. Since the war only twenty-four men, and one woman, have known. Experienced the torture. The terror this endless night won't go your way. The terror it will.

Winston Churchill slept through the Blitz. Then woke up on election night in 1945 with a terrible, stabbing pain. It was his body bringing him the premonition he'd lost. But there were no exit polls in those days. So he was sitting soaking in his bath when Captain Pim came and told him it was Clement Attlee who'd be going back to Potsdam.

Margaret Thatcher was driving to Conservative Central Office at 3.30 in the morning, with the results still coming in, when three escort cars and a police motorcyclist suddenly glided out of the darkness and moved into position around her own vehicle. That was when she finally knew she'd won.

When Harold Wilson sat down to watch the results on election night in 1970 he already knew he'd won. A Marplan poll in the *Times* the day before had given Labour a nine-point lead, enough for a majority of 150 seats. Then he looked on in silence as the returning officer in Guildford (still in black and white, even though the main BBC studio broadcast was now in revolutionary colour) announced Edward Heath had won for the Conservatives with a four per cent swing.

The twenty-five knew. How you veer from depression

to optimism. Feel the panic starting to rise inside you. Force it back down. Retreat into your safe space.

Nick Clegg's safe space is guarded by a man called Ryan Coetzee. Ryan's been brought in from South Africa, where he's been working for the Democratic Alliance. Knows how to play hard politics. Wrestled the Western Cape from the ANC. Put on a million votes in the 2009 election and turned the DA into the official opposition.

And Ryan's told him it's going to be OK. They're going to survive. Twenty-four seats are solid. Another sixteen are in play. A difficult night. But they're still in the game. And depending on how things break elsewhere, probably still in government.

David Cameron is looking to Lynton Crosby, the Australian consultant who masterminded John Howard's successful campaigns in Australia and Boris Johnson's two triumphant runs at the London mayoralty. Lynton believes in tough love. Before the election he sat down right in front of Cameron and told him, 'I'm not going to be sharing our polling data with you. Because if it's good you won't be able to resist telling someone. And then it will get out. And we don't want people thinking we're cruising to victory. We need them to think every vote counts.'

But last night Lynton relented. The polling and canvass analysis showed they were going to win 300 seats, give or take a few. He was going to make it. Come Friday lunch-time, he would still be Prime Minister.

James Morris is the person who's protecting Ed. He's

a partner at Greenberg Quinlan Rosner. OK, he hasn't got his name on the door yet. But GQR are serious players. Set up by Stan Greenberg, Bill Clinton's number cruncher. Took Clinton to the White House. And James (who's Stan Greenberg's partner, remember), has told him it's impossible for Labour to poll less than thirty-five per cent. The actual phrase he used is 'structurally impossible'. That's the floor. Thirty-five per cent of the vote. Now, thirty-five per cent won't get you into the White House. But it'll be enough to get Ed Miliband into Downing Street.

So something happens. You catch a throw-away remark – 'Thought turn-out might have been slightly higher.' Or notice someone check a new text message, then get and up and leave the room a little too hurriedly. And that's when you feel the fear starting to rise. The moment you excuse yourself, open that mental door and shut yourself safely inside. 'Calm down. Twenty-four seats in the bag, sixteen more in play . . . three hundred seats in the bag . . . thirty-five per cent in the bag.'

But the problem is, you can't stay in there too long. Because if you do, the space slowly starts to become contaminated. The doubts start to creep under the door. Seep through the walls.

So Nick Clegg eventually finds himself thinking, 'OK, but how can Ryan be sure? We haven't had the money to really drill down with the polling into the constituencies. Basically, we've been flying blind for the past six weeks.'

David Cameron has picked up on the '7pm Wobble'. The moment they realized turn-out was going to be higher than it had appeared in the morning (good for Labour, bad for them). And when some of the feedback from the constituencies started showing the vote wasn't coming out in the numbers expected. And when the betting markets began drifting back towards Miliband as next PM. Which itself became the cue for people to start speculating, 'Shit, has the exit poll leaked? Have those cunts at the BBC dribbled it out to shaft us?'

Meanwhile, Ed Miliband himself finds his thoughts drifting back to Scotland. Reports from up there have been coming in throughout the day. And they're bad. Very bad. OK, they half-expected that. But what if they haven't managed to contain it? What if this Sturgeon-pulling-the-strings crap is hitting them down here as well? They'd started registering it on the doorsteps about twelve days ago. Hoped it had peaked. But what if it hasn't?

So before your safe space gets infected you have to get out. Go somewhere else. Well away from here.

Nick Clegg travels to France. It's warm and sunny, and he's in that lovely tiny cottage just outside Sud Charente. Everyone's there. Miriam and the kids and Dad and the uncles and the aunts and all the cousins. Someone's sitting out the back painting. Someone else has just come riding through the kitchen on a bicycle. And they're all there together. In the same place. And no-one's running away from anything.

Ed Miliband is sitting in the infield grandstand at Fenway Park in Boston. The same part of the ground he sat in when his father – after a bit of nagging – brought him to his first game back in 1981.

Just below to his left he can see the bulky figure of David Ortiz striding towards the plate. Well, he isn't exactly striding, but he's definitely walking with a purpose. It's the bottom of the seventh, and the Red Sox trail the Yankees by two. But Big Papi is back. They wrote him off in '09, when he was only hitting .206. But they're not writing him off now. Not when he's sitting on thirty home runs and 103 RBIs at .309. So here's the pitch, and Papi's trademark knee raise as he leans into the swing, and – bang! – it's gone! It's cleared the Green Monster and it's out of here! Triumph! Redemption!

David Cameron tips back the tumbler. A delicious blend of sweet pear, crushed apples and syrup soothes his throat. In front of him Richard Burton is gazing with cold eyes at Patrick Wymark. He's just handed over the note. The one that contains the name of the top Nazi spy in Britain. 'It's Patrick Wymark's name.'

Samantha's out at a charity reception, and the kids are asleep. The red boxes are safely lined up in the corner. The Downing Street flat is his own. But there's one major problem. Colonel Turner is still holding his Sten gun. Richard Burton and Clint Eastwood can try to rush him, but they'll be dead before they can get halfway across the plane's aisle.

Another sip of the Jura. Why didn't they think of that? Why just hand him the note?

Burton looks at the nozzle of the gun impassively. It was Admiral Roland who had taken him to the plane, wasn't it? And unless he was mistaken, it was Admiral Roland who had handed him the very gun he was holding.

Of course! That's it! They've taken out the firing pin! Colonel Turner has been outwitted again!

All that's left now is for him to do the decent thing. He rises, pulls open the door and steps out into space. No messy court-martial. No embarrassing publicity for MI6.

David Cameron sets down his glass. Richard Burton's plane soars high above the mountains. The plan has worked. The mission has worked. Just like it was supposed to.

But the respite is only temporary. Try as they might, these three men can only escape for so long.

Which is why Nick Clegg suddenly hears a knocking on the kitchen window. He turns, and there's Stephen Lotinga, his Communications Director. Tall, bespectacled, impeccably dressed in his tailored suit and silk tie. It must be thirty degrees out there. What the hell's he doing wandering around the Charente dressed like that?

'Hi Nick. Just to let you know, we've heard that some of Vince's wards are showing slightly worse turn-out than we were expecting. That was about two hours ago, so it may have picked up a bit since then. I'm going to be keeping an eye on it.'

And in that instant the sun-drenched kitchen gradually dissolves, and he's back in the flat in Sheffield. About the same time, the bleachers at Fenway shimmer and vanish. Moments later Richard Burton's plane fades from the screen, to be replaced by a ticking digital clock. 2.03 . . . 2.02 . . . 2.01 . . .

And now there is only one place left to go. In the far corner of the safe space there's a large, steel box. It's about seven feet long, and is just wide enough for a fully grown man to climb inside and close himself away. On the side, stencilled in large white lettering, is a single word. 'Resignation'.

Some members of Tony Blair's old team still remember it. 'The change'. The moment, about ten days out from polling day in 1997, when they saw the tension that had been lurking behind every word and gesture suddenly dissipate. Tim Allen, his press advisor, finally plucked up the courage to ask him about it. 'You look different. More relaxed,' he observed. And Blair just shrugged and replied, 'I've done everything I can now. If they don't want me, they don't want me.'

Resignation. You've done everything you can do. Everything they've asked you to do. Everything you've asked yourself to do. And if it's not enough, well, then it's not enough. The voters are always right? Fine, let's see. If they want to sit there, cradling the phone, hoping for that message saying there's a little bit of work today, good luck. Fancy standing in the hallway, staring at the letter telling them their landlord is throwing them out of their bedsit before the new rent controls come into force? So be it. Actually welcome the idea of perching at the kitchen table, poring over the bills for the twentieth time, trying to work out where the money for next term's tuition fees is going to come from, do you? Then by all means, be my guest.

You've done everything. And if everything doesn't mean anything, then screw them. If these people are too stupid to help you to help them, screw them all.

But again, you're fooling yourself if you think you can save yourself by letting go. It's much too late to let go now.

So to Ed Miliband it comes across as a faint, metallic scraping sound. Has he really done everything? Should he have listened to Greg Beales a bit more, rather than Stewart Wood? They're both loyal. But Greg's a pragmatist, and Stewart, well, Stewart's what you might call an idealist. 'Don't be afraid to compromise,' Greg kept telling him. 'You've made some bold decisions, there's no shame in tacking towards the centre a little.' 'Stay true to yourself,' Stewart kept urging. And so he'd tacked back. A little. On the economy. And immigration. And all that renationalizing the railways stuff. Not too much. He'd stayed true to himself. Mostly. But what if he hadn't tacked back far enough? Or what if he'd tacked too far?

David Cameron hears it too. Only louder. A sound of

metal on metal. It was just after he'd come back from the Euro summit. The veto. The triumph. And they were ahead in the polls, and Miliband was in a mess. They were motoring. For the first time since the election they were properly motoring. George had said it would look bold, that the backbenchers would love it. And George always got the politics right. So he'd gone along with it – the 50p tax cut. And then it had blown up. Not just the tax cut, but the whole fucking budget. The 'omnishambles budget'. It had taken three years to repair the damage. Three years just to get back to where they were. But what if they hadn't got back to where they were? What if they fell short? And what if, back in 2012, he'd just said 'no' to George?

For Nick Clegg, it's a pounding. An ear-splitting, frantic pounding. What if he hadn't done any of it? Stayed out of the coalition all together. Or gone the other way. Taken the gamble on Labour. 'The issue, Nick, is – is there going to be a progressive realignment?' Brown had growled at him during that fateful phone call. Or what if he'd taken a cabinet job of his own. Or found some high position of principle on which to fold the coalition early. Or insisted on AV without a referendum. Or said no to tuition fees. Or said no to the Bedroom Tax. Every day for the last five years he's woken up, and the first thing he's thought to himself is 'what if'?

So now there is nothing to be done. All they can do is sit there. These three boys who are now men. And around them everything is gradually starting to disappear. The distant voices are finally falling silent. The feeling of dryness in the mouth is fading. The tightness in the chest is easing.

And now everything around them is beginning to turn dark. In that tiny flat in Sheffield, and the sparsely furnished front room in Doncaster, and the spacious sitting room in Oxfordshire, an invisible dimmer switch is slowly being turned. Until all they can see is a small screen in front of them. And in the corner of the screen is a clock.

01.20 . . . 01.19 . . . 01.18 . . . 01.17 . . . 01.16 . . .

3. The Unnatural

Chris Rennard leant back in his chair and loosened his tie. In the end it had all been a little awkward. And rather more complicated than it should have been.

Leadership elections were always very tricky things to manage. This one especially, given the way poor old Ming had been so unceremoniously shoved aside.

But he'd dealt with it in the proper manner. He felt sure of it. This was by far the best solution for the party.

Although they probably shouldn't go around broadcasting the fact. The people at the Electoral Reform Society could be relied on for discretion. And Nick and his team. There was nothing to be gained for them in spreading it around.

But then there was Chris. Just 511 votes in it. Nick Clegg 20,988. Chris Huhne 20,477.

This was really going to hurt him. After all, he was supposed to be the senior partner. It was like Blair and Brown all over again. They'd been friends. Good friends. Chris had been at Nick's wedding. One of the lucky few.

But it was Chris who was senior. Like the elder brother. Or at least, in Chris' own mind he was the elder brother. Nick's leader in the European Parliament. Ming's heir apparent. Nick hadn't even bothered to stand last time around. And there he was, snatching it from under Chris' nose a year later by just over 500 votes. Oh yes, this one would really eat away at him.

And that was without this unfortunate business of the late ballots.

It would probably have been better for everyone concerned if the ERS had just binned the lot of them. They knew the rules. Understood the cut-off.

All right, maybe in retrospect holding a postal ballot in the run-up to Christmas hadn't been the smartest idea. But Christmas was something of a fixture. It wasn't as if people didn't know the post got busy around then.

But it certainly was unfortunate. When it had been explained to him as official returning officer that the winning margin was only 500 votes, but that around 1,300 additional ballots had arrived after the postal deadline, he'd been a bit taken aback.

But he hadn't been taken aback for long. The rules were the rules. So there was no doubt in his mind that the result would have to stand.

Then again, it was best not to be too inflexible about these things. You were talking about people's careers. The future of the party. Maybe even the future of the country.

So that's when he'd made the offer to the two camps. He was minded to accept the result as it was. But if they both agreed, then he'd allow a count of the late votes.

And Julia Goldsworthy, for Clegg, had been crystal clear. 'No. Don't count them.'

Which of course was the correct thing procedurally.

And also, he had to admit, the correct thing politically. Chris had been closing in. Quite rapidly. The late returns were showing that. So those final ballots . . . well, Julia had called it right in his view. Very smart woman, Julia. And attractive. She was going places.

But then – and this was where things had got a little sticky – Chris' team had said, 'Yes, we think we should count them.' Awkward.

So for a second he'd had to weigh things up. Nick didn't want them counted. And Chris did want them counted. A margin of 500 votes. Thirteen hundred envelopes sitting there unopened. And two men's careers and the future of the party and the future of the country hanging in the balance.

But the more he thought about it, the more he kept coming back to the same place. The rules were the rules. And he'd been clear. Both teams had to agree. And Julia had also been clear. Don't open them. Sharp girl, Julia.

So that was it. There really hadn't been much of a decision to make. The result would stand.

He looked down at his watch. It would be time to set off to meet his dinner date soon. And anyway, it didn't matter any more. The envelopes had been destroyed. No one would ever know one way or another if they'd have made a difference. All that mattered was that it was Nick Clegg who was the senior partner now.

He put down the receiver. That had been a very strange phone call. A very strange call indeed.

Not least because he always found it a little odd taking calls like that at home. In the office, or even up in the constituency, it felt natural. All part of the political work environment.

But sitting here, surrounded by the bric-a-brac of his life, with the kids screaming in the back garden, it was weird. To have that voice in here.

'It's Gordon.' You could always tell from the introduction what sort of Gordon you were about to get. Today it was urgent Gordon. Insistent Gordon. Won't take no for an answer Gordon.

In other words, the Gordon most people saw. Although obviously most people never actually got to see him at all. It was the Gordon they saw in their mind's eye.

If you did get to know him though, then you would definitely see a different side to him. Not that anyone ever got to properly know him. But those people who got closer – not close exactly, but closer – all spoke of it. Humorous Gordon. Self-deprecating Gordon. Generous Gordon. Even sentimental Gordon.

But there had been no humour, or generosity, or self-deprecation, or sentimentality in the voice on the other end of the line today. Only urgency.

'You have to come in behind Ed now,' he'd said. No preamble. No pleasantries. 'It's Gordon. You have to come in behind Ed now.'

And that's confusing, obviously. It would be confusing for anyone. It's a quiet Sunday, and the kids are in the garden, and the wife's in the kitchen, and the football's on the television, and there's that familiar, gruff Scottish voice telling you, 'Come in behind Ed.'

His initial reaction had been to say, 'Hi Gordon, how are you?' Like you would on any normal call, with a normal person. But there's no space. Urgent Gordon can't let himself get hung-up on stuff like that.

So then he'd been about to say, 'OK, I'll certainly think about it.' That was instinct taking over. Never directly contradict urgent Gordon. Never, ever. But don't just agree either. Because you don't know what you're signing up for. And the way Gordon works, he probably doesn't know what he's just signed you up for either. Tends to all be a bit stream of consciousness. And an hour later the stream will probably be flowing in a different direction. So it's best to give yourself a bit of time. And him a bit of time.

But then, just as he'd been weighing up the best way to respond, he'd remembered. He was already backing Ed. So he'd gone right ahead and said so.

'But I'm already backing Ed. He knows that.'

And immediately he'd realized he'd made a mistake. Because to urgent Gordon this response represented a form of contradiction. Worse, it represented a form of subtle mockery. 'He's asking me to back Ed. But I'm already backing Ed. The old man's losing it a bit.'

So the gruffness had surged into an angry growl. 'No, not Ed. Ed!'

And at last he'd understood. This wasn't about Ed. It was about Ed.

But it still didn't make any sense. He was backing Ed. Gordon was backing Ed. They were all backing Ed. They'd been backing Ed from the beginning. Not Ed. Ed.

'But Gordon, I . . .'

'Look. You can still back Ed, obviously. But then you have to put Ed number two. Not David. Ed.'

And now it was starting to make a bit more sense. A bit. They were still backing Ed Balls. But he was probably going to come up short. So that meant putting someone else at number two on the ballot.

But it was David who was going to be number two. It was all arranged. David and Ed were going to speak. And then David would offer Ed Shadow Chancellor, and that would be it. It was all sorted. Iain, Vernon, Geoffrey. He'd talked to them all in the week. They were going Ed Balls/David Miliband. Not Ed Balls/Ed Miliband.

So again he'd said so. Another mistake. Because now Gordon had to explain. And if there's one thing Gordon hated – especially urgent Gordon – it was explaining. Because explaining took time. And time was the one thing urgent Gordon never had.

So he could hear Gordon taking a deep breath on the other end of the line, because Gordon knew himself well enough by now that if he didn't take that deep breath the growl was going to become a shout, and this wasn't the time for shouting. It was too important. Plus, it was a Sunday.

So Gordon explained. How there was no deal. And how David had got cold feet about offering Ed Shadow

Chancellor because of the Bloomberg speech – 'too Keynesian'. And how it was clear David was just going to renew the Blairites' grip on everything. And what that would mean for their legacy; the 'Brownite legacy'. And what that would mean for the party. And what that would mean for the country. And yes, he knew Ed Balls and Ed Miliband had their differences. And yes, he knew it would be hard for Ed Balls to serve under Ed Miliband, at least in the beginning. But they all had to put those differences aside now. This thing was bigger than any of them. And Tom and Dugher and John and Lindsay were all signed up. And it was vital, absolutely vital, he signed up as well. Because there were only a handful of votes in it.

And then there'd been a brief pause. Not to consider what he was going to do – he'd known what he was going to do from the first moment he picked up the phone and heard that voice. But just to take a second to remind himself, 'This is how it happened.' This is how Gordon got to be Gordon. Chancellor. Labour leader. Prime Minister. Just by willing it. He insisted this is how things would be. And that's how things were.

'OK, Gordon. Let me think about it.'

'Good.'

He was gone. Urgent Gordon, off to make another urgent call.

Out in the garden he could see the kids still playing. From the kitchen he could hear the clank of plates emerging from the dishwasher. On the television the ball was sailing high up into the stands. It was done. Gordon Brown had decided Ed Miliband was going to be leader of the Labour party. So Ed Miliband would.

Michael Howard flicked open the cover again. It was a very good document: 'A Twenty-First Century Party'. In truth, he didn't really think of himself as one of life's natural modernizers. And if the election result was anything to go by, nor did anyone else.

But it was very good indeed. Just what he'd asked for. All the main proposals had been included. A ten per cent threshold for nominations. If anyone secured more than half of the nominations they would automatically be elected leader. If they didn't, then all the candidates would get to address the National Convention. And then the Convention could have a vote. An indicative vote. To test the water, as it were. And then the parliamentary party would have the final say.

Of course, this proposal certainly wouldn't be to everyone's liking. He recognized that. The membership would be very concerned about losing their existing voting rights. Actually, they'd be furious. And they'd let their anger be known to their individual members of parliament. There would certainly be a lot of pressure placed on individual backbenchers. And they were all still feeling quite bruised. So they'd have little choice but to relay those concerns back to the officers of the '22. He quite understood all of that.

There were some people who thought the 1922

Committee wasn't the force it once was. But he wasn't so sure. Michael Spicer was nobody's fool. And it would be quite a controversial move. Especially given it was going to be his final act as chairman, and he'd already announced he'd be stepping down as soon as a replacement had been elected. Let's face it, there wasn't much point pretending someone who'd just taken his party to their third successive election defeat had much political capital left in the bank.

So yes, it was a very, very good document. But it was fifty-fifty whether he could sell it to the party. Probably more like forty-sixty. Maybe even thirty-seventy.

Plus, the whole process would take time. To have the thing printed, get it distributed, have it discussed and debated, and then to finally get it voted on. Quite a lot of time. Probably four or five months, from start to finish.

Some people thought that was simply too long. That it was important to get the leadership election underway now. It was pretty clear who was going to win, anyway. The polls had David Davis well ahead of David Cameron. They argued he should step down now, they'd have a swift contest, Davis would win, and then they could get on with the business of taking the fight to Labour. And even though he'd just been re-elected, Blair was already starting to look vulnerable.

He lifted his eyes from his desk, and looked around the room. He'd never really liked this room. Not that there was anything wrong with it. It was just a room, in that rather drab old Scotland Yard building, just at the bottom of Whitehall.

But he'd never really liked being here. Never really liked the role. Never really liked being leader. He'd quite liked the idea of being Prime Minister. But that had never realistically been going to happen. What had they said about him? 'Something of the night.' Unfair. But politics wasn't fair. And it had stuck.

So he was never going to be Prime Minister. He knew that. And they knew that. Which is why they'd started organizing. David Davis and his friends.

Which was fine. Like he said, politics was politics. Look what they'd done to Iain. And he'd been the beneficiary of that particular assassination. So he could hardly complain.

But what annoyed him a bit was the timing. He'd been on the road when he'd found out that they'd started ringing round for the signatures. And that was with a week or so still to go to polling day. There he was, out on the stump, still fighting for every seat and every vote. And David and his cronies were already sharpening the knives.

Not that he could let that influence his decision. What was done was done. All that mattered now was what was best for the party.

And in his view it was important for the party to properly debate these proposals. Yes, it might have one or two implications for the upcoming contest. Davis was the strong favourite. At the moment. But if the election was strung out it might present an opportunity for his rivals.

George had told him he wasn't running, which was a shame. But David Cameron certainly had something about him. Even if he did seem a touch light ideologically. And Liam was bound to run. Which would probably cause Davis some difficulty on the right. And then there was Ken. Ken would shake things up a bit.

It was also true that Davis had a few enemies. Quite a lot of enemies, come to think of it. And in a long campaign things like that had a habit of coming back to haunt you.

So basically, that was the choice he had to make. He could try and get his proposals adopted. And he felt they were good proposals. Important proposals. But if he was honest with himself, there was only a relatively slim chance of success. If he did push ahead it would put the leadership contest back months. Which would delay the election to find his successor. And that could have all sorts of unseen consequences for the result.

It also meant several more months sitting in this room. The room where he'd been sitting when he'd had all those angry late-night rows with David Davis.

He closed the cover of the document and pushed it to the side. Then he reached forward for the yellow legal pad, picked up his pen, and began to write.

'Draft statement. I am today unveiling my proposals for a twenty-first-century Conservative party . . .'

*

Politics is for the naturals. People with the look. The touch. The gift.

Nobody who works in or around politics really knows how to define it. But they know it when they see it. They call it 'The Thing'.

Thatcher had The Thing. Blair had The Thing. Clinton patented The Thing.

This is how it works. You're in a room. It's quite a large room, and it's packed, and it's hot, but it doesn't matter because there's this electricity crackling through the air. And everyone in the room is thinking the same thing. 'I've made it. I'm in the room.'

The room. And soon, very soon, *He's* going to be in the room. So even though everyone's talking, no-one's really listening. Well, they're listening. But not to each other. They're listening out. For Him.

Not that they'll actually hear Him. That would be too clumsy. Cheap. He won't use mere words or sounds to herald His arrival. Boris – who's got his own thing going on, but not *The* Thing – might do that. You'll hear the distinctive voice, or the conspiratorial laugh. And you'll say to your neighbour knowingly, 'Ah, Boris is here.'

But the naturals have it down. The art of the double-entrance. Just before they enter the room, they enter the room. They arrive a split second before they arrive.

Abruptly, the volume of the chatter dips. Heads tilt – don't swivel, but subtly tilt – as one. And each conversation (although it's only a cosmetic conversation after all) experiences the same microscopic pause.

And then He's there. Actually in the room. With you.

Immediately, the volume in the room increases again, except now it's even louder than before. Heads tilt back, and people begin adjusting their stances, so they can look without looking like they're looking. And the cosmetic conversation has a new intensity. Partly boosted by the adrenalin rush of knowing you're actually in the room with Him, and partly boosted by the fear He won't be seen dead with someone who has absolutely nothing interesting to say.

But people still aren't listening. They're not listening to anything now. They're waiting for the tap. That touch of the shoulder, followed by the exquisite whisper. 'He would like to see you.'

The touch comes and it feels good. Oh, it feels so, so good. Like your first kiss. Then you're guided – it's almost like you're gliding – with swift efficiency to a predetermined spot in the room. And when you arrive you're eased seamlessly into your place, amidst that tight, expectant semi-circle. The circle of the chosen ones.

You smile. The chosen ones smile back. And as they do their eyes dance and giggle. 'He is coming,' the eyes say.

And then, suddenly, He's there. He. Is. There. Everyone falls silent. A crushing, deathly silence. And you go to speak. But you can't. It's as if He has sucked the air clean out of your lungs. And you try to form the words. The words you've been forming again and again in your head ever since the invitation first arrived. The witty remark. The charming anecdote. The line you've prepared. For Him.

But the words won't come. No-one's words will come. It's a disaster! No one has anything to say!! To Him!!!

And then you hear it. At first you don't comprehend. The voice is familiar. So are the sounds. They're sounds you recognize. The sentence that's being formed from them – you recognize that too. But somehow the link between hearing and understanding has been broken. And then you notice – the semi-circle has broken as well. The people standing to your immediate left and immediate right have gone. As if they were never there. And the other people in the room. They've gone too. And the room. It's gone. The building. Gone. The street. Gone. The city. Gone. Everything has gone.

Except you. And Him. It's just the two of you. He's leaning forward, speaking – to you. Looking – at you. And only you.

But of course He's only speaking to you. Of course He's only looking at you. Who else could He be speaking to? Who else could He be looking at? You're the only two people left in the whole wide world . . .

That is The Thing. And none of our three men have it. Oh, they're all good, solid politicos. Each has risen to be leader of his party. One of them is Prime Minister. One of them is Deputy Prime Minister. The third could be two minutes away from becoming Prime Minister.

So they've got game, these guys. None of them are slouches when it comes to shimmying up the old greasy Westminster pole.

But they're not naturals.

Take Nick Clegg. They say when you first walk into the room, he always seems to already be there. As if it's him who's waiting nervously for you.

Then there's Ed Miliband. Everyone agrees, he's a very nice person. He can be witty, self-deprecating and even charming. But when he's talking to you, he always seems to be standing half a step too far back. Like he wants to maintain some distance.

David Cameron looks he could be the part. No doubt about that. He has 'natural potential'. But he's a touch too smooth. Too slick. Too contrived. Not quite natural enough, come to think of it.

At least, that's what *they* say. The Westminster Watchers. The Punditocracy. The Bubble Breathers.

And if *they* say it, well it must be true. Of course it's true. They've got all these little vignettes to prove it.

So there's the story of the journalist who was at the Labour party conference. Up in Manchester – no, up in Liverpool it was. And he walks out of the toilet, and he's got this fringe meeting he's got to cover. So he's rushing, and he's not really looking where he's going, and 'bang!' Who does he run into? Ed Miliband. Slams right into the guy. The leader of the opposition. Walks straight into him. And he's a tall man, so you can hardly miss him. But he didn't see him. Didn't – and this is the point – sense him. Can you imagine that? With Thatcher? Or Blair? Or Clinton?

OK, the story may have gained a little in the telling. He may not have actually run into him. But it was close. Needed a last-minute body swerve. And yes, he was being a bit careless because he was running late. But that's not the point. The point is, if Ed Miliband had The Thing, he'd have known he was there. Felt his presence. But he didn't. Ed's not a natural, you see.

There's another story. Quite a recent one, this one. A couple of the guys are interviewing Cameron. On the train, on the record, big interview, snapper sitting there bored out of his mind. The full shooting match. And Cameron's just pissed with them. Not answering the questions. When he does answer it's all monosyllabic crap. Just doesn't want to be there. Basically can't be bothered.

OK, that's not very Cam-like. People say he's usually too polished. Too on message. 'Hard-working families' . . . 'long-term economic plan' . . . 'Do you want to give the keys back to the same people who crashed the car?' – normally you can hear the autopilot humming into life.

But today he's just fucked off. With these guys who are just trying to do their job. For no reason. Only four weeks to go til polling day and he's stonewalling them.

Can you imagine Blair doing that? Or Thatcher? Or Clinton?

Of course not. Too slick. Too prickly. It's basically all the same, isn't it? He may be PM, but let's not pretend Cameron's a natural.

And then there's that story about Clegg. Come to think of it, no-one ever seems to have any stories to tell about Nick Clegg. Sitting there, in the hotel, knocking back the expense-account Merlot. 'Hey, I heard this great tale about Clegg . . .' Doesn't happen. No-one ever shares a decent yarn about Nick Clegg. Ever.

Can you imagine sitting there and not having a decent story about Thatcher? Or Blair? Or Clinton?

Of course not. But Nick Clegg? The poor bloke's about as far from being a natural as it's possible to be.

And it isn't just about these little sketches. They help illustrate the point. But it's about all of it. The whole package.

For example, everyone knows Ed wouldn't have beaten David if Gordon hadn't stepped in at the last minute. Well, maybe not everyone. Most people think it was the unions that won it for him. Cue the Red Ed meme. But the people who were really in the know — well, they knew it was Gordon. With those last-minute calls. Pulling in those last-minute favours.

The same with Cameron. David Davis had it nailed on. He was the choice. Lived on some sink council estate in south-west London, born to a single mum, raised by his grandparents. Now there's a biography. Proper heart-warming tale of a working-class boy made good.

But he made the mistake of getting on the wrong side of Michael Howard. The wrong side of the Tory establishment. So they nobbled him. All that fiddling around with the rules. Davis just ran out of steam and Cameron snatched it right at the death. But David Davis could have been the real deal.

Nick Clegg shouldn't have won either. In fact, a lot of people say he didn't win. That those thousand votes would have handed it to Chris Huhne. And that would have changed everything.

If Huhne had won that election he'd have known the score. Would never have left Vicky Pryce for Carina Trimingham. And that would have meant no late-night revenge calls from Vicky to Isabel Oakeshott. And no story about the driving points. And no scandal. And no court case. None of it.

Nick Clegg basically got lucky. There was that tiny bout of collective mass hysteria back in 2010. But people quickly came to their senses. And everyone was pretty embarrassed about it all now. Politics' very own death-of-Diana moment.

No, whichever way you cut it they're not naturals, these three men. Not winners. Jesus, Cameron couldn't even beat Gordon Brown. Ed wouldn't have beaten David *without* Gordon Brown. Clegg? They're out in the streets, burning the man in effigy. All over the country, lots of little Nick Cleggs just bursting into flames.

Here's the bottom line. If you haven't won, you don't get to call yourself a natural. And if you're not a natural, how can you hope to win?

That's what they say.

And the three men know they say it. The whispers. The school playground jibes.

Ed Miliband knows there's a group of backbenchers – his own backbenchers – who have taken to calling him 'Milihouse'. After the nerdy *Simpsons* character who's always getting beaten up and pushed around. 'Ed, how could this happen? We started out like Romeo and Juliet but it ended in tragedy.'

David Cameron still remembers the Margaret Thatcher memorial debate. He'd just read out this beautiful, poignant obituary. Then up pops her old consort, Conor Burns, with his black-cab monologue. Talks about the time he pulled up outside Thatcher's house, and the cabbie refused to take his fare. 'I apologize in advance to the Prime Minister for repeating this story. But he said, "Your fare tonight guv is you go in there and you tell her from me – we ain't had a good 'un since."' Oh, how they'd roared at that one.

Nick Clegg is well aware of the cosy chats. The discreet little meetings 'outside the precincts'. Two, maybe three of them, tucked together in the corner of some tiny, cheap Italian just off Soho. 'Have you seen this polling Matthew's done? Doesn't make for pleasant reading does it? Now, look at these numbers with Vince as leader. Quite a difference, eh?'

And the three men know something else. It's shit. It's all a load of shit.

You don't need The Thing to win. You don't need to be 'a natural' to win.

Look at John Major. Arrives for his first cabinet meeting since becoming Prime Minister. Finds his place around Macmillan's famous coffin-shaped cabinet table, settles back in the PM's chair (the only one in the room with armrests) and looks around at his colleagues. Then what does he blurt out for posterity? 'Well, who'd have thought it?'

Or Gordon Brown. A natural? Brown was as politically smooth as a half-brick. He was a maniac. An obsessive. Right from the beginning – even before he was elected an MP – he was intent on grinding his way to Downing Street. Every time he met someone he'd hand them a card, and then he'd ask for their details in return. And when he got them, he'd file them. And over time the file grew. And then it grew some more. And then one day it had became a full-blown database. The HAL of the Brownite machine. 'Who's chair of Mid Worcestershire CLP, HAL?' 'Michael John Foster. Born 14 March, 1963, in Birmingham. Married to Shauna. Interests cricket and economics.'

And then Gordon started to share HAL with Tony. They both used him to run their shadow cabinet campaigns, back in the days when people voted on this sort of thing. Gordon figured Tony might be going places. Plus, Tony really was a bit of a natural. Knew a fair few people himself. So 'whoosh', Tony's people got sucked up by HAL too. And by now HAL was so big, so omnipotent, Gordon needed someone to manage him. So he hired a guy, a guy just to look after HAL. Literally carried HAL around, on this little disc. And then one day Gordon got the call. John Smith was dead. He was distraught, genuinely distraught. But then when he stopped being distraught, he realized there was a leadership contest coming. And he was going to need HAL. Going to need that disc.

But Tony realized he was going to need HAL as well. So the guy – HAL's minder – got called in to see Gordon. 'Where's the disc? This second. Literally, where is it?' And the guy explained he'd just been called in to see Tony. And Tony wanted the disc too.

What the fuck!?! It was HIS disc! HAL was Gordon's creation! Blair was trying to steal HAL! And so Gordon's people were screaming at the HAL guy, and Tony's people were screaming at the HAL guy, and the HAL guy was almost in tears.

But it was all for nothing. Because the party had already made up its mind. They didn't give a monkeys who had HAL. It was time for Tony. Nothing personal Gordon. But Tony had The Thing.

So at the moment of truth Gordon asked HAL to open the pod bay doors. And HAL explained to Gordon that he was sorry, but he couldn't do it. And on the day the disc was finally handed over – the day the fateful deal with Tony was publicly announced – Gordon walked calmly into his office, shut the door and started chucking the chairs around. The ultimate triumph of the political naturals over the political grinders, right?

Wrong. Because thirteen years later Gordon Brown was walking into Downing Street. All that grinding worked. Eventually.

And this is what infuriates each of the three men. They *are* winners, goddamn it. They didn't win the way they were supposed to win. Or – and this is the more important point – they didn't win by doing the things the Bubble Breathers said they had to do to win. But they still won.

At the start of the election David Miliband was 11–4 on to be Labour leader; Ed was 9–1 against. But he took him, took his big brother clean out. And now he's sitting there, on the brink of leading Labour back to power after just one term. A rebound election win. Not been done for forty years.

David Cameron's ushered the Tory party back in to power for the first time in over a decade. They were meant to have been dead after 1997. And he brought them back to life. Won ninety-seven seats in 2010. Ninty-seven at his first attempt. Beat Labour by seven point one per cent. In 1979 the blessed Margaret only managed to beat Jim Callaghan by seven per cent, and take sixty-two seats. And she had the undertakers and the bin men smoothing her path.

Nick Clegg's taken his party back into government for the first time since Stanley Baldwin and his friends passed around the port at the Carlton Club and decided to pull the rug out from under David Lloyd-George. Eighty-eight years. Not a winner? Try telling that to Herbert Samuel and Archibald Sinclair and Clement Davies and Jo Grimond and Jeremy Thorpe and David Steel and Paddy Ashdown and Charlie Kennedy (god bless him) and Ming Campbell. Come to think of it,

Jeremy Thorpe got charged with murder, and he didn't get the abuse Clegg's getting.

And so yes, it angers them. All this crap about how they're not winners, and they're not naturals, and they haven't got The Thing.

But as well as angering them it confuses them. Why does it confuse them? Because they think they *are* naturals.

Why wouldn't they? It has all come naturally to them. Yes, it's required some hard work. A bit of sacrifice. But up until now, the political conveyor belt has been carrying each of them effortlessly forward.

School – Heatherdown and Eton (Cameron); Primrose Hill and Haverstock (Miliband); Caldicott and Westminster (Clegg). University – Cambridge (Clegg); Oxford, (Cameron and Miliband). First real job – Director of Corporate Affairs for Carlton (Cameron); lobbyist, GJW Communications (Clegg); researcher, Channel 4 (Miliband). Jobs in politics – intern to Tony Benn, then researcher to Shadow Chief Secretary to the Treasury Harriet Harman, then Shadow Chancellor Gordon Brown, then Chancellor Gordon Brown (Ed Miliband); head of political section Conservative research department, then special advisor to the Chancellor, then special advisor to the Home Secretary (Cameron); senior advisor EU Trade Directorate then senior advisor to EU Trade Commissioner Leon Brittan (Clegg). First moves into politics – stood for selection as MP for Doncaster North and won (Miliband); stood for selection as MP for Stafford and won (Cameron); stood for selection as MEP for the East Midlands and won (Clegg). Moves in politics – Minister for the Third Sector, then Minister for the Cabinet Office, then Energy Secretary, then leader of the Labour party (Ed Miliband); Lib Dem spokesman on Europe, then Lib Dem Home Affairs spokesman, then leader of the Liberal Democratic party, then Deputy Prime Minister of the United Kingdom (Clegg); shadow privy council minister, then shadow local government spokesman, then shadow education spokesman, then leader of the Conservative party, then seventy-fourth Prime Minister of the United Kingdom (Cameron).

Yes, each of them had experienced the odd bump along the way. Cameron lost Stafford by 4,000 votes. Miliband found himself slowly suffocating in Brown's treasury and needed to take himself out of politics for a year. In late 2005, as it became clear Charlie Kennedy's demons were finally catching up with him, there had been talk of 'jumping a generation', with Clegg touted as a possible successor. Nothing came of it.

But that's all they were, bumps. Minor stumbles on a journey that was pre-ordained. How was it no-one else could see it?

Ed Miliband can see it. It's his destiny to be Prime Minister. He senses it. And once he's there, it's his destiny to show everyone there is a parliamentary road to socialism. Well, maybe not socialism per se. But social justice. The sort of social justice his dad used to talk about, and write about, and dream about.

David Cameron can see it. He's sat down and mapped it out for people. The history books are going to record that it was David Cameron who saved Britain from the Great Recession. And saved the Union from splintering apart. And then anchored Britain – on her terms – at the very heart of Europe. The natural order. Not just restored, but secured and safeguarded for a generation. The Cameron generation.

Nick Clegg can see it too. He's led his party out of the political wilderness. And now he is going to lead his party home. 2010 was seen as an electoral aberration. But he knows better. The two-party system is dead. No one is going to win a majority in 2015. That means another coalition. And that means liberalism – his own personal brand of compassionate, hard-headed liberalism – is going to be locked into government. For today. For tomorrow. For all time.

So maybe they don't have The Thing, these three men. Perhaps they're not political naturals, like a Thatcher or a Blair or a Clinton. But it doesn't matter. Because destiny is on their side.

Or it was on their side. Most likely still is on their side. But it's just that . . . well . . . things don't seem quite so pre-ordained any more. All the old certainties, all the old realities. They don't feel as real, or as certain. Nothing feels real or certain tonight. Everything's moving. Floating.

Except for that clock. It's still sitting there. And it's still counting.

01.15 . . . 01.14 . . . 01.13 . . . 01.12 . . . 01.11 . . .

4. The Cell, The Salon and The League of Extraordinary Advisors

Nick Clegg shifted the receiver from his ear. David Cameron was properly angry this time. To be honest, since the coalition started he'd never heard him this angry. Which was odd if you thought about it. Afghanistan. Libya. All the terror threats.

And here he was, screaming down the phone about a £1.99 Waitrose bag.

All right, it wasn't the bag itself that he was worried about. It was what had been in the bag that was the problem. His daughter had been in that bag.

If you took a step back and looked at the whole thing, it was actually quite funny. But he wasn't stepping back. The opposite, in fact. At the moment he was talking about calling in the Metropolitan Police, and having Nick's chief political spokesman James McGrory arrested. Which wouldn't be funny for anyone.

So this is what happened. The Camerons' nanny, a very nice lady called Gita Lama, likes to take the Cameron kids out to play in the Downing Street garden. Pretty garden it is too, quite long and wide, with sculptures and trees and a little pond. Cameron's kids love it, and the Osbornes' kids love it as well.

And one of the games they all like to play involves

carrying Florence, who's five, around in this hessian Waitrose bag. She sits in the bag, and Gita or one of the older children picks her up, and Florence gets carted around, laughing and squealing and having a great old time.

But then one morning the Downing Street press office gets a call from the *Daily Mirror*. They've been told the Prime Minister is in the habit of letting his daughter get carried around the Downing Street garden like a sack of old spuds, and would anyone care to comment?

Kabooom!

So who blabbed? Not Gita. No chance. Not any of the Downing Street staff. They know if they so much as whisper a word about any of the kids they're for the high-jump.

So Special Operations are called in, and the records are pulled from Switch, and people start wandering around doing line-of-sight analysis, like it's Dealey Plaza.

And this is what they discover. They discover that a few minutes before the *Mirror* phoned Downing Street, the paper got several calls from James McGrory. They also discover that there are several offices with a vantage point looking into the Downing Street garden. One of them is occupied by James McGrory. It's James who's been caught standing at the window of the book depository with gunpowder on his hands.

Now, what Nick Clegg wanted to say is, 'Don't be

silly. This is preposterous. He wouldn't do something like that.' The trouble is, it was precisely the sort of thing James would do.

James McGrory is not exactly your daddy's Liberal Democrat. He's young. Wiry. Brash. If you first met him – and you didn't know who he was or what he did – you'd think maybe he was a licensed fish porter. Or maybe a City floor broker.

Which is exactly what he'd want you to think. He speaks fluent mockney. He hasn't really got time for anybody, but makes enough time for everybody. He's a ducker and a diver, a bobber and weaver.

A spinner. Not a press officer. A proper, dead-eyed Westminster gun-slinger.

And this presented Nick Clegg with a bit of a problem. Because Nick wasn't supposed to like spin. Or spinners. Or SPADs. He'd said so countless times. Politics had to be different. Westminster had to be run differently. Government had to be run differently.

But that was before he was actually in government. Back when pledging to cut the number of government advisors in half didn't matter. When calling for the government's political appointees to be paid for by the political parties seemed like sound, populist politics. Before he hired James McGrory.

And James was good. Very good. Everyone said it. He had an eye for a story (and let's face it, the Prime Minister's daughter being lugged around the Downing Street garden like an Ocado delivery is a good story). He knew how to place a story. Normally. And – this is the crucial thing – he didn't want to become the story.

Well, he did a little. Nick Clegg had noticed how James had perfected the spinner's art of just managing to appear in a background shot at an event, whilst making it look like he was trying to get out of it. But that was fair enough. This was still the age of the celebrity media handler.

And James wasn't just good. He was loyal. In fact, the word loyal didn't do him justice. Nick Clegg knew James wouldn't just walk through a wall for him. He'd walk through the wall, pick himself up, light himself a fag, go off and find himself some bricks, get himself a cement-mixer, buy himself a trowel (a good trowel, with a proper wooden handle, none of that plastic rubbish), mix the cement, lay the bricks, wait for the whole lot to set, then walk through that wall for him all over again.

So no, James McGrory wasn't your daddy's Liberal Democrat. But he was Nick Clegg's Liberal Democrat. And at the end of the day, that's what mattered.

Nick Clegg slid the receiver back adjacent to his ear. 'OK, David . . . look . . . David, just . . . will you please listen a moment. I know James. He makes mistakes, like we all do. But honestly, this is preposterous. James simply wouldn't do something like that . . .'

In reality, of course, there aren't just three men. There are dozens of men. Hundreds of men, in fact.

And women. Increasingly, there are women. But not quite as many women. And the women don't tend to be quite as senior. But they are there. If you look closely, you will spot them every now and then.

And they are The Team. The Team is a select group. An elite group. It works day and night, seven days a week, fifty-two weeks a year, every year. Until the clock finally reads '00.00'.

OK, they don't work every day. They will take a break now and then. Though they won't call it a break, they'll call it a 'getaway'. If you ever overhear a member of The Team talking about taking a few days off, you'll assume you're listening to someone planning a bank heist. 'It's all arranged. My getaway's planned for a week's time. Little cottage in Tuscany. Miles from anywhere. Somewhere he'll never be able to find me.'

In theory each member of The Team works for one of these three men. He is *their* man. That's what they tell themselves.

But he isn't their man. They are his man. Or woman. His possession. His object. Something that comes with the job. Like the office. And the car.

As soon as each of the three men was elected leader, it was the first thing they heard. 'One piece of advice. You need to pick a decent team. Most important thing you'll do.' Of course, what they really mean is, 'You need to pick a decent team. And I need to be part of it. Choosing me to be part of your team will be one of the most important things you do.'

So the men nodded thoughtfully and said, 'Anyone good you can suggest?' And the person opposite them was thinking, 'Of course there bloody is. You're looking at him.' But they couldn't say that. So they chucked out a couple of names of people they knew. People who they trusted to say, 'Thanks for calling me. I'll certainly think about it. But did you think about X? It was very kind of him to recommend me to you, but actually, he's the person you're after.'

But the men knew all this. They knew the game that was being played. And they knew how to play it. Because there was a time, not so long ago, when they were playing it themselves.

Nick Clegg was on Team Brittan. Back when Brittan was EU Trade Commissioner. Nick wanted to work in Europe. So he spoke to one of his neighbours who knew Lord Carrington. And the neighbour put in a word. And then Lord Carrington put in a word. And the next thing you knew he was sitting there chatting with Leon Brittan. And Leon Brittan was star struck. 'The brightest young man I've ever come across,' he told friends. And a couple of years later they were sitting there together, negotiating trade deals with China.

Ed Miliband was on Team Brown. One minute he was making tea for Tony Benn, who was good friends – ideologically and socially – with his father. And the next he was at the heart of the New Labour project. Benn couldn't ever quite get his head round it. Notes in his famous diary after a visit to see Ed's mum, 'The boys live entirely in the world of the Prime Minister's advisors.'

David Cameron was on Team Major, Team Lamont, Team Howard, Team Everybody. And he didn't like it much. Yes, he liked the politics. But he quickly got bored floating around in the back room. Drifting from one patron to another. He knew from pretty early on he wanted to get out of the back room, and into the front room. Start being his own man. Or having his own men.

So they knew what they were looking for in The Team, these three men. And just as importantly, they knew what they were not looking for.

So people told Nick Clegg he needed to build his own cabinet. Though they pronounced it 'cab-ee-nay'. They told him that partially because they thought that's what he needed, and partially because they knew he used to work in a 'cab-ee-nay' himself. This pronunciation, they surmised, would help him recognize the wisdom of their counsel. And help him recognize he needed to offer them a job in it.

But whilst they remembered Nick Clegg worked in a 'cab-ee-nay' they forgot one important thing. Nick Clegg worked in a 'cab-ee-nay'.

So he knew its limitations. He knew, for example, that it was too small for his purposes. There had only been a handful of people working alongside him in Brussels. All that stuff he was spouting before the 2010 election about getting rid of the advisor culture was all well and good. But if he was going to deliver what he wanted to deliver he had to find a way of circumnavigating two major obstacles. The Civil Service – that rolling, ebbing, meandering bureaucracy that hadn't served a Liberal master for almost a century. And the Tory machine. Actually, it's not so much a machine as a muscular, ravenous attack dog, stalking the corridors of power, guarding them proprietorially on behalf of its master.

The other problem was that the 'cab-ee-nay' system was too pedestrian for his purposes. He'd sit there working on some new trade initiative, waiting for all the necessary cogs to slowly move into alignment. And he'd think to himself, 'Patience, Nick. This is just the way the Chinese work.' And then he came home from Brussels. And he realized that wasn't just the way the Chinese worked, it was the way Brussels worked as well.

There was one other problem. The 'cab-ee-nay' system was just that, a major part of the European governance system. And Nick Clegg knew he couldn't afford to become part of the system. As soon as he did, he was dead. The system would crush him.

No, what Nick Clegg needed was not a 'cab-ee-nay'. What he needed was a Cell.

Obviously, he wasn't going to describe it quite in those terms. But that's what it amounted to.

If he was honest with himself, he made some mistakes in the first few months. He should have kept more distance. The Rose Garden statement, for example. A great moment. The sun shining. Him and Dave standing there doing their routine:

Journo: 'Prime Minister, do you now regret that when once asked what your favourite joke was, you replied Nick Clegg?'

Nick: 'Did you say that?' (comedy frown)

Dave: 'I'm afraid I did once.' (comedy grimace)

Nick: 'Right, I'm off!' (starts to walk away from the podium)

Dave: 'Come back!!!' (Nick comes back. Cue laughter)

But it was bad politics. If they were going to survive in government, they were going to have to do it on their own.

That's why he needed his Cell. It would start small, but gradually grow. As they began to find their feet and get a feel for how things worked, it would expand. And as it did, so would their influence. Their powerbase would build. They would be able to protect and promote their own, distinct agenda. The Clegg agenda.

Or that was the theory. So they began small. Richard Reeves got poached from the think tank Demos. Richard liked to think deep thoughts, stuff along the lines of 'What would JS Mill think?' (the answer, as it turns out, is not all that much). He would be Nick's intellectual in residence, with licence to think giant, humungous thoughts.

Next there was Jonny Oates. An ex-lobbyist – he

would prefer the term 'political consultant' – Nick's 'fixer'. He'd smooth feathers when they need to be smoothed, and ruffle them when they need ruffling.

Polly Mackenzie was Clegg's policy supremo. She's so bright she hasn't just got two brains, she's got 'two brains that are the size of two planets'. Her job would be to take the bits of the coalition agreement and turn it into something they could actually govern the country with.

Lena Pietsch was his first press officer. And she was a good press officer. German. Dependable. Efficient. Basically, a walking, nationalistic cliché.

John Sharkey is the guy who ran the election campaign. Former ad man at Saatchi and Saatchi, he helped run Thatcher's '87 campaign too. Although no-one mentions that now. The Shark's job was to tell Nick the things he didn't want to hear. Before the debates he told him he lacked passion, spoke too fast, was too repetitive, looked too uptight, rambled, was too verbose and too intellectually highbrow. Clegg listened, and hey presto, Cleggmania was born.

So that's The – embryonic – Cell. And in the beginning they played it straight. Richard thinking his deep thoughts. Lena running her stuff past Cameron's press guys, Polly liaising with his policy guys, Jonny keeping it tight with Cameron's own chief-of-staff Ed Llewellyn, and with Andy Coulson, his communications director. Andy even helped Clegg out with a spot of bother surrounding Miriam, after the press uncovered a little bit of discreet work her company DLA Piper had been doing for Colonel Gaddafi.

So on the surface, everything was running smoothly. But Nick Clegg knew this couldn't last. Couldn't last because it wouldn't last – politics doesn't work like that. And couldn't last because he couldn't afford to let it last. There was already a backlash growing within the party about how he and Cameron were becoming too chummy (OK, they had to work together, but did they really have to play tennis with each other? And if they did, how come Cameron always won?). And if they didn't do something, the Whitehall machine was just going to swallow them up and spit them out.

So The Cell slowly began to expand. James was brought in, after working – ironically enough – for Chris Huhne. But that's OK, because he was Nick's guy now. Sean Kemp and James Holt also came in to boost the press team. Julian Astle and Chris Saunders arrived to help Polly with the policy development. Ryan Coetzee flew in to help manage the election campaign. And Stephen Lotinga arrived in his rather dapper suits to keep an eye on everything.

All the while The Cell kept expanding and the big white Cabinet Office room overlooking Horseguards where The Cell was housed kept filling up. And the Tory advisors noticed that every time they arrived for a meeting there seemed to be a new face in the room. And that stories were suddenly popping up in the papers that they hadn't been aware were coming. And that policy options started appearing in the papers too. Options that weren't exactly to the letter of what they thought they had written down in the coalition agreement.

And still The Cell was growing. A whole new raft of junior advisors could be seen disappearing into the white room every day. The Tory advisors dutifully reported this back to their ministers, and their ministers said to themselves, 'What on earth is Nick Clegg doing with all these people?'

What Nick Clegg was doing with all these people was covertly infiltrating The Cell into the Tory ministers' own departments. Each secretary of state gets to appoint their own advisors. But there were seventeen Conservative secretaries of state, and only four Liberal Democrats. So Nick Clegg and the ministers in the non-Lib Dem departments didn't have political support. Which is where the people in the white room came in. They were shadowing these departments from afar. Monitoring them. Safeguarding the Clegg agenda.

So Theresa May would turn up to a meeting on her latest drugs crackdown, and there was Norman Baker sitting at the end of the table with this bloody great briefing note. She was planning to be in and out like Flynn and deploying the sniffer dogs by close of play. But Norman kept popping up with all these questions about cannabis-based medicines, Portuguese 'dissuasion commissions' and the potentially beneficial effects of diamorphine injections. And two hours later she'd find she's had to commit herself to a full-blown report on the international impact of drug-use legislation just to shut him up.

So The Cell was growing and expanding and extending its reach. And what's more it was working. People in the party were noticing. And by now the Tories were starting to notice. The backbenchers were beginning to get a bit angsty. Who was supposed to be running this government, David Cameron or Nick Clegg?

And then, in the spring of 2012, The Cell had its biggest coup to date. The budget was approaching, and the boys and girls in the white room had been in overdrive. They'd been drawing up these detailed plans on an increase in tax thresholds, and a load of other financial nuggets. Nick Clegg and Danny Alexander had been in there with Cameron and Osborne, driving it all hard. And the Tories thought they were just involved in normal pre-budget negotiations, like you would be with an ordinary Minister, in any other run-of-the-mill spending round.

But they weren't. Because The Cell wasn't negotiating with them, it was preparing to ambush them. And back at Lib Dem HQ (a very nicely appointed suite of offices they'd just moved into on Great George Street), a whole campaign was being mapped out. It involved leaflets, emails, mailshots. All calling for a rise in tax thresholds.

And then it began. George Osborne was sitting up in the flat at Eleven Downing Street. At 10.30 he got a call from Mesh Chhabra, his own press guy. 'They had the story on the new tax thresholds. It's all over the papers.' The next night, 10.30, Mesh was on again. 'They've got the cut in the 50p tax rate.' The night after that, 'They've got the clampdown on tax avoidance.' The night after, 'They've got the guarantee of zero point seven per cent spending on overseas aid.'

It was chaos. The Speaker was going bonkers – 'An insult to parliament, the budget is supposed to be announced in the House of Commons chamber, not on the front of the *FT*.' The papers who didn't have any of the leaks were going nuts, 'Treasury in meltdown.' And the papers who were getting the leaks were getting so much detail they were actually praising this new, open style of government.

But for Osborne it was a disaster. If all the good stuff was leaked in advance, then on Budget day itself all the press were going to focus on was the bad stuff. Or they'd be so bored with not having any new good stuff to report, they'd report the old good stuff as if it was new bad stuff instead.

So on the night before Budget day Osborne and his team were sitting in his office in the Treasury. And there was still some hope. They had one or two juicy nuggets left. Enough to just about get through it. And then they heard Big Ben strike 10.30. A moment later the door opened and in walked Mesh. And he just shook his head. 'They've got everything.'

Catastrophe for Osborne and Cameron. But a triumph for The Cell. Because if you looked closely at the leaked stories, you'd notice a pattern emerging. Buried in the body of the story on the new tax thresholds were several lines explaining how they were all the brainchild of Nick Clegg and his team, and a vindication of the high-profile campaign the Lib Dems had been mounting on the issue in the run-up to the Budget. The 50p tax cut would be incredibly explosive, all the papers agreed. But if it hadn't been for resistance from the Lib Dems, the rate would be cut to 40p, not 45p. Reportedly, it was Nick Clegg and Vince Cable who had been urging George Osborne to get tough on tax evasion. The overseas aid commitment? Nick Clegg had been personally lobbying David Cameron over it apparently.

It was a slam-dunk. The Westminster Watchers. The Punditocracy. The Bubble Breathers. Everyone agreed – The Cell had played a blinder over the 2012 budget.

Well, nearly everyone. One or two Lib Dem Ministers, and a couple of other people around the party, were just a tiny bit nervous about some of the coverage that had been generated. Yes, they had their spin on just about everything that could be spun.

But maybe George Osborne did have a point. There hadn't been much new to come out on Budget day itself. And as a result the press had focused on the bad stuff. And some of the headlines were very bad. Awful, actually. They were calling it the 'Omnishambles Budget'. So on the one hand people were reading how heavily the Budget had been influenced by the Liberal Democrats. And on the other they were reading about how the whole thing was an utter dog's dinner. Wasn't that possibly going to cause them a political headache down the road?

And they'd noticed something else. The Tories they were working alongside (and that's what they were all supposed to be doing, wasn't it, working alongside each other for the good of the country and all that?), were becoming cooler. Nothing too heavy. But they were starting to distance themselves. And that was beginning to make things just that little bit harder to get things done. And if they couldn't get things done, well, wasn't that going to cause them a political headache down the road as well?

And there was one other thing. The Tories knew about The Cell now. They finally realized what Nick Clegg was doing with all those people. They understood what was going on in the big white room.

And they weren't happy about it. In fact, a lot of the Tory backbenchers were demanding action over it. Some of them were even going as far as to say they wanted to see The Cell crushed. They wanted to see Nick Clegg and the Lib Dems taught a lesson they'd never forget.

Of course, a lot of that was just macho talk. The coalition still had another two or three years to run. But still, couldn't that potentially cause them a political headache at some point down the road too?

Nick Clegg heard these concerns. He understood them. But the thing is, he didn't really have much of a choice. He needed The Cell. They all needed The Cell.

Because if there was no Cell he knew what the end result would be. They wouldn't be crushed. They'd just be slowly subsumed. Sucked up by the Whitehall machine. Until all that was left of their party was a plaque saying, 'Office of the Deputy Prime Minister.'

So the day after the Budget the door opened. And a new figure walked expectantly across the threshold into the big white room.

David Cameron slipped on his glasses and scanned the resumé a second time. He essentially knew it all anyway. But he wanted to see how it looked set down on paper.

It looked good. Outstanding, in fact. South East Asia correspondent for the *Telegraph*, before being promoted to EU correspondent and then Diplomatic Editor. Appointed Asia editor for the *Economist* in 2000, covering China, India, Japan and the other thirty countries of the Pacific rim. Promoted in September 2006 to be the *Economist*'s US editor.

There was no doubt about it. Chris Lockwood was the worst possible man for the job.

Oh, on paper he was perfect. Any other Prime Minister would have leapt at the chance to bring in someone like that as deputy – only deputy, mind – of their policy unit. 'Alistair, I'm thinking of bringing Christopher Lockwood in to do some work for us.' 'Tony, who the fuck is Christopher Lockwood?' 'US editor of the *Economist*.' 'Shit, *that* Christopher Lockwood. Grab him quick.'

But there was one major problem. Chris Lockwood was David Cameron's friend.

Well, not exactly a friend. The Bubble Breathers had decided he wasn't allowed to have friends. He had 'Chums'. In fact, he had an entire 'Chumocracy'.

He had got Andrew Feldman, an old chum from Oxford (and a Notting Hill neighbour), who he'd appointed joint Tory party chairman. Katie Fall, another Oxford chum (and Notting Hill neighbour), was his deputy chief of staff. Ed Llewellyn, his actual chief of staff, was also a chum from Oxford and Eton. As was Seb James, his education advisor. And Jo Johnson, the head of the policy unit, and Brother of Boris. A chum of a chum.

So this was the decision David Cameron currently had to make. Did he bring in another chum, or not?

He could hire Chris. But then he knew what was going to happen next. He'd get another round of headlines attacking his inner circle of Chumocrats. And the attack would be taken up by Labour, who were starting to make some serious headway with the charge that the Tories were just a bunch of Bullingdon Club toffs who loved nothing better than spending an evening chucking bread rolls around a restaurant and then smashing the place up. And the attack would then be taken up by his own backbenchers, who were starting to worry that Labour's bread roll line was beginning to cut through. Or that's how they'd rationalize it to themselves. Though in reality the thing they hated most about the Chumocracy was that they were not a part of it.

And he couldn't afford that. The polls were dire. The local elections were in a week's time. Some people were even whispering that if the results were really bad he could be facing the prospect of a leadership challenge.

So in truth, there was only one decision to be made. Chris would be perfect for the job. But the politics were the politics.

Which is why David Cameron put on his glasses, reached for the keyboard in front of him, and started to type, 'Ed, let's go ahead and hire Christopher Lockwood . . .'

From the start people had been telling David Cameron he needed to hire some more 'ordinary people' for The Team. People with slightly rougher edges. Spent a bit of time north of Banbury. Got some dirt under their fingernails.

But David Cameron wasn't interested in ordinary people. He wanted special people. Extraordinary people. So Nick Clegg had his Cell. And Cameron had his League of Extraordinary Advisors.

The League may have been of a type. But they were of the right type. They went to the right schools – good schools. They came from the right families – good families. They had the right views – sensible, modern, progressive Tory views.

These were the sort of people David Cameron wanted in his inner circle. Not just people he could rely on. Or even people whose judgement he could trust. He wanted people he *knew*. People he could look *into*. People like him, in fact.

And all those other people, the ones who kept telling him he must disband this likeminded League of Extra-ordinary Advisors, could basically shove it. He was the Prime Minister, and he was going to pick who he wanted for The League. His League.

Now to those who were not part of The League, this may have come across as a trifle arrogant. And elit-ist. And, given the current political climate, some might have argued dangerously out of touch. Well, as far as David Cameron was concerned, they could all shove that as well.

There was a story that had done the rounds of White's club – the all-male bastion in St James', where David Cameron's father was chairman – about what Cameron Snr told a few of the members a couple of days after his son had been elected Prime Minister. 'No one's been able to tell David anything since he was eight.'

Now, it might just be a story. They're not big on Cam-eron Jnr in White's. The old man was OK, but the son's a bit too urban for their tastes. Resigned his member-ship in 2008 too.

What is definitely true is Cameron Jnr saw up close what happens to a Prime Minister who lets the Bubble Breathers push him around. Back in 1992 he was work-ing for Norman Lamont when Black Wednesday blew the government apart. And Lamont came back from another crisis cabinet meeting, and told him, 'Major said this weird thing. He told the cabinet, "I'm not going to let people use Norman as an air-raid shelter."'

Which was definitely a weird thing to say. But that was John Major for you. And the meaning was clear. 'I'm sticking with Norman.'

Nine months later Cameron was sitting in the Treasury, frantically typing out a resignation statement on behalf of his boss. Major had sacked him. Or tried to demote him to Environment, and Norman politely invited him to combine sex with travel and walked out. No traditional resignation letter, nothing. Which is why David Cameron was now sitting there hammering out this short goodbye.

That set the pattern. The Bubble Breathers would call for someone to resign. John Major would refuse. The Bubble Breathers would accuse him of being weak. Then a month later he'd cave in and throw that person to the wolves. At which point the Bubble Breathers would accuse him of being both weak and indecisive. And for once, the Bubble Breathers were right.

That wasn't going to be happening in David Cameron's government. It wasn't going to be happening to his ministers. And it certainly wasn't going to be happening to the members of his League.

There was one other explanation. A small but important rationale for the creation and elevation of the mercurial League of Extraordinary Advisors. They were there because they were meant to be there.

What the hell else were all these people supposed to be doing? Chris and Andrew and Katie and Ed and Seb and Jo and all the others. This was their place and their time, too. They'd all done what they were supposed to do. What was expected of them. What was asked of them.

They'd gone to a good school and good university and worked hard (hopefully not too hard), and got good exam results and good jobs and good careers and become good, clever, thoughtful, compassionate people. They'd played by the rules, more or less. And now they were in politics the rules of the game would get a whole lot tougher.

That's why they'd been selected to join The League. That's why there was a League. It was how things were supposed to be.

So yes, when they announced Chris was joining them there would be another mini-media storm. And yes, Labour would pounce on it. And yes, the green-eyed back-bench malcontents would stir things up.

But that was tough. They'd just have to handle it. The League of Extraordinary Advisors would have to sit down together and come up with a way of getting through it. It was the only way of demonstrating to people that the system worked. That the world worked. That life worked.

Ed Miliband leant back into the sofa and glanced around him. The Sunday morning sunshine was streaming through the tall half-Georgian window, and the smell of fresh coffee drifted across the room.

And there was that sound. The hypnotic staccato of words again drumming out their timeless rhythm.

It was perfect. This was exactly what he wanted.

The men around him – and they were all men this morning, they'd have to look at doing something about that – were currently talking across each other. But that was OK. That was what he wanted too. He needed to see ideas zipping through the air, slamming into one another, then rebounding away, generating fresh ideas, a whole new chain reaction of thought.

It was also important that everything was on the table. In fact, there wouldn't be a table. There would be no shibboleths in this room, or sacred cows. It would be an intellectual free-fire zone. No concept could be too outlandish, no suggestion would be deemed out of bounds.

That was the way things had to be now. He'd realized it from the moment he'd stood and watched Gordon walking out of Downing Street for that final time. In fact, deep down, he'd known a long, long time before that.

The old politics was dying. The old words, the old ideas, the old policies. They just weren't relevant any more. They'd tried them. He'd tried them. He'd been tasked with writing the election manifesto. With trying to give the old politics one final kiss of life.

And he'd failed. 'A Future Fair For All', the document had been called. What did that even mean? What did any of it mean?

It had meant defeat, that's what it had meant. And if he was honest, they'd deserved that defeat. By the end they'd not really had anything left to offer. They'd stopped thinking. They'd stopped governing. They'd just stopped.

And that was his job. Or his mission. To start things again. To go right back to the beginning and start all over again.

And this time it wouldn't be enough to just build a new party. Not nearly enough.

Which is why they were all sitting here in his front room on this glorious sunny morning. They were going to spend the next few hours building a whole new politics.

And they were making good progress. Well, some progress. Maurice Glasman, the campaigning academic who had been the driving force behind the London Citizens living wage campaign, had just been holding forth on the need to 'kill the Brownite rat'. Which wasn't exactly the tone he'd been hoping to strike with these early sessions. But then in fairness, he had said there were to be no sacred cows.

Neal Lawson, the director of the Compass think tank, had spent quite a lot of time talking about Zygmunt Bauman, the octogenarian Polish sociologist, which in turn had set off quite a lengthy discussion on the need for a shared human life anchored around the basic concepts of emancipation, individuality, time, space, work and community. It had been an interesting dialogue, but perhaps a little on the abstract side.

John Harris, the *Guardian* writer, had been more tightly focused, suggesting that they needed to begin talking about, and exploring, the concept of a 'New Socialism'. He quite liked that idea, although he did have some concerns that officially branding their strategy 'New' may set a few alarm bells ringing. And publicly embracing 'Socialism' would be quite a bold gesture so early in his leadership. Especially after all that 'Red Ed' nonsense. Might be best to stick with 'the new politics' (lower case new) for now.

Marc Stears – a professor of political theory at Oxford, and one of his closest friends – had tried to guide the conversation away from the political and back to the personal. Whatever strategy they pursued had to be one that he – Ed – was comfortable with, and felt he had complete ownership of. If the leadership election had shown anything, it was that the best way for achieving success was when he – Ed – was true to himself. In Marc's view he – Ed – was his own best sounding board. And at the end of the day the most important thing was that he – Ed – trusted his own instincts.

He – Ed – had liked that intervention, because it chimed with some of his own thinking. Meetings like this were important. But it was equally important – as Marc had said – for him to be his own man.

Stewart Wood, his closest advisor from the campaign, hadn't really contributed all that much. He'd nodded now and then, agreeing with most of the other contributions. But Stewart had told him that at this stage he was content to keep a watching brief. He wanted to take time to absorb some of the ideas that came out of these sessions.

Which was precisely what he intended to do himself. This was the start of a long process. Some people were trying to hurry him along, already warning he was taking 'too long to define himself'. Well, they would just have to be patient. He wasn't going to be rushing any of this.

That was a big part of the problem with the old politics. It was all 'Now! Now! Now!' Get this statement out – now! Get this new policy up and running – now! Take this decision – now!

Ed Miliband wasn't going to be taking *any* decisions for a while. He'd already publicly explained that as far as he was concerned they were starting with a blank piece of paper. And he'd meant it.

He was going to be using these early months to think. To listen. Weigh up the options.

The next general election was over four years away. They had time. The clock counting down to polling day had barely started ticking.

In the beginning there wasn't The Team. There was The Salon.

Ed Miliband didn't want to be surrounded by spinners. Or strategists. Or pollsters. Or image makers. At least not at the start.

They were all there, of course. Waiting in the wings. At his beck and call.

But he wanted to keep them at a distance, if he could.

Because the way he saw it, if you really wanted to build the new politics, then it meant you also had to try to live the new politics.

Plus, Ed Miliband had more than his fill of the old politics. He'd seen plenty of it, up close. Too close.

He'd been right there in the room when the punishment briefings were being meted out. He'd watched the machine grinding people into the ground. Grinding them down until there was so little left it would be impossible even for their next of kin to identify them. He'd seen careers ended on a whim. Political assassinations ordered just so an example could be set.

And he hadn't just witnessed it.

There was no way you could exist in that world without it touching you. Without it gradually starting to contaminate you. However hard you tried, you couldn't keep yourself clean.

And he'd tried harder than most. To keep his distance from the spinning and the plotting and the smearing. It was the reason he'd escaped to Harvard for a year. But you couldn't shut it out for ever. It was all around you, all of the time.

That was why, somewhere out there, there were the emails. Not emails he'd sent himself. Emails he'd been copied into. Perhaps he'd responded to one or two of them. Not a lengthy response. Just an acknowledgment. Probably a word of caution. 'Do we really want to be doing this?' 'Is now a good time to be putting this stuff out?' That sort of thing.

It was hard to remember now. What he'd seen, or hadn't seen. What he knew, or didn't know. What he'd been part of. What he hadn't been part of.

And to be honest, he didn't want to remember. All that mattered now was that he had the opportunity to put distance between himself and that time. As much distance as he could.

Hence the creation of The Salon. The Salon would begin to wash the stain away. And it wouldn't just be cleansing him personally. They'd be cleansing the entire party. It would be a renewal. Not New Labour. Born Again Labour.

And for a while, everything was working quite well. At least, that's how Ed Miliband saw things. The Salon met fairly regularly – still usually on a Sunday – at his house in Dartmouth Park. Stewart Wood was made a peer, appointed to the shadow cabinet, and made Ed's chief consigliere (although nobody within The Salon used terms like that any more, obviously). Marc was taken on with Ed full time, as his speech writer. Maurice – who Ed had also made a peer – could be spotted regularly wandering in and out of his suite of offices (the old Scotland Yard offices that Michael Howard never really warmed to). And Neal Lawson and John Harris would send over the occasional idea, or briefing note or other intellectual nugget.

But from the perspective of one or two other people – one or two other people in this context being the entire parliamentary Labour party – things weren't working well. Actually, they were a total clusterfuck.

When you tried to contact the leader's office you couldn't get hold of anyone. In fact, you were never entirely sure who you were supposed to be getting hold of in the first place. When you did get hold of someone they couldn't ever tell you anything. And when they did finally get back and tell you something it was complete and utter rubbish. Not that it mattered, because the next time you spoke to them they'd be telling you something completely different. And that would be complete and utter rubbish too.

So finally – once they'd managed to get through the shambles that was the appointment system – people had sat down with Ed. And they'd told him, 'Sorry, but things simply can't go on like this. Your political office is a shambles.'

And Ed Miliband had listened. He hadn't really liked what they were telling him. He was still quite taken with the idea of all those ideas zipping around, generating a chain-reaction of thought. But he'd been in the game long enough to know this – any political office that lets a bunch of people through the door who are hell bent on telling the leader how crap his political office is, has issues. Serious issues.

So reluctantly, Ed Miliband began to ring the changes. Tim Livesey, a former civil servant who'd worked in the foreign office and Downing Street, was pinched from his current job advising the Archbishop of Canterbury. Bob Roberts – a former political editor at the *Mirror* – and Tom Baldwin – a former political editor at the *Times* – were handed more prominent positions in dealing with overall strategy. Greg Beales, who pulled off the trick of working for both Tony Blair and Gordon Brown, was elevated to a more influential advisory role sitting alongside Stewart Wood. Jon Cruddas, the MP for Dagenham who used to be Tony Blair's union fixer, and Torsten Henricson Bell, a former Treasury advisor, were given responsibility for policy development. Spencer Livermore, another old Brown advisor, was brought in to beef up the election planning.

And people started to notice a difference. Things started getting better. Not completely better. But a little bit better.

And they also began to notice something else. There was a small but noticeable up-tick in the number of negative briefings that started appearing in the papers. Not Labour/Tory briefings, but Labour/Labour briefings (Blue on Blues, as they're known in the trade). Ed Balls. Douglas Alexander. Jim Murphy. Each one got a sharp slap across the face. No bones were broken. Nothing compared to the bad old days.

Rumours were also beginning to circulate about tensions within the Miliband camp itself. About how Spencer was angling for Tim's job, for example. Again, nothing too over the top. Not when you thought about what used to go on.

There were even some people who said the Miliband inner circle had now started encouraging the Bubble Breathers to take pot shots at a few of their own. One story doing the rounds had it that Torsten (apparently angry that Jon Cruddas had muscled in on *his* policy brief) had been laying stuff off to the press in an attempt to make it look like *Cruddas himself had been doing the briefing*. The old-Brownite Gleiwitz radio station ruse. Anyway, Cruddas was long enough in the tooth to nip it in the bud before things got out of hand. He fronted Torsten straight up and said, 'Look, I can spend fifteen minutes walking you through what you've been up to here, or you could just stop.'

So yes, things were getting a bit better. But no-one was talking about The Salon any more. And to be honest, they weren't really talking about the new politics that much either.

Which from Ed Miliband's point of view was a shame. He'd very much enjoyed those sunny Sunday mornings in his front room in Dartmouth Park. And he still felt he'd been right to try and mop up the bloodstains from the Blair v Brown gang wars. And that they needed to show the party was moving on from the past.

But that polling day clock really was counting down now. And at the moment it read:

01.10 . . . 01.09 . . . 01.08 . . . 01.07 . . . 01.06 . . .

5. The Queen and the Hedgehog

Ryan Coetzee was loving the optics. The famous door swung open and there was Nick. Striding out – upbeat, confident, looking every inch the statesman.

Dark blue suit, light blue shirt, gold tie. This man looked so sharp you could cut yourself on him. The ministerial car was idling in Downing Street (important man on important business. Can't waste time waiting for the ignition). Quick wave to the waiting cameras, slight pause as the protection officer pulled open the door, Nick slipped smoothly inside. Door slammed shut behind him, bullet-catcher jumped into the front left, and away they glided. Off to Buckingham Palace to tender his resignation to the Queen.

Or that's how they were selling it. Nick wasn't actually resigning at all. He was technically still Deputy Prime Minister throughout the election, in the same way David Cameron was still Prime Minister. So they'd had to come up with a little bit of constitutional chicanery. Got him to resign as Lord President of the Privy Council, or something like that.

Ryan didn't really understand the technicalities, and he didn't need to understand. All he knew was there'd been a Sky chopper buzzing Nick all the way up the

Mall, broadcasting the pictures live. Pats on the back all round. The first stage of the first day of the election had gone like clockwork.

Stage Two had gone like clockwork as well. Nick standing on the steps of the cabinet office, making his statement to the nation. Still looking every inch the statesman, but now he was out there punching as well. 'The very last thing the country needs [leans in for emphasis] is a lurch to the left or the right. Yet that's *exactly* [doesn't just hit 'exactly' for emphasis, he smashes it halfway down Whitehall] what the Conservative and Labour parties are threatening. Why should the British people be forced to choose between too much cutting and too much borrowing? What kind of choice is that?'

Nick Clegg knew what kind of choice it was. It was a '*dismal* choice'.

On Stage Three they'd hit their first minor snag. The plan had been to take him to a school. Lots of smart, well-behaved kids, beavering away on their exam prep. Young minds, their whole future ahead of them. A bright future, thanks to Nick Clegg and the Liberal Democrats.

Then just as they were about to set off, the school bailed on them. Head had got cold feet. Concerns about being seen as politically partisan. Disruption to the school day. Risk of a protestor or two.

But that was OK, this shit happens. So they'd quickly rung around, and they'd got a new venue. Some sort of wildlife sanctuary in Solihull. Probably be some nice pictures of Nick standing next to a herd of deer. All very majestic and green and environmentally sound. Mother nature and Bambi have a bright future thanks to Nick Clegg and the Liberal Democrats.

Anyway, Stage Three wasn't really that important. Just a bit of window dressing. On the BBC Six, which was coming up in five minutes or so, the meat of the package would be the trip to the palace and the statement outside the cabinet office.

This was just what they needed. A good first day. Ryan knew that each day of the election campaign would be a mini set-piece battle. And that during each battle they would have three main objectives.

The first would be to secure 'cut-through'. They had to get Nick and his message on the news bulletins. In an ideal world they'd have him 'leading the bulletins', i.e. appearing in the first political story the viewers saw, the one they actually sat through before they got bored and switched over to *Deal or No Deal*. Second – they had to try to get 'cut-through' on their 'grid-issue'. Each day of the campaign was mapped out in advance on a big grid, a sort of giant Excel spreadsheet. They needed to make sure the journalists were talking about Nick Clegg's Excel spreadsheet, not David Cameron or Ed Miliband's Excel spreadsheet. Third – under no circumstances could they allow Nick to 'go off grid'. Leave him standing there, looking like a rabbit trapped in the headlights, trying to talk about something that was Cameron or Miliband's grid issue, rather than his own grid issue. If they did, then someone senior in the campaign team would turn to someone else senior in the campaign team and say in a low voice, 'This is not good. We're off the grid.'

But today had gone well. Apart from the hiccup with the school, they'd remained rigidly on the grid. He knew they probably wouldn't be leading the Six, because the BBC always defaulted towards the two main parties at the start of the campaign. But they'd get some decent coverage. Solid grid coverage.

And then Ryan Coetzee glanced up. He'd become lost in his thoughts. It was 18.05. The Six had started. And there, on the screen in front of him, was Nick.

But Nick wasn't stepping out of the car at Buckingham Palace. And he wasn't standing on the steps of the cabinet office, talking about the vital choice facing the British people at this general election. He was stroking a hedgehog.

Still wearing the nice pale blue shirt. But the killer suit and the tie had gone, replaced by a worn-looking jumper that emphasized his paunch, a pair of dark canvas trousers and a pair of dirty green wellington boots. The Deputy Prime Minister of the United Kingdom looked like he'd just wandered off the set of *The Good Life*.

And he was stroking a hedgehog.

The commentary was fine. What there was of it. A couple of minutes explaining what Nick had done earlier in the day, and paraphrasing his cabinet office statement. But it didn't matter. Because no-one would be listening to the words.

All they'd notice was that Nick Clegg was stroking a hedgehog.

And Ryan Coetzee thought to himself, 'We had the perfect grid. We had the Queen on our grid. How the fuck did we manage to end up with a hedgehog?'

And behind him a low voice whispered, 'This is not good. We're off the grid. I never saw a hedgehog on the grid.'

So now each of the three men had a team. They'd spent years assembling The Team. And they had their political mission. Spent years – decades even – refining in their own minds exactly what their personal political mission was. But they'd nailed it down. Eventually.

Maybe they even had destiny on their side. That's certainly how it felt. That fate was gently nudging them forward.

But now they needed a plan. A strategy. A big map that had lines and contours and arrows and little red pins sticking out of it. Something that reassured each of them, 'This is not going to end up a suicide mission, Colonel. We have left nothing to chance. We've checked out the position of the moon, and the time the sun rises, and the time the sun sets, and the ebb and flow of the tides. And we know exactly where the beach obstacles are, and the minefields, and the machine gun nests. And we've got a plan for neutralizing each and every one of them. Don't worry, we'll have you and the boys on that beach and up those cliffs without a scratch. Well, there'll be a scratch or two. But you'll make it.'

That's what each of these three men had demanded – their own battle plan. And that's what each of these three men had received. It was literally all written down, in this huge folder (regardless of party, it's usually a red folder for some reason) that they called The War Book.

Then, about a year out from the election, someone pulled out The War Book, and the party suddenly moved on to a War Footing. No-one really knew for sure precisely when or why or how this official move to a War Footing took place. Except for the fact that one day, in the middle of an otherwise mundane meeting, someone dramatically clapped their hands and shouted, 'Come on people! We need to sharpen up! The election's only a year away! We're on a War Footing now!'

At which point the battle plan went live. And what a plan it was.

For example, here's what Labour's battle plan involved:

The 'Weekly Look Ahead Meeting' every Monday or Tuesday, between 12.00 and 13.00. This, as the name implies, involved a 'weekly look ahead'.

The 'Weekly Meeting' every Monday at 14.00. This meeting was used to agree the 'strategic overview of the week ahead'.

The 'Campaign Planning Meeting' every Tuesday or Wednesday, at 14.30. This meeting was to bring people up to speed on what had been agreed at the 'Weekly Look Ahead Meeting'.

The 'Quarterly Look Ahead Weekly Meeting', every Thursday between 12.30 and 13.30. This meeting was used to look ahead a few weeks further than the look ahead that had just taken place at the 'Weekly Meeting', and the 'Weekly Look Ahead Meeting'.

The 'Weekly Catch-Up Meeting' (not to be confused with the 'Weekly Look Ahead Meeting'), every Monday, between 10.30 and 11.30. This meeting 'reviewed progress, decisions, etc' that had been taken in the 'Weekly Meeting', the 'Weekly Look Ahead Meeting', the 'Campaign Planning Meeting' and the 'Quarterly Look Ahead Weekly Meeting'.

The 'Weekly Core Catch-Up' (not to be confused with the 'Weekly Meeting', the 'Weekly Look Ahead Meeting' or the 'Weekly Catch-Up Meeting'), every Thursday at 10.00. This meeting 'reviewed decisions taken' in the 'Weekly Meeting', the 'Weekly Look Ahead Meeting', the 'Campaign Planning Meeting', the 'Quarterly Look Ahead Weekly Meeting' *and* the 'Weekly Catch-Up Meeting'.

Then there was the 'Weekly Polling Meeting', the 'Weekly General Secretary's Meeting', the 'Weekly Chief of Staff's Meeting', the 'Weekly Attack Meeting', the monthly 'War Book Meeting', the 'Monthly Campaign Update Meeting', the 'Monthly Strategic Message Discussion Meeting', the 'Monthly General Election Strategy Group Meeting', the 'Monthly Ed Balls Meeting', the 'Monthly Alistair Campbell Catch-Up Meeting', the 'Monthly Harriet Harman Catch-Up Meeting' and the bi-monthly 'Sunday Group Meeting'.

But then someone went and leaked the whole lot to Toby Helm at the *Observer*. And the world went mad. 'Why am I in the "Monthly Campaign Update Meeting", not the "Quarterly Look Ahead Weekly Meeting"?' 'What the hell do you mean I'm excluded from the "Weekly Core Catch-Up"?' 'How come Ed Balls gets a full Meeting and I only get a Catch-Up Meeting?'

And some people in Ed's office were trying to clean up the mess by saying Tom Baldwin had just made the whole plan up. And others were saying it was Douglas just trying to bounce people into his master plan. But whatever the real reason, the upshot was they had to rip the whole thing up and start all over again.

So each of the three men cast an eye over their battle plan – with all its meetings to check on meetings that had taken place to double-check previous meetings. And they said to themselves, 'Now *that* is a plan.'

But there was just one problem with the plan. Actually, as it turned out, there were several problems with the plan.

The first problem with the plan was that over time people started to spend so much time poring over the plan, they could no longer see the plan. Take, for example, the mysterious case of the five Labour pledges that became 3,250 Labour pledges.

Back in the mid-nineties – when some Labour strategists still worried the voters might confuse Tony Blair with Michael Foot – someone decided it would be a great idea for him to cement his bond of trust with the British people by writing down five promises to them on a little plastic card. A bit like the sort of thing kidney donors carry.

So they sat down and came up with what became known as 'The Five Pledges'. 'We will cut class sizes to thirty', 'We will cut NHS waiting lists', 'We will get 250,000 under twenty-fives off benefits and into work', 'We will commit to no rise in income tax rates,' 'We will ensure young thugs get fast-track punishment'.

In the end the one about the young thugs got toned down to 'persistent young offenders'. But the cards were a great success. And because Labour won with a majority of over 100, the 'Five Pledges' came to be seen as a core part of Tony Blair's all-conquering battle plan.

So in one of the meetings (probably the 'Quarterly Look Ahead Weekly Meeting', or whatever its latest incarnation was), someone suggested resurrecting the pledge cards. At which point someone else pointed out this wasn't 1997, and they might not have the money to spend on hundreds of thousands of little plastic kidney donor cards. And then someone else suggested they simply ditched the cards, and stuck with the pledges. All of Labour's candidates could put them in their general election mailings, and in one fell swell swoop cement a new bond of trust with the voters. Whilst simultaneously proving Ed Miliband wasn't anything like Michael Foot either.

Everyone in the 'Quarterly Look Ahead Weekly

Meeting' thought this was a great idea, and promptly ran off to claim it as their own. And then they began working on the new pledges.

At the 'Weekly Look Ahead Meeting', and the 'Campaign Planning Meeting', and the 'Weekly Catch-Up Meeting', and the 'Weekly Core Catch-Up Meeting', people sat down and began brainstorming what the new pledges might look like. Some argued for the economy. Others argued for the NHS. A couple for crime. There were suggestions for pledges on immigration, the environment, jobs, a living wage, housing, child-care, zero-hour contracts, payday loans, banking reform, energy prices, media regulation, regional devolution, rent control, tax credits, industrial policy, tuition fees, the Bedroom Tax. Then finally, after vigorously batting these ideas back and forth for an hour or so, the meetings would break up, and everyone agreed to come back the next week and start brainstorming all over again.

The exception to this process was the General Secretary's meeting that took place at Labour's Brewer's Green HQ, just off Victoria Street. Iain McNicol was the General Secretary in question, a relatively young but level-headed former national political officer from the GMB union. His job was to run the Labour party day to day. He signed off the month's cheques, tried to find the money to sign off the next month's cheques, and basically kept the whole operation ticking over.

And now that Labour was on a war footing (it would

have been nice if someone could have sent him a memo about that), he found himself sitting down for his regular meeting with Spencer Livermore and Douglas Alexander – who, when he wasn't dabbling as Shadow Foreign Secretary, was Ed Miliband's general election coordinator – as they brought him up to speed with how the battle plan was shaping up. And Iain McNicol listened, and nodded, and took a few notes, and then chipped in with a bit of practical advice on how the national party could help pull the plan together. Then, at one meeting, they dropped in the fact they were resurrecting the 'Five Pledges'. And Iain McNicol listened, and nodded, and took a few notes, and told them he thought it was a great idea. But then he said to them, 'Make sure to keep an eye on the Freepost deadline. If you want the pledges to go on the candidate mailings you're going to have to sign them off in time to get the artwork over to the Royal Mail.' And now it was Spencer and Douglas' turn to nod. Very good point. And of course, they'd be very careful to ensure the pledges were signed off in time for the Freepost deadline. At which point they jumped up and hurried off to their next meeting.

And each week or so (so long as Douglas wasn't off having to be shadow foreign secretary somewhere), he and Spencer arrived for a new General Secretary's meeting. And they brought him up to speed on the battle plan. And Iain McNicol listened, and nodded, and jotted down some more notes. And then he said to them, 'You're keeping an eye on that Freepost deadline, aren't you? We need to make sure we get the artwork over to the Royal Mail in time.' And they nodded back at him. Yep, it was all in hand. The pledges were coming along nicely.

Which was true. Kind of. They'd all agreed they needed a pledge on the economy. Something about the deficit, or not borrowing, for any of their manifesto commitments. But some people worried that sounded excessively austere. And anyway, weren't they committed to investing a lot more in the NHS?

And they did have to have an NHS pledge. That's something else they'd all agreed on. The problem was, they couldn't quite make their mind up what it should be. More nurses and GPs? GP appointments? Social care reform? Cancer test deadlines?

It was the same with education. Everyone had signed up to having an education pledge. But what should they go with? The tuition fee cut? Apprenticeships? Smaller class sizes again?

They still had a little way to go on the final two pledges. At the moment it was a toss-up between something on welfare, something on immigration, the energy price freeze, zero-hours contracts, the minimum wage or childcare. But there was another meeting to go to now. So they could pick it up the next week.

And then, in the midst of the 'Weekly Catch-Up Meeting' (come to think of it, it might have become the 'Weekly Core Administration Meeting'), someone had a brainwave. Why didn't they just include *everything*. Come up with some broad, vague, over-arching principle, brand it 'a pledge', then chuck everything in underneath.

Brilliant. That's precisely why they had these meetings, so someone could eventually come up with a corker like that. And before you knew it Vague Over-Arching Principle One – sorry, Pledge One – was now 'A Strong Economic Foundation'. It contained a pledge that none of the manifesto commitments would require additional borrowing, a pledge to cut the deficit every year, a pledge to balance the books *and* a pledge to secure the future of the NHS while they were at it.

Pledge Two was 'Higher Living Standards for Families'. That included the energy freeze, a ban on zero-hour contracts, a rise in the minimum wage *and* twenty-five hours' free childcare.

Pledge Three was 'An NHS With the Time to Care'. OK, nobody was sure that even came under the heading of a vague principle. But it didn't matter because it included the new nurses, the new GPs, a joined-up service from home to hospital (whatever that meant), the new GP appointment system, and a range of new cancer tests.

Pledge Four was 'Controls on Immigration', which promised that people who come here wouldn't be able to claim benefits for at least two years. Brilliant. An immigration pledge and a welfare pledge *all in the same pledge*.

Pledge Five was 'A Country Where The Next Generation Can Do Better Than The Last'. Again, more of an aspiration than a principle. But again, who gave a damn when you could shoe-horn in an apprenticeship for every school leaver who got the basic grades, smaller class sizes and a cut in tuition fees of £6,000.

And that was it. They'd done it. In the end they'd managed to cram in eighteen pledges. Eighteen. Blair could only come up with a measly five.

But there was one small issue. They'd gone and missed the Freepost deadline.

The pledges were signed off too late for the candidates to get the artwork over to the Royal Mail for sign-off. So each of them was told to design their own artwork and come up with their own pledges – 650 candidates. Each with their own five pledges – 3,250 pledges in total.

And the original five pledges (or eighteen pledges)? They'd make an appearance in the manifesto. But who read the manifesto? All that time spent debating them in 'The Weekly Look Ahead Meeting' and 'The Weekly Meeting' and 'The Campaign Planning Meeting' and 'The Quarterly Look Ahead Weekly Meeting' and 'The Weekly Catch-Up Meeting' and 'The Weekly Core Catch-Up Meeting' (or whatever they were calling them by then). All that time just wasted. It was as if some people didn't understand they were on a war footing.

And a few days after the five pledges finally got signed off, Douglas and Spencer turned up for their General Secretary's meeting. And Iain McNicol sat there, and nodded, and jotted down a few notes. And nobody so much as mentioned the word Freepost.

*

The second problem with the plan was that the people responsible for drawing up the plan were never, ever happy with the plan. Or rather, they were never happy with their bit of the plan. Actually, that's not true. They were happy with their bit of the plan. They thought their bit of the plan was far and away the best bit of the plan. It was the other bits of the plan they weren't happy with. Actually, that's not true either. They couldn't be unhappy with the other bits of the plan, because they couldn't see the other bits of the plan. Only the people who had responsibility for those other bits of the plan could see those bits of the plan. And that's what the people who weren't responsible for those bits of the plan were *really* unhappy about. 'Why am I only dealing with my bit of the plan?' they said to themselves. 'My part of the plan is good. It must be. That's why David/Ed/Nick gave me responsibility for my part of the plan. But that other part of the plan, well it can't be very good. Because if it was, I'd be working on that part of the plan as well.'

And sooner rather than later – usually sooner – no-one was thinking about their part of the plan at all. All they were thinking about was the other part of the plan. The invisible part of the plan. *Why was it so invisible?* And they began talking to other people, people who also couldn't see the part of the plan they couldn't see. And because none of them could see what was going on in that part of the plan, and because they couldn't understand *why they weren't able to see that part of the plan*, they all started to begin guessing about what was going wrong with that part of the plan. Because something must have been going wrong with that part of the plan, right? Otherwise they'd all have been working on it.

And before you know it everyone was talking about how the plan was falling apart. 'Have you heard? Something's gone badly wrong with the plan. No, I don't know either. No one's talking. Tom doesn't know. Dick doesn't know. Sally doesn't know. Must be really bad. For them to be so worried they're keeping it from *everyone*.'

And that's how you end up with another mystery. The mystery of Ed Miliband's disastrous winning polling numbers.

Every couple of weeks a small group congregated in one of the meeting rooms in Brewer's Green for the Polling Meeting. Douglas was there, Spencer was there, Greg Beales was there, James Morris was there. And they started crunching through the latest polling numbers – the public polls, the private polls, the party's private focus group data.

Now, this was sensitive stuff. Everyone – from Ed Miliband down to the cleaning lady – understood how sensitive these numbers were. Not the public polls so much, but the private figures. Lynton Crosby wasn't even letting the Prime Minister of the country see *his* numbers.

Because these weren't just any old numbers. These were the POFs. The Party's Own Figures. And, as such, they had an almost mystical significance. Ordinary polls could be easily brushed aside. Polls go up, polls go down.

But not the POFs. If the POFs somehow managed

to get loose, there was no escape. 'The Right Honourable Gentleman talks to me about leadership. I'll tell him about leadership. I have in my hands his party's own focus group findings. Their *own* findings Mr Speaker. And do you know what they show? They show the Right Honourable Gentleman opposite is viewed as "uncool", "hapless", "out of touch" and "gormless". When people were asked who he reminded them of, they replied Mr Bean or Elmer Fudd. When asked, "What sort of drink would he be?" they replied, "A glass of crème de menthe". Honestly, Mr Speaker, do we really want a glass of crème de menthe running the country?'

So everyone in the party understood why the circulation list for the internal polling had to be kept to a bare minimum. Until they found out they weren't on it.

At which point the rumours began. 'They had the polling meeting yesterday. Apparently, it's bad. Really bad. That's why they're keeping the circulation list so tight. They daren't let people see it.'

Which in turn created something of a dilemma for all those people who were senior players in the party, or who thought they were senior players in the party, or who wanted other people to think they were senior players in the party. But who weren't on the list.

Because what were they to do? They could do and say nothing. Thereby giving the impression they didn't know what was happening, and weren't actually players at all. They could help give the rumours a shove. At which point people started saying, 'Have you heard?

Even Jane Doe is now admitting the private polling's bad. Proves just how bad it really is.' Or, they could pretend to have seen the figures, even if they hadn't seen the figures. 'Yes, I've heard the rumours, but I've had a look at the focus group data myself, and it shows Ed isn't a glass of crème de menthe, he's actually a nicely chilled glass of Krug Clos d'Ambonnay.' At which point the people who *really were* on the list said to themselves, 'Hang on. What's this stuff about polling showing Ed's a glass of Krug? I haven't seen this, and I'm supposed to be seeing everything. Have they started hiding stuff from me now?'

So finally, to try and get a grip on the polling rumours, someone who was actually on the list – James Morris in this case – was tasked with sitting down with a few more people to give them a bit of an insight into what the polling actually said. And he sat down with some people from the shadow cabinet, and some people who were working on the battle plan (but not people who usually see the part of the battle plan that includes the polling), and he carefully ran them through some of the numbers.

And off went the rumour mill again. 'Hear what happened yesterday? They had a polling meeting. Yes, *on a Monday*. I know, the Polling Meeting is supposed to happen *on a Thursday*. It was a *special crisis meeting* about the polling. You don't hold a crisis meeting on the polling unless it's bad, do you? God, the numbers must be awful.'

And then someone who was shown the new numbers

emerged from the meeting, and said, 'They showed us the numbers. According to James Morris we're holding steady on thirty-five per cent.'

Which was the cue for a whole new set of rumours. 'Have you heard? You know that special crisis meeting on the polling? They only went and showed them a bunch of made-up figures. The figures they had showed us holding steady on thirty-five per cent. I know, *thirty-five per cent*. Why would they need to hold a special crisis meeting on the polling if we were really holding steady at thirty-five per cent? They must think we're all idiots. Imagine what the real numbers must actually look like?'

So in the end, in a final, final bid to get a grip on the rumours about the polling numbers, they decided to open up the circulation list. Now it wasn't just Douglas and Spencer and Greg and James who were on the list, it was all the individual Task Force heads who were on the list as well. And because they were now on the list, but hadn't been on the list before, some of these people decided to show other people who still weren't on the list what the numbers were. Just to prove to them that they really were on the list.

Which meant a whole lot of people were suddenly seeing the numbers who didn't really understand the numbers. They were looking at cross-tabs of sub-samples of subsets. And before you knew it, some guy from digital outreach was sitting at lunch telling one of his mates, 'I saw the polling numbers yesterday. They're not looking good. The Green switchers really do think Ed looks like a glass of crème de menthe.' And away the rumour mill went again.

So what did the numbers actually look like? What would the people not on the list have seen if they had been on the list. Or if they'd just said, 'Fuck it,' snuck up to the meeting room one Thursday and peeked in through the keyhole?

What they'd have seen were Ed Miliband's disastrous winning polling numbers. If they'd peeked six months from polling day, they'd have seen some shockingly bad figures. If they'd peeked a couple of months later, they'd have seen them steadily starting to improve. If they'd peeked immediately after one of the early debates, they'd have seen his numbers soaring. If they'd peeked a couple of days later, they'd have seen them falling back. If they'd peeked fourteen days from polling day they'd have seen a three and a half per cent swing to Labour in the marginals, enough to see Ed Miliband into Downing Street. If they'd peeked eight days out they'd have seen a one and a half per cent swing to Labour in the marginals, enough to see David Cameron into Downing Street.

Because as it turns out, there's nothing special about the POFs at all. They go up and they go down. Just like the ordinary polls go up, and then go down.

Which begs the question, is there really any point in having the POFs in the first place? All this worrying about the polls, and worrying about who's seeing the polls, and worrying about who's not seeing the polls. Do they really have time for all of this? Aren't they supposed to be on a war footing?

And it begs one other question. If Ed Miliband's ratings fall, but there's no-one in the Thursday meeting to see it, do they actually make a sound?

There's one other problem with the plan. And this is quite a fundamental problem. The plan won't work.

It can't work. Just think about what the plan involves.

Each of the three men would say, 'I need a plan.' So the people immediately below them – The Cell, The Salon, The League of Extraordinary Advisors – would go off and start working on the plan.

But the plan was far too big for them to work on alone. So they went and got a lot of other people to work on the plan with them.

Now there was a whole new tier of people working on the plan. They were the people running in and out of the 'Weekly Meeting', the 'Quarterly Weekly Look Ahead Meeting', etc. And eventually, they came up with the plan.

But now they had to actually implement the plan. So that's when they turned to Iain McNicol, or Grant Shapps (Conservative party chairman), or Tim Farron (Lib Dem president).

And the party General Secretary or the Chairman or the President had to put in place their own tier of people to help implement the plan. And they in turn had to put in place their own tier of people. Who in turn put in place their own tier.

Which is how you end up with a third mystery. The mystery of the Labour candidate in the marginal seat who voted Tory.

In fact, Warwickshire North isn't just a marginal. It's a teeny-tiny, wafer-thin, super marginal. In 2010 the Conservatives won it by just fifty-four votes, or zero point one one four two four nine per cent of all votes cast.

If Ed Miliband wanted to walk into Downing Street he had to – absolutely had to – win Warwickshire North. If David Cameron wanted to stay in Downing Street he had to try to stop him. And to do that, David Cameron had to find that zero point one one four two four nine per cent of voters again, and convince them to stick with him.

But how? How did David Cameron find these zero point one one four two four nine per cent? Who were they? What were their names? How would he have recognized them if he saw them?

There were a number of ways. One was that he already had a rough idea where they lived, based on how people in Warwickshire North voted in the past. So let's imagine a little scenario in Fillongley. Nice little village, with a lovely parish church. Good bunch of people in Fillongley. Solid, hardworking Midlands' stock. Always vote Tory at local election time. Or Curdworth, which nestles just between the M6 and M42. Site of one of the first skirmishes of the Civil War – the Battle of Curdworth Bridge. The Cavaliers ended up routing the Roundheads, which may or may not be a good omen. Anyway, they're true blue loyalists in Curdworth these days.

So David Cameron has a general idea about where the zero point one one four two four nine per cent may be lurking. But a general idea isn't really good enough. So he's gone and got himself this whizzy, hi-tech computer system called 'Merlin' to help him zero in on them. Lots of little worker-bee type people in Conservative HQ, and the local constituency party, have been running around gathering all this information about the residents of Warwickshire North – such as their shopping habits, what sort of house they live in, their credit rating, what sort of car they drive, what type of mobile phone they carry, etc.

And on the back of that, everyone in Warwickshire North has been sorted into their own special socio-economic group, with special names, like 'Golden Empty Nesters' or 'Corporate Chieftains' or 'Provincial Privilege'. Merlin will then analyse the data, crunch it and deliver his verdict. Something like, 'Based on the information you've given me, Mrs Edith Smith, of 158 Coppice Drive, Dordon, is a Golden Empty Nester and is likely to be a Strong Tory voter.'

Likely. But not definitely. Merlin is clever, but he's not a mind-reader. He can't be absolutely, cross-his-microprocessor-hope-to-die certain Mrs Edith Smith is going to vote Tory. She might be impressed by that nice Mr Farage this time. Or still annoyed about that 'men being able to marry other men' business. Imagine all that rigmarole carrying on in the Church of St Nicholas and Peter Ad Vincula. So Merlin can make an educated guess. But he can't know for sure.

He also has a frustrating tendency to break down every now and then. Most notably when he's having to deal with large volumes of data. Slap bang in the middle of election campaigns, in other words.

So Merlin is good, but a touch temperamental. A bit like the Golden Empty Nesters of Warwickshire North, come to think of it. Which means David Cameron really only has one concrete option. If he wants to find his zero point one one four two four nine per cent, he's basically going to have to just knock on their door and ask them, 'Excuse me, but are you by any chance one of the decisive zero point one one four two four nine per cent who voted Conservative in 2010, and are you likely to be doing the same this May?'

But obviously David Cameron can't knock and ask himself. He's too busy running the country and campaigning and stuff. So he asks if – as part of the battle plan – someone can go and knock on Mrs Smith's door for him. At which point one of the campaign's Big Dogs – Lynton Crosby, or Barack Obama's old campaign guru Jim Messina – picks up the phone to Grant Shapps, and says, 'We need to find out for the PM how Mrs Smith is going to vote in Warwickshire North.' And Grant Shapps says, 'OK, I'll find out.' So he picks up the phone to one of his regional chairmen, and says, 'You need to find out for me how Mrs Smith is going to vote in Warwickshire North.' So he gets on the phone to the

Warwickshire North election agent and says, 'I need to know how Mrs Smith is going to vote.' So the agent walks out into the election committee rooms and says, 'Do we have any info on Mrs Smith? She's that Golden Empty Nester on Coppice Drive.' And someone else says, 'Oh, Harry's just finished canvassing Coppice Drive. Hang on.' And he picks up this big sheaf of papers, each of which has a lot of names and addresses with a little tiny box next to them. And in the boxes are all these letters scrawled in fading blue biro. So he finds Mrs Smith's name, and he looks at the box beside it, and in the box is the letter 'C'. At least, it looks like a 'C'. It's a bit indistinct, but he's pretty sure it's a 'C'. So he says to the agent, 'She's a C.' And the agent nods, picks up the phone, calls the regional chairman and says, 'She's fine. She's a "C". Strong Tory.' So the regional chairman phones Grant Shapps, and says, 'All good. She's Tory.' And Grant Shapps phones the Big Dog and says, 'She's one of ours. It's all holding up well in Warwickshire North.' And the Big Dog nods, and passes Mrs Smith's name on to one of the worker bees, and the worker bee puts her name into Merlin, and Merlin does a bit of crunching and says, 'Based on my calculations, the Conservative party is going to win the seat of Warwickshire North by zero point one one four two four nine per cent.' And so the Big Dog picks up the phone to David Cameron and says, 'We've just had the latest returns back from Warwickshire North. It's tight, but we're going to hold on.'

Unfortunately, what David Cameron and the Big Dog and Grant Shapps and the regional chair and the agent and the committee room worker and the worker bees and Merlin don't know is that Harry has made a small mistake. He's seventy-two and his hip is playing up a bit. And it was a hot day. And he'd been out for the best part of two hours.

And then he'd knocked on Mrs Smith's door. She'd been very nice, and said she had always voted Conservative. But this time she was having a few doubts. Quite a lot of what Nigel Farage was saying made sense to her. Not all of it. But a fair bit of it. And she still wasn't happy about the gay marriage vote. She was a parishioner at St Nicolas. And the congregation there were still very upset about it all. So no, she was sorry, but she couldn't promise she'd be voting Conservative this time.

Which made things a little bit confusing for Harry. He could mark her down as an 'A', which means she's 'against'. But she hadn't gone quite as far as to say she was *definitely* against. He could put her down as a 'U' for Ukip. No, that was wrong. It was 'I' for Ukip. 'U' was 'Undecided', or something like that. But again, she hadn't *definitely* said she was voting Ukip. Probably best to put her down as a weak Tory. Now, what was that? Was it a 'W'? No, a 'P'. Why a 'P'? It didn't make much sense. But that was what they'd told him to write, so a 'P' it was. Damn it, he wished he could stop his hand shaking like that. And the bloody pen was running out of ink already. There. Mrs Smith. The soft Ukip voter of

158 Coppice Drive, Dordon. Who was about to become the Strong Tory voter of 158 Coppice Drive, Dordon.

And back in the committee rooms, someone is busily typing up another batch of canvass returns that Harry brought in yesterday. Real trooper Harry. Despite his hip he'd be out there on the doorsteps, rain or shine. But some of his writing was getting a bit hard to read. What was that letter? Was it an 'S'? Looked a bit like an 'S', but the last stroke had been cut short, making it appear as a kind of back-to-front question mark. No, on second thoughts, it looked like a 'C'. Harry's hands were a bit shaky. It was definitely a 'C'.

Which is how Mike O'Brien, former Labour Immigration Minister, former Labour Trade Minister, former Labour Solicitor General, former Labour Pensions Minister, former Labour Energy Minister, former Labour MP for Warwickshire North and current Labour party candidate for Warwickshire North, ended up being marked down by Merlin as one of the decisive zero point one one four two four nine per cent of the electorate who would go out on 7 May in Warwickshire North, vote Conservative and send David Cameron back to Downing Street.

So each of the three men has his vision. And they have their team. And they have destiny on their side. And now they have their plan.

But it's not *their* plan. Not really. The plan belongs to the handful of people who they've tasked with designing the plan. And the dozens of people below them. And the hundreds of people below them. And the thousands of people below them.

So Nick Clegg would turn up to a meeting, sit down at the head of the table and say to those around him, 'OK, so the campaign launch on Monday, have we got the grid all sorted?' And the people around the table would nod, and someone would say, 'Yep. The Queen. The cabinet office. The school. All nailed down.'

Ed Miliband would take a sip of his coffee, look around the room and observe, 'The polling. It's looking quite good isn't it?' And everyone would murmur their approval. 'Oh yes Ed, the polling's looking very solid.'

David Cameron would take off his jacket, slip it over the back of his chair and declare confidently, 'I understand the canvass returns are showing everything's going to plan in the marginals?' 'Yes Prime Minister,' they'd all respond, 'everything's going to plan.'

But they don't really know. They can't know. The plan has too many variables. Too many moving parts. Too many things that can go wrong, and will go wrong.

And in his tiny bungalow in Warwickshire, Harry is settling down in his old, frayed armchair, with the cat on his knee, a small glass of whisky by his side, and the television on in front of him. In the corner of the screen he can see a clock. And to his old and slightly tired eyes, it looks like it's counting backwards.

01.05 . . . 01.04 . . . 01.03 . . . 01.02 . . . 01.01 . . .

6. How Many Hens?

The question was, how many hens? One of the hens? Some of the hens? All of the hens? None of the hens?

This much was clear, the hens were not on the grid. And that really should have been the clincher. 'Sorry girls, but if you're not on the grid, you're not getting in.'

Or on. They weren't on the grid, so they shouldn't be getting on Ed Miliband's bus. Or anywhere near Ed Miliband's bus.

But the reality was, they were near Ed Miliband's bus. There were at least twenty of them, all in their little black dresses with their pink sashes, currently standing right outside Ed Miliband's bus, screaming and chanting for Ed Miliband.

What to do? They could just do nothing and hope they would all get bored and go away. But what if they didn't? It wouldn't look very good if he just hid inside. There didn't appear to be any crews about at the moment, but that didn't mean there weren't *any* cameras out there. There was always a camera out there these days.

They could apologize and cite 'security reasons'. But that would make him look ridiculous. What were they supposed to be doing, protecting Ed Miliband from the crack Al Qaeda hen suicide brigade?

No, assuming it was a real hen do (not one of those Channel 4 spoofs), they'd have to let at least some of them on. After all, this was what his campaign was supposed to be about, right? Getting out of Westminster, leaving the Bubble Breathers behind, taking his message out to the people. 'Four million conversations in four months,' they'd said.

Well, at least some of those conversations were going to have to take place right here, right now, in the middle of Chester. The issue was, how many?

They couldn't let them all on. It would be utter chaos. Hens in the toilet, hens running up and down the aisle, hens running amok all over the next Prime Minister's battle bus. 'Stand up to Putin? Ed Miliband couldn't even cope with Nicola and her mates from Knutsford.'

Maybe they should just let a handful of them on. But which ones? There were bound to be some Tory voters in amongst them. Or worse. Ukip. God forbid, Ed ends up splashed all over the papers with his arm round a hen who's been on Facebook bad-mouthing Muslims or Poles.

They could try to vet them. 'Labour hens only.' No, they couldn't. That would just look insane.

In any case, this wasn't primarily a political dilemma, it was a presentational one. These women were off on a hen do, not on their way to a party compositing meeting. They'd been drinking (even more than your average Labour delegate on their way to a compositing meeting). They were up for partying. If they weren't careful, there'd be a photo on the front of the *Sun* of a hen vomiting in Ed's lap. Or presenting him with a giant dildo. And what would Putin and the rest of the world think of that?

There was only one answer. Let Nicola, the bride to be, on.

Bob Roberts had already managed to find out she was a solicitor. That probably ruled out any extreme Facebook postings. Knutsford was a Tory area. But she seemed genuinely excited about bumping into Ed. They could make sure she didn't bring a bag on with her (security), which would eradicate the dildo danger. And anyway, if she was the only person on the bus, even if something daft did happen, there would be no one there to see it. Or more importantly, take a smart-phone snap of it.

So that was the answer. One hen. If your name was Ed Miliband, and you were two weeks from polling day, and you wanted to become Prime Minister of your country, then one hen on your battle bus was all you could afford.

There was a time – not such a long time ago, actually – when these three men would open their front doors, walk out into the street, and all they would see were people. Rushing to work, taking the kids to school, popping to the shops. And they would join them. They would step out of their front door and disappear seamlessly amidst the throng. Because they were people themselves.

Then they stood for election and things changed a little. They were no longer people but politicians. They still felt the same. They still did all the same things, in almost exactly the same way. But now when they walked out of their front door they noticed it was slightly more difficult to disappear.

Most of the time it was fine. But every now and then they would be at the school gates and someone they knew wouldn't be talking about sports day, they'd be talking about something they'd seen on the news. Or someone in the supermarket queue who they didn't know would share a little joke with them.

And where once there had just been people, now there were *The People*.

Then, over time, things changed again. Each of the three men was promoted. They started to appear in the papers a lot, and on the television a fair bit. They were all 'senior spokesman' for their parties.

They'd still walk out of their front doors, and join The People going about their business. But they were a little apart from them now. When they were at the school gates, they noticed how parents they didn't even know were coming up and saying hello. Now when they were in the supermarket, they'd hear a burst of laughter, they'd turn round and it would suddenly stop.

And they'd begun to compensate for it. When they were out alone, they'd find themselves walking just a touch faster, with a gaze that remained locked on some fixed point directly ahead of them.

Because The People were no longer The People. They'd become *The Voters*.

And then it had all changed again – a big change this time. Each of the three men had become leader of his party. Now when they walked out of their front door, there'd be a car waiting for them. They couldn't make it to the school gates as often as they used to. And when they did, the conversation with the other parents seemed more stilted and awkward than they'd remembered.

And The Voters had ceased to be The Voters. They had become this amorphous blob called *The Electorate*.

Then there had been the final change. The change each of the three men was living through now. There were no school runs. Or trips to the supermarket. Or walks alone.

When they opened their front door, there would be a car waiting. But now the door would be opened for them by a broad-shouldered man, with alert eyes.

And The Electorate had itself been replaced. It had become *Britain*. All those people they used to see scurrying past their front door had been reduced – nationalized you might say – down to a single noun. *Britain* was about to go to the polls. *Britain* was preparing to deliver its verdict.

Its verdict on them. Their exile was complete. They no longer had a say. Britain. The Electorate. The People. They all had a say. But not these three men. They had to stand back. And just wait for Britain's verdict.

*

How had this happened? When had it happened? Why had it happened? Where was it written that when you became a politician you had to resign your membership of the human race?

Ed Miliband certainly didn't know. He was the person who had won the Labour leadership election campaign using the slogan, 'Ed Miliband, he talks human.' OK, he hadn't personally signed off that slogan. It was a poster one of his supporters had knocked up himself. But it was indicative of how he was perceived at the time. He was a good communicator. He could talk to people. He could empathize with people. Everyone in the Labour party said so.

When he was working for Gordon, and the civil war with the Blairites was raging, it was him keeping the lines of communication open. 'The emissary from planet fuck' they'd called him. But he was chosen as the go-between for a reason. He could connect with people, even when they didn't agree with him. The Blairites understood that, and they respected him for it. They may not have voted for him, but they all respected him.

This reputation even went as far back as his days at school, at Haverstock. Haverstock was tough, with a lot of hard, working-class kids. To survive there you had to know how to get on, and mix with people. And he had. The education he'd received had been about so much more than passing exams. It had been about learning how to look after himself. About understanding that the world was a complex place, with people of all kinds of nationalities and cultures and races. He had understood. He'd fitted right in there. Which is why the other day they'd put out a party political broadcast, and his old school friends Socratis and Lucy had been in it. They'd both said it. How well he'd got on with everyone. Socratis had told people, 'He was a very bright guy. Picked everything up, so, so quickly.' Lucy had said he was someone who you felt you could trust. 'He was someone who quietly but determinedly was getting on with what needed to be done. Not being influenced, not needing to change who he was,' she'd said.

But then the Bubble Breathers had got to work. There was something a bit strange about Ed Miliband, they'd decided. You couldn't quite put your finger on it, but there was. Perhaps it was the way he talked. Not just what he said – though that was a bit odd as well, like you'd always caught him in the middle of a PPE lecture. But the way he said it, that rather peculiar nasal twang. And there was the way he looked. Awkward, like he'd just rented someone else's skin for the day. And that distracting little white patch on his hair, that really stood out at PMQs, and made it seem as if he'd just fallen foul of a seagull. And what about when you saw him with people, real people, not other politicians like him? He had this disconcerting way of staring intently at them when they were speaking. And whilst he was doing it, he wouldn't blink. Not once. He'd just stand there, unblinking. Staring at them. Staring through them.

So no, it was hard to quite put your finger on it. But

there was definitely something a bit *weird* about Edward Samuel Miliband.

And that was it. They hadn't been able to make 'Red Ed' stick. So now it was 'Weird Ed'. And The Salon – even though it wasn't really The Salon any more – had come to him and they'd said, 'Ed, we need to do something about this "weird" thing.'

So they'd started to take him out to places. Places where he could meet The People, to show he knew exactly what to do when he came into contact with them. That he wouldn't freak out, or anything. It would show The People he wasn't that weird after all.

They took him down to Billingsgate fish market at half-five in the morning. He met the market porters, people like Lenny 'Apples' Appleton, and 'Mad' Dickie Barrett. And it went OK. But it was supposed to be a private trip, and someone in The Salon leaked it to the papers. And it all sounded a bit weird. Who spends their time hanging around Billingsgate fish market at half-five in the morning? Unless they're buying some fish?

Then they decided to take him down to meet the anti-austerity protestors who were camping out around St Paul's. It would show he could connect with all kinds of people. Old people, young people, black people, white people with dreadlocks. But then it emerged in the papers that it was all getting a bit hippyish down there. The protestors were using drugs. There was a bit of free love about. Some people had started using the entrance to the Cathedral as a toilet. So The Salon decided it would probably be best if he didn't go down there after all. But then the fact he'd been thinking of going also got leaked. And people said, 'Why's Ed Miliband thinking of hanging out with a bunch of trustafarians on the steps of St Pauls? Fish markets first thing in the morning. Protest camps late at night. What is it with this guy?' It all sounded very, very weird.

And it quickly became clear to The Salon That Was No Longer a Salon that the trips weren't having the desired effect. So they decided on a more conventional response to The Weird Problem. Ed would give a speech. He'd stand up, and he'd say to The People, 'Some people think I'm a bit weird. But they're wrong. I'm not weird.' And then he'd sit down. And at that point The Weird Problem would go away.

Or that was the plan. So he sent out a twitter message to his followers (or The Salon That Was No Longer a Salon sent out the message on his behalf), announcing 'Later today I'll be speaking about all of this.' And the tweet contained four photographs. A bacon sandwich. David Cameron with a huskie. A bunch of photographers. And a pint of beer.

And then he gave his speech. He was not 'chiselled', he said. He was not 'square-jawed'. He looked a bit like 'Wallace' from the Wallace and Gromit cartoons. But that didn't matter. 'My true test of leadership is not just whether you look the part but whether you can retain your soul,' he said.

A couple of the Bubble Breathers thought it was quite

a good speech. But the rest pointed out that this was a man who wanted to be Prime Minister. And yet there he was on national television, talking to the country about his own jaw. And how he had trouble eating a bacon sandwich. And how he resembled a little plasticine man from Wigan. And how he sometimes worried about losing his soul. It was all a bit weird, to be honest.

And then The Salon That Was No Longer a Salon had a new idea. To show Ed Miliband wasn't weird they should stop taking him to weird places, and they should stop getting him to make weird speeches. Instead, they should start taking him to normal places, where he could meet normal people. Then he could give normal speeches about meeting those normal people. After which The Voters and The Electorate and Britain would then say to themselves, 'That Ed Miliband is always going to normal places and meeting normal people. He's not that weird after all. I think I might vote for him.'

So that's what he did. He gave a speech in which he talked about all the normal people he'd met. There was Gareth, a software developer, who Ed had wandered up to on Hampstead Heath. And Xiomara, a bar manager who he'd started chatting to in his local pub. And two young students, Helen and Beatrice, who he'd also met on Hampstead Heath. And Colin, who he'd met in hospital. But who had then died shortly afterwards.

And if you'd sat through the whole speech, it might have sounded all right. But by the time the Bubble Breathers had got hold of it, it sounded horrific. Ed

Miliband likes cruising the local pub scene, chatting up the barmaids. Or cruising around on his own on Hampstead Heath, accosting young women and men at random. Or creeping around hospital wards, pouncing on dying patients. Jesus, this guy isn't just weird, he's the new Jimmy fucking Savile.

And Ed Miliband was sitting there watching all this. Living through it all, like it was some sort of nightmarish out-of-body experience. And he was thinking to himself, 'What the hell is going on here? How did any of this happen? I'm exactly the same person I've always been. The same normal person I've always been. Just ask Socratis and Lucy.'

David Cameron remembered now. He'd been speaking in Bristol, and it had finished quite late, and they'd all been starving. So they'd gone to Nando's.

He didn't mind Nando's, actually. Chicken. What's not to like.

OK, it wasn't exactly his destination restaurant of choice. 'The Chiltern Firehouse or Nando's tonight, Prime Minister?' That was one of the small perks of the job. You got to make choices like that now.

But it had been a long day, and there were five or six of the team with him, and someone had spotted a Nando's just round the corner. So why not?

Yes, people would notice him. And the iPhones would be out, and the pictures winging their way round Facebook before anyone had finished their first bite of Peri

Peri. But there was no harm in that. David Cameron in Nando's with The People. Nice little bit of free publicity.

Not that publicity was the reason they were in there. They were in there because they were hungry.

And that's when she started coming over. The girl in that ridiculous print dress. It was her friend's birthday and they were all out celebrating, and would he come over and pose for a selfie. Yes, of course he would. Happy to. Let him just have a bite to eat first, and he'd be over.

Then she came back a second time. And then a third time. Yes, don't worry, he hadn't forgotten. Honestly, he'd be over, just give him a second.

So he finished his chicken, and over he went. Said hello to her, wished her friend a happy birthday, had a little chat — that awkward little chat he often had with the kids, who were always torn by the dilemma that they were hanging with the Prime Minister (cool), but also hanging with that evil Tory toff Prime Minister who despised poor people and wanted to bomb lots of innocent Arabs (decidedly uncool).

Then he posed for the selfie (she did some ludicrous gaping grin), and they all left.

But there it was. That stupid, gaping grin, beaming out from the front pages of the *Guardian*. A news story, 'Student who took Nando's selfie with Cameron criticises him over tuition fees,' *and* a full-blown 800-word article in which she'd been moved to explain, 'I didn't want to smile. I couldn't betray myself that much.'

Well, good for her. She'd shown him. Coming over again and again, badgering him for a photo. Pretending it was for a friend's birthday, when it had obviously been for her. But she'd turned the tables at the end. Not a smile, but a gormless, open mouthed, grimace. That had really stuck it to the man.

How many people did he meet? At receptions, charity events, campaign events, party events, political meetings, government meetings, head of state gatherings. Not including the people he'd meet off-duty, on those occasions when he and Sam managed to duck out of the bubble and get some time for themselves. Thousands. Hundreds of thousands, perhaps.

Say he met fifty people a day. There were a dozen or so just sitting outside his office. There were over thirty people in every Cabinet meeting. Every time he went over to the Commons there were 650 MPs wandering around. And at one time or other he'd bumped into almost every one of them. And they all had their own staff. And the House of Commons had its own staff. The cooks and the cleaners and the postmen and the clerks and the librarians and the attendants and the policemen and the security guys. Most of the time he'd be breezing past them, but every now and then he'd nod and say hello. Good politics. And the right thing to do as well, of course. Then say he went to a factory. He'd meet the owner and the manager and all his or her junior managers. And then he'd be walked round the business – the boardroom, out on to the shop floor, off into the canteen. He'd meet another fifty to sixty people on a trip like that. If he chaired a committee meeting, that would be another fifteen to twenty. He might do two or three of those a day. Then he'd usually go off to another public event. A school visit perhaps. There he'd meet the head and heads of department and the governors and the pupils and maybe a few parents. That would easily be another thirty to forty. Actually, forget that, a single class would hold about thirty (maybe a few less, Michael had been successful in getting the sizes down a little). Then in the evening he would normally be over to the House again for a vote or two (bumping into another thirty or forty people along the way). And then back to Downing Street for a charity function – he could meet as many as a hundred people at a time at one of those.

So fifty people was a conservative estimate. A ludicrously conservative estimate. But he saw a lot of the same people every day, so best to stick with fifty for the sake of argument. That meant as Prime Minister he'd meet 350 new people a week. Around 1,400 a month. 18,200 a year. By then end of his first term as PM he'd have met 91,000 people. That's 91,000 new people. A whole Wembley stadium full of new people. And most of them would be ordinary people. Teachers, factory workers, charity workers, small businessmen, nurses, policemen, soldiers, farmers. The People.

And they'd vanish. Disappear. Not even a footnote to a footnote in history. The only people who anyone ever remembered – who the Bubble Breathers made sure anyone ever remembered – were people like the Gorm-less Gaper. And she wasn't even one of The People. Ordinary people didn't come up and keep badgering him, then go running off to the *Guardian* pretending to be the La Pasionaria of Nando's. They'd take a nice dis-creet snap from a distance, shove it round to their friends on Twitter, and leave it there.

No, it was the oddballs that people remembered. The two-bit activists. The wannabe prisoners of conscience. The ones who *didn't* act like *normal* people. Who tried to make some great political point about bumping into him whilst he was eating a plate of chicken and coleslaw.

And this was the thing. The more Gormless Gapers he ran into, the more the Bubble Breathers pumped out their favourite narrative, 'the out-of-touch political class'. And the stronger the narrative ran, the harder he had to work to combat it. Which meant The League of Extraordinary Advisors had to come up with ever more normal, spontaneous yet ludicrously contrived photo-ops. 'We've got a problem with the out-of-touch-Tory-toff narrative again. Better get him in the hard hat, hanging off the side of a moving JCB, whilst talking to a bunch of guys in blue overalls on a building site in Crewe.'

And the more he did, and the more normal, spontan-eous people he exposed himself to amidst these normal, spontaneous, utterly contrived photo-ops, then the greater the chance of bumping into yet another Gorm-less Gaper. It was like a form of Russian roulette. Except he was playing with 91,000 bullets in the gun.

And how the hell had all this happened? It wasn't that long ago he'd been walking out of his front door in Notting Hill as an ordinary person himself. Jesus Christ, all he'd wanted was some chicken.

Theresa May had told Nick Clegg she'd ring him back. And she'd better fucking ring him back. Fast.

When they gave him the protection officer he'd half expected it. Deputy Prime Minister might sound important enough to a lunatic, or a bunch of terrorists who thought the actual Prime Minister was too tough a nut to crack. The Cell had thought it was great – a sign they'd all finally arrived. But then The Cell didn't have this guy padding round after them eighteen hours a day.

It was bearable, though. Then they told him he'd have to have a car. A proper bomb-proof car, with run-flat tyres, and CS gas canisters, and all the rest of the chrome. The sort of car Cameron had. And Netanyahu.

That had made him think a bit. But what could he do? This was what he'd signed up for. Well, it wasn't quite what he'd signed up for. But it was what it was.

This shit he hadn't signed up for, though. It was all getting too fucked up now. They'd turned his street into a zoo. Almost 200 of them. Protestors. Anarchists. The St Paul's mob. They called it a street party. But it wasn't a party. It was intimidation, plain and simple. Yes, there were banners and jugglers and musicians and poets.

But they weren't there to spread love and joy. They were there to scare him. And Miriam. And the boys.

Well they'd got their wish, these street heroes. Fortunately, he and the family had been out. But they'd managed to scare a lot of the young kids who lived in the houses next door. And their parents. Which was the point. They were trying to divide him from his neighbours. Trying to get them to turn on the Cleggs and drive them away. Again.

That's why he'd picked up the phone to Theresa May. He'd had enough. Being spat at in the street. Getting shit through the letterbox. Now this. He wasn't going to be forced to start running. Not again. Not now. Not by them.

She'd been sympathetic enough. In that cold, distant way of hers. She understood how threatening it must all have felt. Looked very different when you were the target of that sort of thing than when you read about it in the papers. She'd have an immediate look into what had happened, and see what could be done. Of course, the officials had made it clear it would be difficult to provide complete security unless he moved into one of the official residences. And as far as she understood it, he'd rejected that suggestion. Publicly. And there was the issue of resources. She was locked in a battle with Downing Street at the moment over police numbers. There may be presentational issues if it appeared special treatment was being given to members of the cabinet. And he did already have quite a high (and costly) protection classification for a DPM. No, she understood that. He couldn't really ask his protection officer to pull out his gun and start blasting away at a couple of beat poets. Give her a couple of hours and she'd get back to him.

But he knew what she'd say. He could already see far enough beyond his own sense of anger and injustice to know what her response would be. A couple of uniforms outside the house for the next few days. An increase in mobile patrols up and down the street. A new set of instructions to the area commander.

But he wanted more than that. For a start, he wanted the whole bunch of them thrown in jail. Although he knew they wouldn't be. They'd been 'peaceful', in their own very deliberate, insidious, passive/aggressive way. And he knew once his anger subsided he'd have to acknowledge that. Put out some statement about people having every right to protest peacefully. He was a liberal after all.

And he wanted it to stop. He wanted to be able to walk along his street, knock on every door, and say, 'I'm really sorry. You shouldn't have had to put up with any of this. But I've dealt with it. I've spoken to the Home Secretary. Nothing like this will ever happen again.'

And he wanted to look Miriam in the eye and say, 'I'm sorry. Nothing like this will ever happen to you or the boys again.'

And there was something else he wanted. He wanted to understand why. How. How had it come to this?

The usual crap about politicians being out of touch, separated from the people. He got all that. Hell, it wasn't so long ago he was spouting it himself.

But this? This was insane. Two years ago he was the most popular politician in the country. They were mobbing him in the street. In fact, he wasn't a politician. He was *one of them*. Nick Clegg was One of The People.

And now it was hot saliva and dog shit and mobs on his doorstep. *He* was the one who was supposed to be out of touch? *He* was the one who didn't get it? Some of the people sitting down in the middle of his road had brought their own kids to the protest. *Their own kids.* To sit outside the house of a man they didn't know, trying to scare his wife and scare his own children? Is this what The People had become now?

How had they become that? Why had they become that? He didn't know. All he knew was that Theresa May had better fucking ring him back.

It's another of those strange paradoxes these three men face. They are accused of being out of touch with The People. But the more they reach out to them, the more distant they seem from them. They are accused of not understanding The People. But what they really don't understand is when they stopped being one of The People. Every single day they are forced to prostrate themselves at the blessed feet of The People. And each time they do they see those feet are in fact made of clay.

But they can't say that. Not just because the politics dictates they can't say it. But because they daren't say it. If it's The People who are ignorant and narcissistic and shallow and fickle – rather than the politicians – then what's it all for? What are these three men doing? The spit and the shit and the bile. Who's it all been for?

So they sit there, staring at the clock in the corner. But The People aren't sitting there. They haven't experienced the tightness in the chest, or the dryness in the mouth, or the sensation they are swimming underwater. They're down the pub, or watching another channel, or getting ready to go to bed. They don't have to wait. Their verdict's already been delivered.

So they can't see the clock counting down:

01.00 . . . 00.59 . . . 00.58 . . . 00.57 . . . 00.56 . . .

7. The Bubble

The first hour of the day was the best. It was the hour David Cameron still owned. Straight up or another five minutes in bed? Cereal or toast? Shave first or brush his teeth first? His decision.

The rest of the day belonged to The League of Extraordinary Advisors. And the Big Dogs. And the Bubble Breathers. And The People. He would be going where they told him to go. Saying what they told him to say. Doing what they told him to do. Acting the way their focus groups told him they wanted and expected him to act.

But not for this first hour. The League of Extraordinary Advisors and the Big Dogs and the Bubble Breathers and The People did not yet have a settled view on cereal or toast.

But as soon as he stepped through that door with its little coded keypad, he belonged to them. And he knew it immediately. A commute from home to work constituting a single step.

Down the narrow Number Eleven staircase (the flat in Number Ten was too small for three kids), lined with the cartoons of dead politicians. A nice reminder of his personal and political mortality.

Then out of the front door, and into the idling car. Downing Street could be surprisingly peaceful at this time in the morning. Too early for any protestors. Not too early for the snappers, they never slept. But it wasn't worth hanging around outside just to get a shot of him walking to the car.

There were some days when it would be worth it. 'A terse-looking David Cameron left Downing Street this morning, the strain of the crisis that has engulfed his government etched across his face.'

But there was no crisis today. Today was just another day inside The Bubble.

Though that sort of depended on your definition of The Bubble. To some people Westminster was The Bubble. The freaks, the fortune tellers, the exotic dancers, the forbidden animals. To them, the whole political circus was The Bubble.

For others the general election was its own Bubble. Those five frenetic weeks once every five years when the freaks and the fortune tellers and the exotic dancers and the forbidden animals took the show on the road.

And for others this was The Bubble. This air-conditioned Jaguar, making its serene progress through the congested streets of central London. Not that he'd actually wanted his progress to be quite this serene. One of his first acts as Prime Minister had been to dispense with the motorcycle outriders. But then he'd got stuck in traffic on his way to Buckingham Palace. After which they'd explained to him that a stationary target presented quite a tempting target for an RPG. Which had been another, rather more graphic, reminder of his mortality. He'd agreed to have the outriders reinstated soon afterwards.

So there he was, gliding towards Euston Station, in his little convoy, with the tail-car flashing up its electronic V-sign to The People behind – 'Keep Back'. A Bubble within a Bubble within a Bubble.

And now he was on their dime. Every minute of his day was mapped out by the LOEA and the BDs with military precision. The Grid? Pah. When it came to managing The Bubble the grid was a piece of old parchment, with a few dotted lines scrawled on it, and a big cross marked 'here be treasure' on the back. The Schedule on the other hand. The Schedule was The Bubble's GPS.

Not just where David Cameron would be, and what he'd be doing, minute by minute. But where he'd be and what he'd be doing street by street, doorway by doorway, staircase by staircase. '13.35 PM arrives Turner Road entrance. Met by Mr John Smith, director, ABC Holdings and wife Jane. Enter through first set of double doors. Turn right, up first flight of stairs, turn left, through set of double doors, then right, into the boardroom. 13.37 PM meets directors of ABC Holdings. Mr Brian Smith, Mr Graham Smith, Mr John Smith Snr. Ms Emily Smith. 13.45 PM exits boardroom, turns left, moves along corridor, turn right SECOND set of doors, move down the stairs, turns left through large steel doors, on to factory floor. Met by Mr Reg Smith, Mr Tommy Smith and Mrs Val Smith . . .'

And that was just the main schedule. The bullet-catchers had their own schedule, with primary entry and exit routes, and secondary entry and exit routes, and super expedited entry and exit routes. In fact, the bullet-catchers' schedule was so detailed it basically tracked his movements down to the nearest yard. One guy's job was to stand by the kerb at *exactly* the spot where the car needed to stop. Literally he'd stick out his arm, and whoosh, there'd be the Jag's bumper, parallel to his arm. The arm got overshot once, and boy, was there a fuss. Next visit the guy brought his arm down in such an exaggerated fashion he looked like he was auditioning for a part in a Bruce Lee karate movie.

But that's how detailed The Schedule was. It mapped the progress of The Bubble right down to the very last arm.

And now he was at Euston. '07.45 Arrive Euston Station, Melton Street car park entrance. Cross paved concourse, turn right, through automatic double entry doors, up escalator (left hand side), turn left, ahead across main concourse, then left at walkway, then right through ticket barrier (Platform 11 and 12, right hand side barrier), on to platform 11 (right hand side), enter first Virgin Trains carriage (buffer side), at first door (buffer side), PM party occupies seats A1, A2 . . .'

That's how it worked. As smoothly as that. No swearing at the ticket machine because he'd forgotten his booking code. No arguments at the ticket barrier because he'd got an off-peak ticket, and the train left before 09.26. Just levitated on through.

So the train was no longer the 08.01 service to Manchester Piccadilly. It had now become the 08.01 Bubble to Manchester Piccadilly. Or the final carriage had. Or half a carriage.

No point in The Bubble being any larger than it needed to be. 'Sorry Mrs Tanner. Your seat has been commandeered by the Prime Minister. I know, very inconvenient. What, you're heading up for your grandson's birthday. And you were going to vote for the Prime Minister, and now you're not? And you're going to write to Virgin Trains to complain? And your local paper? Totally understand. All most unfortunate.'

This was a trip to Manchester, not the Finland Station. No need to seal off the whole train. About a dozen seats should do it. Bit of space for the PM to work. Couple of seats for the bullet-catchers. Press guy. Body guy. Couple of general logistics wizards. That should be it. Every time Obama goes to the shops there's a twenty-vehicle convoy. David Cameron's Bubble is discreet by comparison. A very British bubble.

But of course, that's just the PM and his party. Down the other end of the train – tucked safely away in steerage – were the Bubble Breathers.

There were about ten BBs on this trip. It was expected to be a relatively low-key visit, to a school, so it was essentially the PM's regulars – the broadcast journalists and wire service scribblers and a couple of photographers who would be tasked with covering him for the duration.

Nothing ever happens on the school visits. A school is, by definition, a tightly managed environment. Or the schools prime ministers visit are. They have good results and well-behaved pupils and are run by head teachers who combine all the best attributes of General Patton and Mother Theresa. 'The Prime Minister visited a school in Greater Manchester today and was stunned after a fight broke out in a classroom, two teachers were caught in flagrante in a stockroom cupboard, and the head prefect was apprehended selling pot behind the bike sheds.' No one has ever read a story like that, and they never will. A school provides its own ready-made Bubble within a Bubble within a Bubble.

But the BBs weren't especially bothered by that. They displayed an easy camaraderie, born of the knowledge this would be a lengthy campaign, and that they were destined for many long days and dangerous nights together before this was all over.

It was the same at the other end of the train. David Cameron and his team were already slipping into the rhythm of life on the road. The League of Extraordinary Advisors were taking the opportunity to dress down – Alan Sendorak ('Senders'), his head of political press, was sporting slacks, an open-neck shirt and moccasins – and were deporting themselves with a languid confidence. For the Road Crew the Bubble within a Bubble within a Bubble actually represented a form of escape. A release. This was the moment they'd been working towards for five years. They were – finally – living through the days of decision.

So The Bubble moved steadily northwards. David Cameron contemplated taking the time to doze. Or simply think. He could have gazed out of the window, watched the countryside drifting by and just floated away for a couple of hours. But opposite him sat his famous red ministerial box. And in it was the final draft of the manifesto. Red for danger. Red to remind him, 'You could float away. But then you'll have less time to study the manifesto. And then you'll miss something. A single word or sentence. A misplaced table, or a skewed line on a graph. And then they'll pounce. They'll seize on it and run with it and hammer you with it. They'll hammer you again and again and again until there's nothing left. Nothing left of your precious manifesto. Nothing left of your dreams of an historic second term. Nothing left of you.'

So David Cameron didn't doze. And The Bubble continued northwards.

Meanwhile, down in steerage, there was a little frisson of excitement amongst the Bubble Breathers. The Labour party had set a trap. Or tried to set a trap. They'd announced they would abolish the tax-free status of non-domiciles living in the UK. How would the Tories respond? Agree with the policy, and look like they were dancing to that weirdo Ed Miliband's tune? Or oppose it, and make it look like they were dancing to the tune of some oligarch from Kiev who comes to London twice a year to visit Harrods and Stringfellows?

But suddenly there was Senders, doing a bit of insouciant spin. Some worker bee back at head office had dug out a clip of Ed Balls from a year ago, saying abolishing non-dom status was a daft idea that would cost the taxpayer billions. Or something along those lines, the clip had been edited a bit. But here it was.

So Senders' phone was passed around, and then the Bubble Breathers started to toss it about. The story, not Senders' phone.

Labour had got a hit, yes. But not a clean hit. That clip of Balls was embarrassing. But it was also going to be awkward for David Cameron if he was seen sticking up for Stringfellows' Dmitri, rather than the hard-pressed British taxpayer.

Not that it really mattered either way, because they had their line for the day. They didn't have to bother about boring themselves and everyone else to tears with a bunch of worthy questions about education. All anyone would want to know was whether the Prime Minister thought Dmitri should be getting another lap dance courtesy of HMRC.

The problem was, they'd have to wait a while to put it to him. He was tucked away at the back of the train, and they were stuck down here at the front. Ten carriages and an entire Bubble away.

It was another ninety minutes or so before they finally

pulled in to Manchester. Ninety minutes in which David Cameron's had the opportunity to work out his LTT (line-to-take) on Dmitri. In fact, he was going to have another thirty minutes or so to get it smoothed out.

Because the Bubble Breathers weren't going to get the chance to breathe that rarefied prime ministerial air that nourished them so, quite yet. They were being ushered by The League of Extraordinary Advisors towards their waiting Battle Bus.

The Battle Bus was the press's very own Bubble within a Bubble within a Bubble. Actually, it wasn't so much a Bubble as a large, four-wheeled prophylactic. Inside it was cold and sterile – lots of smooth black leather seats, and pristine, Teutonic engineering. But emblazoned on the outside, in huge lettering, was the enticing promise of 'A Better Future For You, Your Family and Britain.' The Battle Bus had one function, and one function only. To insert the press into the prime ministerial Bubble, and then withdraw them as quickly and safely as possible.

On rare occasions David Cameron rode the Battle Prophylactic himself. But not today. Today he needed that extra thirty minutes to get Dmitri clear in his head and double-check that table on page twenty-seven of the manifesto. So the Bubble Breathers were herded by Senders & Co across the station concourse, towards their waiting chariot.

This was important. The BB's had to be herded on to the bus *before* David Cameron got off the train and levitated to his car. Why? Because who knows who he might have bumped into on his way. '11.33 Exit train, second door (engine side), turn right across platform, through ticket barrier (left hand side), turn left, down escalator, turn right at group of twenty Bedroom Tax protestors screaming, "Fuck the Tory scum," turn right, at group of people in wheelchairs chained across entrance, turn left at man dressed in *Daily Mirror* chicken costume, turn right at people wearing fox masks chanting, "blood, blood, blood on your hands!" . . .'

The fucking of Tory scum is most definitely not on the grid. Plus, imagine if the BBs *did* get sight of Cameron getting off the train. Cameras rolling, snappers snapping, scribblers scribbling. It really didn't matter what they saw. At that point The Bubble ceased to be The Bubble. Or worse, The Bubble was still The Bubble, but they were *inside* The Bubble. *They'd penetrated The Bubble!* Before anyone was ready for penetration! And the penetration would be taking place *at a train station!* And a train station was not, by any stretch of the imagination, *a tightly managed environment!*

So off the BBs went, shepherded (moccasin first), on to the Battle Prophylactic, as veteran Press Association photographer Stefan Rousseau (who's covered everything from Rear of the Year to the war in Iraq) muttered to no-one in particular, 'Unbelievable. They wouldn't let me get a shot of him getting off the train. Unbelievable.'

You'd better believe it brother. This wasn't any old

Bubble. It was a League of Extraordinary Advisors' Bubble.

And now The Bubble was moving again, heading North by North West. Or, for those with slightly less romance in their hearts, along the A666 towards Bolton.

In the back of the Jaguar David Cameron was preparing. Getting his game face on. Running through his head, word by word, exactly what he was going to say, and how he was going to say it. 'What we've seen from Labour this morning is frankly pretty shambolic.' No, not 'shambolic', 'chaotic'. Chaos was better. The threat of Labour chaos was one of the key attack lines. 'What we've seen from Labour this morning is frankly pretty chaotic. On the one hand saying they want to get rid of non-dom status, but on the other hand saying if they did so it would cost the country money.' That sounded good. This wasn't about him. It wasn't even about Dmitri and his lap dancers. 'This goes to a bigger issue. Which is, when you see such confusion over a policy like these . . .' Cut. Do over. 'This goes to a bigger issue. Which is, when you see such confusion over a policy like this, are these people really capable and competent of running an economy?' Classic deflection. They asked about non-doms. You responded with your own question about Ed Balls and Ed Miliband. And then you supplied your own answer. 'I think people will conclude they're not.' Very nice. But the pay-off wasn't quite strong enough. 'I think people will conclude "they're not".'

Better. David Cameron speaking for The People. But it needed to be slightly punchier. 'I think people will conclude, "no, they're not".' That's it. Take a beat after 'conclude', lean in knowingly. It's there. Now, that table on page twenty-seven . . .

On the Battle Prophylactic they were preparing too. 'Yes, we're about twenty from the school . . . no, of course . . . non-doms . . . no, nothing on education . . . you've got the Balls clip . . . no . . . Tories are still on the back foot . . . what . . . no, sorry, I'm not being precious, but I'm not standing up doing a piece to camera while we're doing 60mph . . . what . . . no . . . if the driver touches the brakes I'll be all over YouTube.'

Twenty minutes later – an hour in Bubble Mean Time – the BBs were pulling up outside the Sacred Heart Roman Catholic Primary School. All around the streets were quiet. Apart from the giant bus, and the posse of outside broadcast vans and the police vans, nothing was stirring. It was as if Bolton could sense a showdown was coming. Or possibly it's just that Bolton was enjoying the Easter break, which is why the visit to Sacred Heart was actually a visit to a holiday study camp. The need for a tightly managed election backdrop was something the drafters of the fixed-term parliament act had failed to factor in.

So the assorted cameramen and snappers and anchors and hacks were ushered off the bus, and finally guided through the outer membrane into the pristine and hygienic confines of The Bubble. The Bubble Breathers were where they belonged, at last.

Well, some of them were. Senders was patiently but firmly explaining that a 'pool' system would be in effect. In this context 'Pool' is a polite term for the introduction of a form of Bubble Breathing Apartheid. A new Bubble within a Bubble within a Bubble had been created (the classroom just down the hall), which was where the Prime Minister would meet a small number of pupils and join them in the reading of a short story, the *Paper Bag Princess*, by Robert Munsch. Munsch . . . 's-c-h'. Obviously the entire pack of Bubble Breathers couldn't be allowed to descend en masse on these unsuspecting infants, it would be too disruptive to the lesson (even though this was not a real lesson, and everyone knew the whole thing had only been put on for the benefit of the cameras). So a small, hand-picked number of BBs would be allowed in, and they would then share their pictures/words with everyone else.

Sometimes the Bubble Breathers accepted this pernicious form of separate but equal development, and sometimes they raged against the machine. Today they weren't fussed about the *Paper Bag Princess* (no one ever gets a story from a school visit, never mind a holiday study group), so long as they got their opportunity to get their clip with David Cameron on non-doms. Senders assured them they would. *Paper Bag Princess* first. Then Dmitri the West End lounge lizard.

So a couple of snappers and a cameraman and another couple of scribblers were prized away from the main pack and led by Senders & Co along the hallway and into the classroom. In the middle of the room were four young children and a teacher, all of whom were sitting around a table and self-consciously trying to act as if a gaggle of still photographers and TV cameramen and print journalists and press advisors and assorted other aides and protection officers and prime ministers pop in to their reading lessons every day. Which is precisely how The League of Extraordinary Advisors advance team had told them to act. 'Just be yourselves.'

And the Pool, apologetically but ruthlessly, encircled the table. 'That's OK darling, don't look at me, you just carry on with what you're doing.' 'Can I just ask you what you're name is? Lucy? Lucy's a lovely name. And what's your surname? Sorry, I mean what's your second name. Howarth? Can you just spell that for me? H-O-W-A-R-T-H. Great. Lucy Howarth. Fantastic name.'

And all the while one of the LOEA's had started a methodical countdown. 'The PM's five minutes out.' 'The PM's two minutes away.' 'OK, they've arrived. Right, can we all move back please. Can we give the PM and the children some space.'

Dutifully the Pool moved back, creating a semi-circle around the sides of the room. And though they didn't know it, in that instant Lucy Howarth and her three friends were sitting in a Bubble within a Bubble within a Bubble within a Bubble within a Bubble.

Then the door opened, and there he was. Tall, dark

and handsome, in his dark blue suit and burgundy tie. The Paperbag Prince.

'OK, are we going to do a little reading?' David Cameron looked down at the children. The children looked up at him, looked across at their teacher, then let out a nervous giggle.

He moved around the table and settled down in the empty chair that had been left for him next to Lucy. 'And what's your name? OK Lucy, do you want to start?' Lucy looked up at him and smiled.

He picked up the book. 'What are we reading? *The Paperbag Princess*. I'm not sure I've read that one to my children. Would you like to read a little bit of it to me?'

Lucy looked at him, looked back at her teacher, and smiled again. From the fourth Bubble the snappers and the cameramen and the scribblers and the press guys and the advance guys and the bullet-catchers and the headmaster peered into the fifth Bubble, expectantly.

'How about if I help? I'll do a line, you do a line.' Lucy just smiled.

He turned and looked at her. Her teacher looked at her. Her friends looked at her. The fourth Bubble looked at her.

Lucy Howarth glanced up at David Cameron and smiled one last time. Then with a little groan, she leant forward and gently let her head fall, face down, on to the table in front of her.

And the snappers snapped. And the scribblers scribbled. And the cameras whirred.

*

The first hour of the day was the best. But David Cameron didn't really mind all the other hours. The Grid. The Schedule. Creating a Bubble within a Bubble within a Bubble. It was the way the whole thing worked. The way things were supposed to work.

If you had a structure, if you had a plan, if you had rules – and you stuck to them, more or less – then most of the time things would work out. You just had to trust in the system, and trust in yourself.

Look at when they went up to Bolton. What was supposed to be a day trumpeting their education reforms had ended up being all about non-doms. He'd stuck to the line on it, and he'd stuck to it well. But the story had still got away from them. 'Ed Miliband's stand on non-doms shows whose side he's on.' 'Ed Miliband seizes the agenda.'

Then that little girl had put her head on the desk, and it had become the image of the campaign. 'Cameron's awkward school photo-op.' 'David Cameron visits school and one girl sums up how we'll all feel if Tories win General Election.' 'Cameron fails to impress schoolgirl with reading skills.' That wasn't how it had been at all. She'd just been a little overwhelmed by all the attention. Understandably. If people had been in the room, they'd have seen what actually happened. But they hadn't been in the room. That was the whole point of creating a Bubble within a Bubble within a Bubble within a Bubble.

And yes, after that there'd been a few minor wobbles.

A bit of muttering about how things were being managed. But they'd pulled a few moves to get the non-dom issue parked. And they'd stuck to The Grid. And The Schedule. And The Plan.

They'd got back on track. Or at least, he thought they'd got back on track. Tonight, as he stared at that screen, he had to believe they'd got back on track.

So he's sat there, in Oxfordshire, in his own private Bubble of one. And 150 miles away, in Bolton, Lucy Howarth is sound asleep. Tucked up safely outside The Bubble. She's dreaming of dragons and knights and fairytale princesses. And she's blissfully unaware of the clock that's counting down on her Paperbag Prince: 00.55 . . . 00.54 . . . 00.53 . . . 00.52 . . . 0.51 . . .

8. Willy Wonka, Ralph Miliband and the Big Idea

That had everyone stumped. When he first bounced it off a couple of members of The Salon That Was No Longer a Salon it had stumped them as well.

Well, that was good. Now they'd all have to think for a second. And thinking never did anyone any harm.

Not that everyone on the team agreed with that proposition. When he first said he wanted to do a PowerPoint presentation, there were a few raised eyebrows. And then when he said he wanted to build it around his father, there were one or two people who inserted a note of caution. And then when he said he wanted to introduce some slides of Willy Wonka and Margaret Hodge, those same people came right out and said they thought it wasn't a very good idea.

And he listened to them. It was always important to listen. But whilst he was listening he gave them The Look. The Look involved him twisting his body ninety degrees and placing his right elbow down on his desk, with the palm of his right hand on the side of his cheek. He'd still be listening, but he'd be looking at a spot somewhere just over their right shoulder. And whenever the person opposite saw the look, they knew.

So Ed Miliband had given everyone the look. And now he had his audience well and truly stumped.

And it was a smart audience. Yes, the Bubble Breathers were in attendance. Along with some of the usual political padding. But there were a lot of sharp cookies out there as well. Ed Miliband's type of cookie.

Because this was none other than a Google audience. Or at least, it was a Google event. A Google 'Big Tent' event. Actually, a Google 'Big Tent Hang Out'.

And they'd invited him to hang with them. The Bionic Nerds. And did he know something about being a nerd in a world of cool kids? Oh yes, by God, Ed Miliband knew all about that.

Which was why he had decided this was the moment. The moment he'd been waiting for. The moment to unveil his VISION.

Ever since he'd made that throwaway remark about how he was starting his leadership with a 'blank piece of paper' they'd been on at him. 'What is Ed Miliband's big idea?' 'What does Ed Miliband really believe?'

And like all the other questions they'd directed at him since he'd become leader, they were rhetorical questions. Who was he kidding, they weren't questions at all. They were sneers. Put downs.

'Ed Miliband doesn't have a big idea.' 'Ed Miliband doesn't really believe in anything.'

They couldn't be more wrong. He didn't have one idea, he had dozens of ideas. Hundreds of ideas. Small ideas, big ideas, some ideas as big as your face.

That's because ideas were his life. When he was young, he'd sat there looking up at his father and his friends – literally and rhetorically – absorbing ideas. At first it was their ideas. But then over time he'd started taking his own thoughts and his own arguments, slowly piecing them together and crafting ideas of his own.

He remembered one occasion when some of his father's friends had stayed for dinner. They'd been debating some pressing political issue or other, and he'd stepped in with an opinion of his own. And one of his father's friends had attempted to dismiss it. Just rejected his statement out of hand. Bang! His father had come storming on in. He'd angrily defended his idea. Defended his right to have an idea. Defended *him*. And David. David might have been there too.

Yes, Ed Miliband had plenty of big ideas. A blank piece of paper? He could fill a thousand pieces of paper with his ideas. Whole volumes. Entire libraries.

So this was the question. The one that had them all stumped. Who was the odd one out?

- a) His father, the Marxist Professor Ralph Miliband
- b) Margaret Hodge, chair of the Public Accounts Committee
- c) Willy Wonka
- d) Google

Tricky? Well, they'd asked for ideas. So he was going to present them with an idea. A rather niche idea, admittedly. But they'd wanted an *Ed Miliband idea*. And now they'd got one.

Although it wasn't actually that complicated an idea. And it wasn't even that complicated a question that he was using to frame his idea. The answer was fairly obvious.

The answer was his father. His father was the odd one out. Why? Because his father was the only one of the four who didn't believe in capitalism.

It was easy really. When you took the time to think about it.

He'd even inserted a little clue, by stressing 'Marxist Professor'. That had really got The Salon That Was No Longer a Salon chaffing. 'But we're trying to kill off this Red Ed stuff aren't we?' Tough. They'd wanted an idea. Here was an idea.

Although technically he'd started with a question, not an idea. But that was his little test. Once people knew the answer to the question, they'd be able to see what the Big Idea was as well. Just like when he'd sat listening to his father and his friends. It would suddenly all click into place. They'd just have to work at it a little. Like he'd had to work at it.

And when they did work at it, then they'd finally get to his Big Idea. Which was this.

Willy Wonka believed in capitalism. Margaret Hodge believed in capitalism. Google believed in capitalism. And they were right to believe in capitalism. Sort of.

The thing Willy Wonka and the others had missed

was that because capitalism was here to stay, it didn't mean people didn't still have choices about what kind of society they needed. Ed Miliband believed people did have choices. He believed that deep down Willy Wonka also thought people had choices – just look at the way that at the end he'd handed his chocolate factory over to Charlie and Grandpa Joe. And he believed that deep down the British people thought that too.

Some people had said the opposite. Not about Willy Wonka or The People, but about him, Ed Miliband. That because he had this blank piece of paper, he didn't actually believe in anything.

Well he did. Passionately. He believed it was possible to build a *more responsible* sort of capitalism. A society that was more equal, not less equal. Where power was spread to the many, not concentrated in the hands of a few. Where people showed their responsibilities to each other.

And there was something else people said. 'What is he actually *for*?' Again, they didn't mean Willy Wonka, they meant Ed Miliband. 'What is Ed Miliband actually *for*?' they'd ask.

This was what Ed Miliband was for. He was for showing his father had been right.

Not right about everything. Nobody was right about everything. But right about this.

His father had come to Britain when he was sixteen. He'd joined the Royal Navy. And he'd talked to his son about those days. He'd sat down opposite him – in that same room where he and his friends brandished words like clubs and wielded them like rapiers – and he'd talked about how people from all walks of life had come together for a common purpose. 'This is how Great Britain succeeds,' he'd said.

OK, he may not have phrased it precisely like that. His father had some ambiguous views on patriotism and nationalism. But that was the gist of it. When people came together and worked together responsibly, that was how they secured success. It was how Willy Wonka had ultimately secured success. And it was how the nation would secure success when he, Ed Miliband, son of Marxist Professor Ralph Miliband, was Prime Minister.

This was his Big Idea. Only one of his Big Ideas. What he believed. What he was for.

And yes, for the moment he had them all stumped. He could see the Bubble Breathers raising their eyebrows and giving each other these silly little grins. And he could see the Political Padding looking ahead blankly. Although that was what the Political Padding was primarily there to do. And even the Bionic Nerds were looking a bit perplexed. Although they'd all stiffened up a bit when he'd criticized Eric Schmidt for quibbling over his taxes.

Well that was OK. Willy Wonka and Ralph Miliband and the Big Idea. They just needed some time to work through it. To process it. They'd get there in the end. All they had to do was work at it a little.

*

So they were all agreed. David Cameron. George Osborne. The League of Extraordinary Advisors. The Big Dogs.

They'd finally got it nailed down. The Big Idea for the election.

There would be no big idea.

And no one was more relieved than David Cameron himself. He'd had a Big Idea once. A really big, really brilliant idea. And it had turned out to be a disastrous idea.

They'd called it The Big Society. With a capital 'B'. A bold, upper-case, 30-point 'B'.

It involved harnessing the powers of the state to help stimulate social action. Social enterprises would be handed responsibility for delivering front-line public services. New community organizers would help every citizen to become a member of an 'active neighbourhood group'. Funding would be directed to those groups that could demonstrate ways of strengthening communities in deprived areas. A 'National Citizen Service' would be established to help bring the country together.

It was Big. Really, really Big. So they'd written it all out in this gorgeous little blue book. Not one of those glossy, soulless, corporate style manifestoes you usually see at election time, but a proper, tight-weave, hardcover book, with 'An Invitation To Join The Government Of Britain' on the front.

And people had loved it. 'An impressive attempt to reframe the role of government and unleash entrepreneurial spirit.' 'We demand vision from our would-be leaders, and here is one who offers a big one, of a society rebuilt from the ground up.'

But although people had loved it, The People hadn't loved it. They were decidedly cold on it, in fact. It turned out they weren't keen on signing up for active neighbourhood groups. Or enlisting in any National Citizens Service. They were too busy doing stuff like going to work, and doing the shopping, and putting the kids to bed. And they were pretty cold on the idea of the Salvation Army taking over the running of their local GP's surgery. Or whatever it was these Big Society advocates had in mind. Actually, they weren't all that sure what the Big Society was. And if they were honest, they didn't really want to know. They didn't want to join the government of Britain. All they wanted was the actual government of Britain to clear up the mess the bankers had left, as efficiently and painlessly as possible.

The Big Idea was why David Cameron had lost the election. Or why he hadn't won the election. At least, that was what David Cameron told David Cameron.

He'd broken his own golden rule. He hadn't trusted the system. Quite the opposite. He'd literally promised to break up the system, then rebuild it again from the ground up.

When what he should have been doing was sticking with the plan, and working hard, and playing by the same old rules. Economy. Leadership. Economy. Leadership. That was what won elections. That was what the Big Dogs kept telling him. It was what The League of

Extraordinary Advisors kept telling him (or what they told him most of the time. The League liked to dabble with ideas now and again, some of them quite big ideas. But they always had the good sense to return to first principles when their ideas became so big they threatened to get out of hand).

And they were right. Not that winning elections was all it was about. Power for power's sake was meaningless. Though not quite as meaningless as no power for no power's sake.

But he knew he had to be careful. There was a perception – primarily fashioned by the Bubble Breathers, but not without its other adherents – that there was something a bit light-weight about David Cameron. Or if not light-weight, then a bit false. Phony.

'Dave the PR man', they branded him. As if his time working as Director of Corporate Affairs at Carlton was something he should be ashamed of. Yes, he had been a PR man. A bloody good one.

A good enough PR man to know this line about him just being a PR man was potentially damaging. Which is why he'd been prepared to embrace the Big Society. And also why he'd been prepared to quietly drop the Big Society when he realized it had become a political albatross.

It's also why he'd been prepared to embrace some of the other Big Ideas people had foisted on him. Iain and his welfare reforms. Michael and his education reforms. Andrew and his health reforms.

Each of these proposals stood on their merits. Of course they did. And it was vital to show coalition with the Lib Dems hadn't blunted the party's radical edge. That the intellectual cupboard wasn't bare now the Big Society had been dumped.

But it was also important presentationally. Important to show there was more to David Cameron than just image and presentation.

And again, it had worked. For a while. 'The most radical programme of education reforms for a generation.' 'Reforms to our welfare system that bear comparison to Margaret Thatcher's great economic reforms.'

But again, while many people had been impressed, The People had not. Michael was at war with the teachers. Iain was at war with the disability lobby. Andrew was at war with everyone who had ever watched an episode of *Casualty* or caught a cold.

And that just wasn't how you won elections. Through waging war on people. Certainly not through waging war on The People.

So he'd had to step in again. Michael had been pushed sideways, with his thanks. Iain had been invited to move sideways, then told he could stay, but that he'd have to tone things down. Andrew had just been pushed. No thanks, nothing.

But that was what had to be done. They'd all agreed. No more big ideas.

What they needed were little ideas. Better still, no ideas at all. Or at least, no new ideas.

But they couldn't say that, of course. 'Vote for us for more of the same.'

That would have broken another of the rules. Which was that you had to present your programme as representing bold, radical change. Even if that wasn't what The People wanted. And even if that wasn't what you were offering them. 'Dependable old Zad. The washing powder that's not new, and not improved. Washes just as white as it's always washed.' No PR man worth his salt would come up with a pitch like that.

So that was the dilemma. How could David Cameron sell his programme of bold, radical consistency?

Which is why they were now all gathered in his modest office in Downing Street (only dictators had grandiose offices), with him perched on the edge of his favourite armchair that was tucked neatly in front of the fireplace, and GO and the BDs and the LOEAs arrayed in front of him.

It was here where they were finally going to work it out. How to sell their VISION. How to convince The People that by doing exactly the same thing for another five years they'd end up in a very different place.

And it was here, by the fireplace, that they saw it. David Cameron had been in a car. He'd been in a car, and the car had broken down. Actually, it wasn't David Cameron who had been in the car. Someone else had been in the car. He'd just been wandering along the road, and he'd come across the car. What had happened to the car had nothing to do with him. It was all the fault of some other guy who'd been driving the car.

Anyway, there's this car. And in this car is a family. And they're petrified. Why wouldn't they be? They'd been roaring along the road at God knows what speed, and then they'd gone swerving off the road and into a ditch. And the guy who'd been driving them, he'd just leapt out of the car and done a runner.

And that's when David Cameron turns up. He checks everyone is all right, and tells them, 'Don't worry, I'll fix this, and then we'll have you on your way.'

And the people in the back of the car are relieved. He looks like the sort of person they can trust. Not some hustler. Or worse.

So Dave the Mechanic pops the hood, and goes in. And he's under there for what seems like an age. He's hammering away, and pulling at the battery, and prodding the distributor and juggling with the alternator. And after a while the family are beginning to think, 'Maybe we were wrong. Maybe Dave the Mechanic *is* a hustler. Maybe he doesn't know anything about cars after all.'

And then just as they're starting to get properly worried, up pops Dave with a confident smile, slams down the hood, and says, 'OK, why don't you try starting her up.'

So Mum gingerly manoeuvres herself into the front seat, and turns the key. But nothing happens. 'Try her again,' says Dave the Mechanic. She tries again. Again, nothing. 'Give her another go,' says Dave with a confident smile. She tries a third time. Nothing.

And now Mum's starting to think, 'Oh, God, he really is a hustler. Or worse. And we're stuck out here all alone, and . . .'

And Dave says, 'It's OK. You can trust me. Give it one last go.' So she takes a deep breath, and turns the key one last time. And with a rasping cough, the car splutters into life.

So now the car's running again. But Mum can't drive. And the kids can't drive – they're only three and five. Sweet kids too. So Dave the Mechanic says, 'That's OK, you budge over. I've got her.'

And Mum thinks about it for a second. But really, what's to think about? They're stuck in the middle of nowhere, and that waster of a father has run off and abandoned them, and Dave the Mechanic did get the car going eventually, just like he'd promised.

So with a nod, she shifts across to the passenger seat. And Dave clambers in, and off they go.

They're driving. And the sun's rising high in the sky now, and it's a sweltering day, and all around them is emptiness. Nothing but scrubland as far as the eye can see.

And the car's running OK. Not getting up much speed, but that's fine. After what's just happened, they don't mind cruising along at a nice, steady pace.

But there's just one thing. Dave the Mechanic is chatting away, amiably. He's telling them all about how he fixed the car. He's going into great detail about how he pulled at the battery, and prodded the distributor and juggled with the alternator.

Which is fine. It's clear he does actually know a bit about cars. And he did get them back on the road. And Mum and the kids are very grateful.

But there's only one thing they need to know from him now. And it's not how he fixed the car.

What they want to know is, 'Where is this guy taking us?'

Dave the Mechanic looked around his office. And George Osborne nodded. And the Big Dogs nodded. And The League of Extraordinary Advisors all nodded.

That's it. They had it now. They knew how to sell it. The No Vision Vision. The No Idea Big Idea.

They'd spent all their time in government either with their head under the hood, or trying to explain what they'd been doing under the hood. Now they had to stand back and take a little time to explain to The People where it was they were actually planning to take them.

And it didn't need to be some grandiose place. A mansion with palm trees and marble floors and peacocks sauntering around the grounds. If they did tell The People that's where they were taking them they wouldn't believe it anyway. It just needed to be somewhere neat and tidy and cosy and safe. Somewhere familiar, that they recognized.

*

And now the sun has reached its zenith in the clear, blue sky. The deserted road pulls away in front of them, glistening and flickering in the heat.

And Dave the Mechanic turns to Mum and he says, 'Anyway, that's enough about how I fixed the car. You're probably wondering where we're going.'

Mum gives a nervous smile and nods.

'There's this little town about fifteen minutes up the road. There's not much there, but there's a store and a pay-phone, and the bus to the big city pulls in there twice a day. Will that be OK for you?'

And Mum goes to respond. But before she can, she sees Dave the Mechanic is now looking at her, with that reassuring smile on his face.

'Or, I could just pull over. And we could wait for your husband to come back.'

At which point Mum turns away and looks out of the passenger window. And all she can see, as far as her tired eyes can see, is that same endless expanse of nothingness.

The thing that bothered Nick Clegg about 'Equidistance' was that it was a great idea, but a lousy word. It was too mechanical. It lacked passion. It smacked of compromise.

He was trying to sell a VISION here, not a brand of washing powder. In fact, he wasn't trying to sell anything. He was trying to build something. Something that would stand.

Or that's what he had to get across. That idea that he was trying to do what he thought was right. That he didn't have a mysterious portrait hidden away in the attic, ageing a little more every time another starving student flunked their finals.

And 'Equidistance' didn't do the trick. It was a lawyer's word. Even worse, a politician's word. A word dredged up straight from the putrid, fetid heart of The Bubble.

And yet 'Equidistance' was a very good idea. As a way of encapsulating what he wanted from a second Liberal Democrat term of office, it really did do the job.

Though in theory what he wanted from a second term was what was in his manifesto. He knew he would have to be very, very firm on that point. What Nick Clegg *wanted* was every dot and comma that had been painstakingly written down in that funky-looking, psychedelic document promising 'Opportunity For Everyone'.

But he'd also have to be clear that what he *wanted* and what he *could have* were two entirely different things. Nobody could have *everything* they wanted, *all* of the time. Even though a document with a title 'Opportunity For Everyone' didn't exactly point a potential reader to a series of hard decisions ahead.

But there were hard decisions ahead. Whatever the outcome of the election.

And this was the essence of Equidistance. There were only two realistic outcomes on 7 May. One was a hung parliament with the Conservatives as the largest party. The other was a hung parliament with Labour as the largest party.

Either way, a hung parliament was all but inevitable. What wasn't inevitable was which way it would be hanging.

And that meant he had to be ready. As soon as the result was in (probably even before the result was in), and he heard the drum beat, and saw either David Cameron or Ed Miliband being led stoically towards the gallows, he'd slip on his domino mask, come galloping into the square on his trusty white steed, strike down their captors and whisk them to safety. Don Diego de la Clegg – The People's Champion – would again save the nation from political deadlock.

But to do that he had to be prepared to act without fear or favour. He couldn't be shown to be surreptitiously aligning himself with either side. If he were seen to be in league with David Cameron, Ed Miliband's supporters would shun him. If he were seen to be in hock to Ed Miliband, David Cameron's supporters would ostracize him. To be a true hero, Don Diego de la Clegg would have to demonstrate he was beholden to no-one, except The People.

Which was how the concept of Equidistance had been born. Or rather, how the concept of Equidistance had been thrashed out in a series of fractious meetings by Ryan and Jonny and Stephen and the rest of The Cell.

At the heart of Equidistance was an acceptance that compromises would again have to be made. That was the nature of coalition government. But this time those compromises would be clearly set out in advance of polling day. Or those issues that Don Diego would never compromise on – so help him, so long as there was breath in his body – would be clearly set out in advance of polling day.

What precisely these inviolate issues would be still had to be ironed out. But they would be designed to place him and his party firmly in the political centre-ground. Don Diego was a fiscally hard-headed man. But he was also socially compassionate. That was what set him apart from those who would seek to oppress or fool The People. Perfectly equidistant from them, in fact.

So Don Diego had his Big Idea. But as he'd confided to some of the occupants of the big white room, it didn't sound like a Big Idea. It lacked the necessary swash or buckle.

And there were some other problems with Equidistance. One was that whilst everyone agreed with the idea in principle, in practice some people wanted to be more equidistant than others.

Like Vince Cable, for example. When he'd sat down to talk Equidistance with Vince, he'd been decidedly cool about the whole thing. True, whenever he sat down with Vince, Vince was cool. He'd settle back, peer down that angular nose of his, and adopt the demeanour of a university lecturer asking a struggling student whether they thought this course was really for them.

But this time he'd been especially icy. Equidistance was all well and good. But did Don Diego understand what was going on out there? The Devil had the peasants by the throat. Governor Camerón was despised. To be seen to be merely 'equidistant' from such a man? How could they hope to win the trust of The People?

Or Danny Alexander. When he'd discussed Equidistance with Danny, he'd put on his serious look. It was quite endearing. Danny would narrow his forehead, and purse his lips, like a young child in a school play who's just been told, 'This is the part when you have to look like you're thinking very, very hard.'

Danny had understood. And he'd said he'd support him, of course he would. But not *everything* Governor Camerón had done had been bad. There were many people who still remembered what things had been like before the Governor and his man had arrived. And what about what they'd been hearing about that hothead Eduardo Zapata? He was roaming the countryside telling The People Don Diego was a charlatan and a fraud. Was it wise to be 'equidistant' from such a renegade?

There was another problem. It was all well and good starting to talk about equidistance a few months out from the start of the campaign. But for the last four and a half years Don Diego had been working side by side with the Governor. Obviously he'd been doing everything he could to undermine his dastardly plans from within. But The People couldn't see that. As far as they were concerned, Don Diego was the Governor's lapdog.

And there was one final problem with Equidistance. The problem was Don Diego himself.

It was almost as if there were two Don Diegos. There was the man who knew he had to do his duty by The People and those who supported him. Who understood he now had an opportunity – a once-in-a-generation opportunity, possibly – to change things for the better. If he stayed where he was, working by the side of the Governor, or Eduardo Zapata if he managed to seize power, then he could make a difference. If he kept doing what he was doing, he might be able to set The People free.

And there was the Don Diego who longed to free himself. Who the people in the big white room referred to as 'one of life's serial outsiders'. The man who wanted to settle, but could never settle. Who wanted to rest, but couldn't rest until he was out alone on the plains, chasing his dreams.

So as he settled himself into his high-back studded leather armchair, and distractedly tapped his foot on the red and green hexagonal carpeting, he could only reflect that it was not just the word Equidistance that was problematic. The whole VISION – the entire plan – was fraught with difficulties. With dangers. And deep down, in his heart, he wasn't entirely sure it was even a VISION or plan he agreed with.

But then he shrugged. What could Don Diego do? It was the only VISION or plan he had.

Now none of the three men can see the VISION. Their VISION.

It had once seemed so clear. So vivid. What they were going to do. How they were going to do it. Everything they were going to deliver. For The People.

But now they can't see anything. Except a clock.

00.50 . . . 00.49 . . . 00.48 . . . 00.47 . . . 00.46 . . .

9. The Loyalty Thing

'I shouldn't be here.' It's the first thing each of them thought when they first walked into the room. They'd just entered a completely unthreatening environment, a nice, middle-class flat in south London.

A group of friendly faces greeted them. Or if they weren't friends as such, they were at least kindred spirits.

And as each new arrival made their slightly nervy entrance, for a moment the mood lightened. 'Thank God. I'm not on my own.'

But then it darkened again. 'How many of us are there now. Eight? Ten? Can we all trust each other? How many more are coming? If we end up with twenty in here there's no way it won't get out.'

Someone cracked the joke. 'Were you followed?' Except they were only half joking. Nothing was in anyone's office diary. No one who was not in the room had been told they were meeting. Even those who *were* in the room hadn't openly discussed with each other *why* they were in the room. 'A few of us are getting together for a chat about where things are heading. You should come along.'

So they'd come. But they knew they hadn't just been

invited along for a chat. Or to chew the fat over where things were headed. They'd been invited along to help plot a murder.

Drinks were offered and rejected. And finally, with a look at her watch, The Hostess brought the meeting to order.

She began speaking with a hard, deliberate tone. It was time to drop the pretence. They all knew why they were here. Each of them could read the polls. They had all had the same conversations on the doorsteps. Every one of them had witnessed first-hand the confusion and chaos that currently passed for leadership in their party.

This could no longer be allowed to continue. They were heading for disaster. Something had to be done.

People nodded cautiously. Partly there was relief that, as she'd said, the pretence was over. They could now start to openly discuss what needed to be discussed. There was also a sneaking sense of admiration. 'Christ, you have to give it to her, she's got some guts. She's got us all here, *in her own flat*, and she's coming out with this stuff. *In her own fucking flat.*' But the sense of foreboding still hung there. 'Jesus, we're actually doing this. We're sitting here actually talking about taking him out. This is crazy. I should never have come.'

The next person to speak, Plotter Number Two, was supportive. In his view they had three options. One was a direct, overt challenge. 'Thanks Ed, for everything you've done. You brought people together at a difficult time; prevented things from fracturing. But now it needs someone else to take the party forward.'

The second was a delegation. The shadow cabinet. One or two greybeards. 'Sorry, but this can't go on. You need to change course. On the economy. On welfare. On everything, basically. And you need to do it quickly and publically. Or else.'

The third was an insurgency. 'Try to start shaking things up from within. Give some more speeches. Ramp up the briefings. Put down markers. Try and give ourselves a fighting chance. Or at least, get ourselves into a position where we can define the defeat. Salvage something from the wreckage.'

Plotter Number Two's own personal preference was for option one. A straight kill. Swift. Humane. Clean.

But everyone knew this was a choreographed intervention. Plotter Number Two and The Hostess were close. They were trying to lead them all down a predetermined path. Well, not so fast. There was potentially more than one life at stake here.

Plotter Number Three joined the discussion. If they did go for option one, how would it work? In practice?

Although it sounded a neutral question, it actually introduced a note of caution. Everyone present already knew how it would be done.

A letter would be circulated. Signatures obtained. Though not a real letter. It would be an email, from an anonymous Gmail account. And there would be no real signatures. Just a series of phone calls. 'OK, I'm in.' Nothing traceable.

Then another call would be made. The chief whip needed to see Ed. No, it wouldn't wait. It was happening. They weren't playing this time. How many? Hard to tell. Fifty. Sixty. No, not Ed or Chuka. Rachel or Harriet? No, not them either. At least, she didn't think so. It was hard to know. None of them were returning her calls. But the word was the junior shadow ministers were about to break cover. Patrick Wintour at the *Guardian* had already started ringing round. She understood they were going to press the button on the *World at One*. Resignations had been lined up for the following morning. Five or six. Timed to drop every two hours or so across the course of the day. The PLP Chair? Yes, she'd tried him. He wasn't answering either. What did Ed want her to do? What was Ed planning to do?

And now they'd all pictured it, it had become real. Viciously real.

Plotter Number Four introduced another word of caution. 'OK, say we do it. What then? Who takes over?'

The Hostess – 'What about Alan?'

Plotter Number Five – 'Alan? He's already been sounded out. Said he wasn't interested.'

And now they're all speaking at once.

Plotter Number Six – 'No, what Alan said was he wasn't interested if there was a contest. But there wouldn't be a contest . . .'

Plotter Number Seven – '. . . There isn't time. There'll

have to be a swift, clean kill, followed by a swift, clean coronation. If we could convince Alan he'd be crowned without a fight he'd probably go for it . . .'

Plotter Number Eight – '. . . But isn't that the problem? We've left it too late. We're less than a year from the election now. If we take out our own leader less than a year from the election who knows how the voters would react. How would the base react . . .'

Plotter Number Nine – '. . . And say we take Ed out, insert Alan, and then Alan crashes in flames. Then it wouldn't be Ed Miliband's defeat, it would be our defeat . . .'

The Hostess could sense which way this thing was drifting. For Christ's sake, she'd got them here, *in her own fucking flat,* and they were still all flapping around. What was wrong with these men?

The Hostess – 'Yes, there are risks. If we change leader this late on, no-one can know for certain how things will play out. But we know for certain how things will play out if we *don't change leader.* Look at the private polling. It's so bad he couldn't even risk sharing it with the shadow cabinet. We owe it to the party to act. We owe it to ourselves to act.'

Plotter Number Five – 'OK. But say we do move against him. How many people are sitting in this room? Ten of us. That's not enough. Not nearly enough.'

Plotter Number Two – 'But it isn't just us. There are others thinking of moving too. Seriously thinking about it. Ian. Simon. They're talking about going to see Dave Watts and saying to his face, "Enough's enough. You've got to tell him to quit." There's even talk that Tom is finally losing patience. If we could get Tom signed up then we really could finish him.'

And there was a moment of silence. It was all becoming real again. And everyone was thinking the same thing. 'Jesus, we're really talking about doing this. We're actually talking about taking out the leader of the Labour party. What if someone talks? What if he finds out? And why hasn't Plotter Number Ten said a word? Why the hell am I doing this? I shouldn't be a part of this. I shouldn't even be here.'

He had found out. Not all the details. He didn't have all the names and the times and the places.

But Ed Miliband knew. He knew it had gone beyond playground jibes. He knew they were plotting. Preparing to move in for the kill.

Or talking about moving in for the kill. The Salon That's No Longer a Salon was still pretty dysfunctional. But not as dysfunctional as it had been. They heard things. Saw things. Now and then people told them things.

So he knew. But the question was, what would he do about it? What should he do about it?

He could move first. Launch a pre-emptive strike. Sack someone. Make an example.

But then what if he was wrong? The Salon That's No

Longer a Salon wasn't as dysfunctional as it was. But it was still pretty dysfunctional.

Not that making an example of someone who turned out to be entirely innocent was necessarily all bad. Still sent a strong signal. But it would also smack of the old politics. And he didn't want to back anyone into a corner. Couldn't have the shadow cabinet starting to think, 'Jesus, if poor old so-and-so's getting the chop, and he wasn't anywhere near the flat, what chance do I have? I wasn't anywhere near the flat either. But I could have been. I was invited to the flat. Might as well help take him out before he takes me out. No point getting canned over a flat I've never set foot in.'

And even if he did want to back people into a corner, who did he have to back them into a corner with? It was all well and good bringing the boys down to the yard. But you had to have some boys to bring. Peter was gone. John was gone. Stewart wasn't even a proper member of the shadow cabinet. Chuka was almost one of them now.

There were no boys any more. If he was going to push back at them, he was going to have to do the pushing himself. Alone.

Of course, he didn't need to push anyone. He could just come out and call them on it. Wouldn't even have to name any names, just make an appeal, a direct appeal. Not even an appeal, a demand. He could demand unity. Go over their heads. To the party. To the country. Demand an end to the briefing. The plotting. The treachery.

But then he'd have to confront The Loyalty Thing. Or the Disloyalty Thing.

The Brother Thing.

The Brother Thing was to Ed Miliband what the boulder was to Sisyphus. Try as he might, he could never quite get it over the brow of the hill. Out of view.

In the end he'd developed a little line for dealing with people whenever they brought it up. Though not many did any more. Not directly.

'I'm sorry, but I don't subscribe to the ancient principle of primogeniture,' he'd say with a smile that wasn't really a smile. 'Especially when it comes to selecting leaders of the Labour party.'

It was a very neat line. A very neat, totally ineffective line. Nothing he'd done, nothing he'd tried, nothing he could ever do or try would make people forget The Brother Thing.

Ed Miliband may not subscribe to the ancient principle of primogeniture. But everyone else did. Which was why they didn't bring it up with him any more. They didn't need to. In the same way they didn't bring up the fact he had that strange white pigment in his hair, or that odd nasal twang. It was just another part of who he was.

Ed Miliband. The guy who had knifed his own brother.

They'd had meetings about it. During the leadership election, back before The Salon had even been a Salon. Whole meetings just to deal with The Brother Thing.

And they'd got it all down. They would explain to people how Ed felt it was important for the party to move on from the New Labour era. Then they'd talk about how he believed – fervently believed – his party needed a 'superior model of leadership' based on 'listening, empathizing and inspiring'. And finally, they would tell everyone about The Visit.

It was dark when Ed Miliband pulled up outside his brother's house in Primrose Hill. He nodded to the armed policeman standing guard outside, rang the bell and waited. David's children – his nephews – were asleep. But his wife Louise was still awake. David opened the door and welcomed him, if that was the right word, into the left-hand sitting room. And there, in the house they had grown up in together as children, Ed explained how he had decided he was going to run against his brother for the leadership of the party.

David listened politely. He'd obviously have preferred it if he'd had his support, he said. But then 'with composure and generosity of spirit that impressed even Ed's most loyal supporters' David had told him, 'I don't want to be the reason you don't stand. I think you should do it.'

It was a compelling narrative. When people heard it, The Salon That Was Not Yet a Salon could see it made them stop and think. Was it really so wrong for Ed Miliband to want to move his party on from the New Labour era? Was it really beyond the pale for a man to form the honest view he possessed different qualities to those of his own brother? And if he'd sought and received that brother's own personal blessing for the course he had chosen, why should it present a problem for anyone else?

So people stopped. And they thought for a minute.

And then they stopped thinking, and they shrugged. It didn't make any difference. Ed Miliband was still the guy who knifed his own brother.

David Cameron thought it was looking quite good. Esther, Helen, Nicky. That would help with the 'Women Problem'. He wasn't quite so sure about Baker at the Home Office. The guy was a full-on conspiracy nut. Theresa certainly wouldn't be happy. But that was up to Nick. It was his side of the reshuffle.

Which left Andrew. And that was the tricky one. What to do with Andrew Mitchell.

The whole thing had become a bit of a clusterfuck, to be honest. First there'd been that horrific shooting in Manchester. Some psycho had gunned down two women cops. Then a couple of days later Andrew had been caught screaming 'plebs' at the cops at the gates at the bottom of Downing Street, because they wouldn't let him ride his bike out. The *Sun* had got it, and the shit had really hit the fan. They'd tried to ride out the storm – Andrew swore blind he'd never said it. Sat in this very office, opposite him and George and Ed and Craig, and told them, 'I did not use that toxic phrase.'

But then they'd got the email. John Randall, one of the whips, had been contacted by a guy who had been outside the gates when it happened. Saw the whole thing. Andrew swearing and carrying on at the police. And Randall was Andrew's own deputy. OK, they didn't really get on. But there it was. In black and white.

He'd hit the roof when they showed him the email. Called Andrew straight up. 'You lied to me.' And yet Andrew was still denying it. Which was crazy, because now they had the proof. An independent eye-witness. But even then, there was something about the way Andrew was insisting that did make him wonder.

But it didn't matter. They had the proof, and pretty soon the papers had the proof, and then they had a copy of the log from one of the cops on the gate, and that was it. Andrew had come down to Chequers and they'd shook hands like grown-ups. And he'd spoken to Sharon, Andrew's wife, telling her to keep her chin up, they'd get through it, and in time he'd look at bringing Andrew back.

And that was it. All very sad. Andrew was a decent man. He'd made a mistake, but he was a good man and a good chief whip. Dependable. Loyal. But that was politics. These things happened. Time to move on.

But Andrew didn't move on. He kept claiming he'd been the subject of some great conspiracy, And then The League of Extraordinary Advisors got wind of some programme Channel 4 were working on. 'Plebgate' they were calling it. And suddenly Andrew was demanding to see the CCTV footage of the incident at the gates. Kept ringing, kept emailing, kept pestering

Ed and George. He even started getting David Davis involved, who of course started getting some of the backbenchers riled up. 'Mitchell's been stitched up. Number Ten are covering things up.' Which was crazy. He'd already asked the cabinet secretary Jeremy Heywood to look into the whole thing, and he'd said the CCTV evidence was 'inconclusive'.

So they got George to have a chat with Andrew, to try and calm him down. Lie low for a bit, let the storm pass. Then they'd see what they could do about bringing him back. No promises, but he was pretty sure they'd be able to work something out.

But he wasn't having it. They were talking about national security and data protection, and Andrew was threatening FOI and questions in the House. So in the end they decided, 'Jesus, OK, just give him the damn tapes. There's nothing on them anyway.'

And then three months to the day after it had all kicked off at the bottom of Downing Street, Channel 4 aired their *Plebgate* programme. Or rather, they detonated their *Plebgate* programme live on the 7.00 pm news.

It was unbelievable. The cops had talked about all these shocked tourists watching Mitchell ranting away. But the CCTV showed there were no tourists. And there was no blazing row. You could see Andrew in his silly helmet and bicycle clips just walking his bike to the gate, cool as a cucumber. And they had this tape of a meeting Andrew had up in his constituency, with these goons from the Police Federation. And they showed this clip of one of the Police Fed guys talking to the Bubble Breathers afterwards, saying, 'Oh no, Andrew Mitchell wouldn't give his side of the story. He wouldn't say what happened at the gate.' And then they played the tape. And you *could hear* Andrew explaining to them exactly what happened and exactly what he'd said. But the most amazing thing of all was the email. The email that had convinced him – or at least had convinced The League of Extraordinary Advisors – that Andrew had been lying to them. *It was a fake.* The guy who sent it made it up. And what's more, the guy who sent it was also a serving police officer, *serving in the very same unit as the cops at the gate.*

Andrew Mitchell was right all along. The whole thing *was* a stitch-up.

And now he was in the clear. Vindicated in the eyes of the public. Yes The People backed their brave police officers. But they didn't like bent coppers. And they had a pretty clear sense of what was right and wrong.

So the way was now open for a return. The final piece of the reshuffle jigsaw puzzle. Put a lid on the whole affair. Draw a line under the Plebgate clusterfuck and move on.

Well, yes and no. It wasn't quite as simple as that. Nothing in politics was ever quite as simple as that.

Which is what he'd tried to explain to Andrew. He'd been treated atrociously by the police, of course he had. Everyone could see that. Even the Bubble Breathers were writing sympathetic pieces about him, saying he was about to be brought back into the cabinet.

Well, they may have thought that, but they weren't making the decision. And if the wrong decision was made they weren't the ones who'd have it hung round their neck.

For one thing, there was the court case. When the Channel 4 film came out, Andrew went a bit overboard. Understandably perhaps, but you couldn't afford to let emotion get the better of you in their business. He'd called one of the cops on the gate a liar, the cop had sued him, and Andrew had countersued. In fact, he'd countersued both the cop and the *Sun*. They'd tried to get the whole thing ironed out – George had been in to try and get the *Sun* to step back, and there'd been some feelers put out to the Fed. But no one was budging.

He also had to think about the reaction of the cops themselves. Some of the Plebgate officers had acted despicably. But the relationship with the police was already strained. Cuts, pay. He didn't want to pour any more petrol on that particular bonfire unless he absolutely had to.

So no, it wasn't as easy as it seemed. Or some of the Bubble Breathers liked to pretend.

And then there was the other thing. The thing about Andrew being right.

Throughout the whole affair, they'd kept telling him how he needed to play it. They'd told him to apologize for whatever words he had used. Whether he'd said 'Pleb' or not didn't matter. He'd sworn at a police officer – Andrew's line that he'd only sworn 'in the presence of a police officer' simply wouldn't cut it. And he'd finally agreed to deliver a disastrous half-hearted apology, though only after he'd unwittingly managed to convince Craig and some of the other members of The League that if he'd been in the habit of speaking to the cops in the same way he spoke to them, he was lucky not to have been arrested. Then they'd told him not to participate with Channel 4. Craig had rung the producers and told them there wasn't a story in it. That it wouldn't do any-one any good to go raking over all this again. But Andrew had kept egging them on. Then they'd found out one of the cops who was being investigated in the programme had flipped. Started taking these late-night walks along some deserted railway tracks. It was looking like they might be about to have another David Kelly on their hands. So once again, they'd got Ed to ring Andrew up, and told him to get Channel 4 to back off. And again, he'd refused. Then they'd warned him not to get mixed up in a row with the *Sun*. Again he'd refused.

And yes, then Andrew had been proved right. But that wasn't the point. Actually, it was precisely the point. If he brought Andrew back now, it would be an admis-sion that Andrew had been right, and they'd been wrong. That Andrew had been right and *he'd* been wrong.

Andrew was dependable. And loyal. And he'd been fucked over. But that wasn't the issue here. The issue was what was best for the government. And was it best for the government, just a year from the election, to get the Prime Minister standing outside Downing Street with an ugly great sign saying, 'I got it wrong'? Or was it best for the government to have him out there holding up another sign saying, 'The way to get on in this government is to do precisely the opposite of everything Downing Street tells you'?

Andrew Mitchell had been right. But if he was brought back into government now, everyone would see Andrew Mitchell had been right. And by extension, they would see that David Cameron had been wrong. And the point of this reshuffle wasn't to show people that David Cameron was a man who got things wrong.

This was the thing about loyalty. People said it was a luxury successful politicians couldn't afford. Well, they were wrong. There was a time and place for loyalty in politics. And a big part of being a good leader was to know exactly when that time and place was.

And it wasn't now. It wasn't a year out from a general election. Esther. Helen. Nicky. They hadn't got where they were through being proved right.

Annette Brooke was excited. Nick Clegg could see from the way she was smiling at everything anyone said to her just how excited she was. 'Annette, it's going to be really tough to hold this seat, isn't it.' 'Yes [broad smile] but we can do it. I know we can.' 'Annette, you must be sad to see your party in such a difficult position.' 'Oh no [even broader smile], I think we're in a much stronger position than people think.' 'Annette, do you know where the toilets are?' 'Oh yes, they're just through that door and on the left [broadest smile of the day].'

And why shouldn't she be excited? She'd been MP for Mid Dorset and North Poole (MDNP they liked abbreviating it to), for fourteen years, and she hadn't seen many days like this. All the photographers and the cameramen and the journalists jostling and milling about, and trying not to trample all over the kids at the Tops Day Nursery. It was a nice, warm sunny day too, with a lovely cool breeze, and that would make for some lovely shots out here in the play-garden.

When she'd first won the seat from the Tories back in 2001 it had been a bit of an upset. Scraped home by 300 votes. But the 2001 election had been a foregone conclusion, so no-one had really made much of a fuss. 2005 was pretty dull as well, and in 2010 people were focusing all their attention on the new seats the Lib Dems would be winning as Cleggmania swept the country, not the seats they already held.

So no, Annette Brooke hadn't seen too many days like this one. Although technically, it wasn't really Annette's day. It was really Vikki Slade's – 'that's Vikki with two "K"'s' – day.

Annette Brooke was the MP, but Vikki With Two 'K's was the candidate. That's because eighteen months ago Annette had announced she was standing down. Nothing to do with what was happening to her party, she'd stressed. But now she was sixty-eight and she'd recently had a fall outside parliament where she'd cracked her hip, and she just knew it was time to call it a day. Plus, she said, she wanted to spend more time with her family. Which was a bit of an unfortunate phrase, given that everyone knew that whenever a politician said they were stepping down to spend more time with their family, what they actually meant was they were stepping down because of some appalling scandal that was about to consume them.

But in Annette's case there was no scandal. She wasn't the sort of MP – or person – to get herself embroiled in any scandals. She was hard working, committed, unflashy. The sort of MP the Bubble Breathers liked to hold up as public service role models, then ignore.

She hadn't held any ministerial office, though that was primarily because he hadn't actually offered her a government job. Annette was dedicated and hard working and unflashy but, as she'd admitted, she was coming towards the end of her career and there weren't that many jobs to go round.

But she'd been a great constituency MP. That was where her talents were. And though he was aware that saying, 'X is a great constituency MP' was the political equivalent of saying, 'X may not be that good looking, but they've got a great personality,' in Annette's case it was true. She'd been a teacher and a lecturer before entering parliament, rather than being part of the activist-special-advisor-MP-merry-go-round. When she'd been elected she'd concentrated on important, but less high profile, issues. Pre-school education. Human trafficking. GMF.

And her work hadn't gone unnoticed. In 2010 she'd been awarded MP of the year at the Dods & Scottish Widows Women in Public Life Awards. And in 2013 he'd managed to help line her up for an OBE for her years of public service. She'd also recently been ranked 641 out of 648 on the website SexyMP (he was ranked 224 apparently, one place below Lisa Nandy, but just ahead of James Duddridge).

Vikki With Two 'K's was very committed and hard working as well. And she would probably come out a bit higher on SexyMP. Younger (some might even say glamorous), Vikki was a local businesswoman who had been appointed chair of the local chamber of commerce when she was only twenty-nine. 'A dynamic and highly motivated individual driven by a passion for her local community,' according to her CV. 'A little atom bomb' was how Paddy Ashdown had described her when he'd come to visit the constituency. Though he'd made sure to make a point of saying that Annette was 'fabulous' as well.

So here they were, Nick Clegg and Smiling Annette and Atomic Vikki With Two 'K's. And the sun was shining, and the kids were running around, and the Bubble Breathers were circling.

And Annette was loving it. Because this was a perfect way to gradually bring the curtain down. None of these people saw her during those long afternoon meetings when she was chairing the all-party parliamentary breast cancer group. They hadn't taken all that much notice when she'd tabled early day motion 213 on the 'school starting age for summer born pupils' and pointed out that according to The Institute for Fiscal Studies, children born in August are six point four percentage points less likely to achieve five GCSEs or equivalents at A*-C and around two percentage points less likely to go to university at age eighteen or nineteen than children born in September. And none of these cameras had been with her when she'd visited that refuge in Moldova and talked to those women with their scarred bodies and minds.

But that didn't matter, because they were here now. Which meant what was happening here today was important. And that meant what had been happening here before today had been important. It meant what she'd been doing here – what she'd been doing with the last twenty years of her life – had been important.

Which she always knew, of course. But it was still nice to have external validation once in a while. To see that, you only had to look at her smile.

And now the photographers wanted to line them all up for a photo. So they all shuffled into line, Vikki With Two 'K's, and the nice lady from the centre, and him and Annette. And he started looking straight down each lens, hitting each one in turn like a pro. And Vikki matched him lens for lens, and the nice lady from the centre was following their lead. And Annette was in her own little world. She had her eyes closed, and she was grinning away at no-one's lens in particular, and having a great old time.

Then someone said, 'Annette, could you just take a couple of steps back.'

There was a brief bit of banter. He did his 'Oh come on, we need Annette in this shot as well' line, and Vikki With Two 'K's was nodding, saying, 'Of course, we can't have the shot without Annette.' But they both knew the score. In fact everyone knew the score, except Annette Brooke, who had got temporarily lost in her own little world. A world where her committee room was packed with hundreds of members of the public, and there were hundreds more queuing up outside. And where the House of Commons chamber was jammed to the rafters, and every member was leaning forward expectantly, hanging on her every word about the school starting age. And when she stepped out of the door of that women's sanctuary, the BBC and CNN and Reuters and a dozen other camera crews were waiting, and then surged forward shouting, 'Ms Brooke, what was it like in there? What did those women say to you?'

And then she came out of her temporary world. Came out of it and looked at him, and at Vikki With Two 'K's. And she could see they weren't protesting any more. They were just looking at her, slightly apologetically. But only slightly.

So she took two short steps backwards.

One.

Two.

In front of her she left the Deputy Prime Minister and his candidate for the crucial marginal seat of Mid Dorset and North Poole (notional majority 269) alone in the shot.

And she hadn't just stepped out of a shot. She'd just stepped out of her life. The life she'd known for the past two decades. And the sun was still shining, and the kids were still playing. But for an instant, and for the first time that afternoon, the smile on Annette Brooke's face faltered.

And he could see it. For a millisecond, somewhere deep inside him, Nick Clegg registered the moment. And then immediately dismissed it, because he'd seen that look and that moment repeated so many times. The end of a politician's journey.

And then he started hitting the lenses again, one by one. And beside him Vikki With Two 'K's started hitting the lenses as well. And the lenses smiled back. 'Hello Nick, hello Vikki,' the lenses say. 'Do you both have far to go?'

One call. That was all it would take, one call. There wouldn't be any fingerprints. He could pick someone reliable, like Nick or Jason. And there were plenty of Ed B surrogates floating around. Or wannabe surrogates. Any one of them could have done it. Around two dozen people. There would be no way of tracing it back to him.

And they deserved it. They'd crossed the line. Now it

was the *Sunday Times*. 'Knives out for "Ed Balls the bungler"'.

Why? Because they'd had a meeting. The Labour leader and the Shadow Chancellor had sat down in the same room to talk about tuition fees. And they'd disagreed. They'd come at things from a different perspective.

Ed Miliband had thought a cut from £9,000 to £6,000 was vital to their election chances. It would wedge the Lib Dems. Put clear red water between them and the Tories. Appeal to their key eighteen-to-twenty-one-year-old demographic. Not to mention their hard-pressed parents, who were currently trapped slap bang in the centre of the 'squeezed middle'.

And his Ed had disagreed. He thought a commitment to tough spending rules and tight fiscal discipline was more vital to their election chances. That they could not afford additional borrowing – economically or politically – and that any cut would have to be funded by additional cuts or an increase in taxes. And ten weeks from polling day neither of those options were electorally palatable.

So they'd talked about it. The leader and his Shadow Chancellor had sat opposite one another and tried to thrash it out. And yes, both of them had been blunt with each other. But they'd stuck to the policy. It hadn't got personal. No one had screamed or shouted or thrown their toys out of the pram. True, they hadn't been able to reach a consensus. But there'd been a bit of progress. And they'd agreed to meet again to finally get it nailed down.

And that was how it was supposed to work. How the grown-ups were meant to do their business.

But then what had those fuckers gone and done? They'd picked up the phone to Tim Shipman and James Lyons, stuck the knife in, and given it a neat little twist. 'Senior figures also expressed frustration and incredulity that Balls has dug his heels in over funding a cut in English tuition fees from £9,000 to £6,000 a year — three years after Miliband first backed the policy and with the announcement due at the end of this week . . . insiders say a meeting between Miliband and Balls last Wednesday, which many hoped would settle the policy, had "ended badly".'

He reached down for his mobile, picked it up from his desk and pressed the small green handset icon. A procession of names sprang up on the screen. Well, if that was the way they wanted to play it . . .

It wasn't the disloyalty that angered him. There was no love lost between the two Eds, everyone knew that. When they'd both been working for Gordon, it had always been Ed B who had been the senior partner. Gordon had valued Ed M. But Ed B had almost been like his surrogate son.

So when Ed M had won the leadership, it had been hard initially for Ed B to make the adjustment. Especially when he'd snubbed him and handed Shadow Chancellor to Alan. But things had moved on. Alan had gone. Ed B was Shadow Chancellor. He was possibly only a few weeks away from becoming Chancellor, the one job in politics he really craved. The leadership had gone for him now, he knew that. It would be Yvette's turn next. But he could still be Chancellor. After all those years sitting in those stuffy rooms in the Treasury, poring over those spreadsheets and tables, making sure Gordon's budgets were locked together. Now he was just a dozen weeks away from unveiling a Budget of his own.

But still they were knifing him. He pressed a second button on his phone, and the names began accelerating upwards. George Eaton . . . George Parker . . . Graham Wilson . . . (he'd have to remember to delete that one now Graham had moved over to Downing Street).

And the thing was, they weren't even good at it. They were so ham-fisted. So clumsy. You could tell who'd done it and why they'd done it from a mile away. 'The shadow cabinet source said Miliband was considering moving Balls from the Treasury brief last autumn.'

Jesus Christ. Hadn't he learned from that fucked-up briefing on Ed's inner-circle he gave to Sam Coates. 'Tom hates Bob. Ed doesn't have much faith in Iain. Tim has a political tin ear. Anna's the fixer who doesn't fix it. Greg is in exile and behaving like it. Torsten wants discipline but puts the Shadow Cabinet's backs up. Nobody is quite sure what Jon's up to, particularly when he's "thinking" in his new place in the West of Ireland. *And there aren't enough hours in the day for Stewart to sort it all out.*'

Actually, it might not have been Stewart. Might have

been someone who actually knows how to play the game a bit just putting Stewart in the frame.

But it didn't matter. It had come from one of those immature, insecure, inept children who was still playing 'let's make a Prime Minister'.

On the screen the names had finally stopped scrolling. Nick Robinson . . . Nick Watt. Nick. The *Guardian*. Hit them where they lived.

He wouldn't just be lashing out in revenge. There would be a practical purpose. 'Ed Balls is reported to be furious at a briefing that has originated from a senior aide to Labour leader Ed Miliband. According to one MP who is close to the Shadow Chancellor, some members of Miliband's team are still opposing his attempts to lock down the party's fiscal stance in advance of the next month's formal campaign launch. According to the MP, "Ed Balls can't believe that with the start of the election just a couple of weeks away, people in the leader's office are briefing against the shadow cabinet like this. It's playing right into the Tories' hands."'

All done in the proper way. Nothing gratuitous. Aim for the advisors, not the leader himself. Make the point you're not briefing against them, but you're briefing against *their briefing*. Make sure to signal a possible non-aggression pact via the Ed quote. Then throw in the line about playing into the Tories' hands. Close down the opportunity for them to brief a comeback.

And it would work. The story would drop, and then they would get the call. Ed Miliband's just seen the

Guardian. No, he hasn't read the *Sunday Times* piece, but he's been told about it. All very unfortunate. Not authorized by him of course. No, he understands the *Guardian* story wasn't placed by Ed B or anyone on his team. Anyway, they needed to shut this all down. So close to an election. Didn't help anyone but Cameron and Osborne. Could he come round later this morning? Then they'd get this whole thing ironed out.

And now his finger was hovering over the button with the green handset icon again. All he had to do was press down. A single push of a button. One quick conversation. That's all it would take.

And then he could hear Ed B's voice. 'No briefing, Alex.' He'd looked at him. No briefing? That could have meant a lot of things. No briefing unless they brief against us. No briefing where the trail leads back to us. I don't want to know about the briefing. You know I have to tell you 'no briefing', but you also know I've been at this long enough to understand there will be times you have to brief. And when you do, I have to be in a position to honestly claim I'd told you not to do it.

So he'd stared at him, trying to divine from Ed B's own face, or his voice, or his posture what 'no briefing' actually meant. He couldn't just come out and ask him. 'You say no briefing, but do you actually mean no briefing?' You don't ask that sort of question in his line of work. It's why he's in this line of work. Because he can read people. Or he can read Ed. Know instinctively what 'no briefing' actually means.

And of course he did know. Which is when the loyalty thing came into play. He had to be loyal to Ed B. And Ed B had just been carved up, by his own leader, in the newspaper. And it was his job to stop that happening. To go all Sean Connery in the *Untouchables* – 'You pull a knife on us, we pull a gun. It's the old Brownite way.'

But he had to be loyal to Ed B. And Ed B had told him 'no briefing'. And because he could read Ed B like a book, he knew he meant it. No briefing. Period.

Which is why the finger was still hovering there over that small green button. He had to press it. He had to press it to finally teach them a lesson. This was not how the grown-ups behave. He had to press it because it would work. They would finally realize they had to get this thing settled one way or another. He had to press it because that's just the way things are. Loyalty begets loyalty. Disloyalty begets disloyalty.

And then he placed the phone gently back down on the desk.

One call. That's all it would have taken. One call.

That's how the three men deal with it. The loyalty thing. They deal with it in basically the same way. In different ways. Depending on what sort of loyalty the situation demands.

Sometimes people have to be actively pushed aside. For the greater good. The government, the party, the wider political project. At other times people need to be sacrificed. They could be saved, perhaps. But the act of rescuing them carries too much risk of its own. And then there are times people have to be just left to fade away. When the natural cycle of politics has to be allowed to assert itself.

That's their job, as leader. To know when and where the loyalty thing has its place.

And the disloyalty thing. Because however you dress it up, ruthlessness has its place as well. In fact, it's a vital component of leadership. You have to show you are prepared to wield the knife. That you have the strength to insist that disloyalty occasionally begets loyalty.

So they sit there, watching the clock counting down. Knowing that soon it will be time for a new sacrifice. That the natural cycle of politics is preparing to assert itself once again.

0.45 . . . 00.44 . . . 00.43 . . . 00.42 . . . 00.41 . . .

10. Juror Number Eight

Come on. Were they being serious? The sleeves and the jacket? No, they weren't serious. They couldn't be.

The private polling. All the constituency data. It was all holding up well. This was a 'no complacency' moment, surely? A 'we're on the right track, don't turn back' moment. Maybe even a 'this is the time to hold our nerve' moment.

But not a sleeves-and-jacket moment.

'We need to change the narrative,' Craig had told him.

Why? The narrative was the election was too close to call. And that was precisely the narrative they wanted. On a knife edge. Once-in-a-generation decision. The most vital election in his lifetime. In anyone's lifetime.

Yes, they'd had the wobble. And that's all it had been, a wobble. The Bubble Breathers had tried to blow it up into a full-blown panic. They'd been ringing round every member of the cabinet trying to make them crack. 'The Conservatives' election campaign was in turmoil this weekend after senior cabinet sources warned the party was heading for defeat if David Cameron and his election team stuck to their current strategy.'

Well, they hadn't been able to find any turmoil. Or anyone who said they were on course for defeat. The best they'd managed to get was 'some jitters'. The odd voice requesting 'a more positive message'. Or 'a more prominent role for Boris'.

And everyone knew. The jacket only came off and the sleeves only got rolled up for a crisis. A proper 1987-David-Young-grabbing-Norman-Tebbit-by-the-lapels-and-screaming, 'You're going to lose us this fucking election!' meltdown. What sort of leader starts rolling up his sleeves over a minor case of the jitters?

'We need to give them licence to change how they're writing about you and the campaign,' Lynton had said.

But why would they want them to change what they were writing about the campaign? The campaign was working. It was working just as it was supposed to work. Labour had crashed the car. He'd found the car. He'd got under the bonnet, rummaged around and got his hands dirty. He'd fixed the car. The car was running again. He was driving the car serenely off into the sunset.

That was the plan. And that was how you achieved success in politics. In everything. You stuck to the plan. If you started bouncing around, jumping from one idea to another, or one line to another, or one strategy to another, you were dead. And you'd deserve to be dead.

Remember what they'd talked about in all those interminable planning meetings? All the clever new ideas they'd thrashed out. And they'd always come back to the same place. The economy. Leadership. The economy. Leadership. Fix the car. Drive the car. That was it.

There had been nothing in any of the strategy meetings about sleeves or jackets.

'What we need is to communicate some passion.' They'd both said that. Craig and Lynton.

Jesus, what was it about passion. That's all anyone ever talked about, 'passion'. Passion was not a good leadership virtue. In fact, it was one of the worst leadership vices. When the guys with business cards containing nothing but a PO Box number were sitting opposite you and saying, 'We have credible information a major terror attack will be launched in London next Wednesday,' the last thing you needed was passion. What you needed was a calm head, and a steady nerve. What you needed to do was trust in the plan.

'We think people need to see you a bit more pumped up.'

He couldn't even remember who'd come up with that one. 'Pumped up'? This was a general election, not a fucking wrestling bout.

What had happened to leadership? What was he supposed to do now, say, 'Don't give the keys of the car back to the guy who crashed it. Give them to the guy who wants to go ton-up with the top down and *Brown Sugar* blaring out of the stereo'?

What was the one thing everyone – even his worst critics – grudgingly acknowledged about him. The Bubble Breathers, the euro-nuts, the jealous guys and jilted girls on his back benches. They all agreed David Cameron was good in a crisis.

The riots. Libya. He'd walk out of Downing Street, stand at that podium, and he'd land it. The right tone. The right look. People would be sitting there, and they'd think, 'OK, someone's in charge here.'

And maybe he wasn't in charge. Maybe he was thinking, 'Shit, what the hell am I going to do about all this?' But he didn't show it. And that was important. It was important people saw someone who looked like they were in charge. Someone who had a plan, and was sticking to the plan.

Not someone who took off their jacket, rolled up their sleeves and started wandering around shouting and hollering about how pumped up they were.

'We think you should give it a focus, obviously. Maybe talk about helping small businessmen. About how that pumps David Cameron up.'

Well, yes, he could. He could talk about risk takers and entrepreneurs and wealth creators. With his jacket off. And his sleeves rolled up. Talk about how all that pumped him up.

But it didn't pump him up. He knew it was important, of course. But it wasn't something he was passionate about. What he really cared about were things like fixing the economy. It would take a lot of small businesses to eradicate a one and a half trillion national debt. Or education. When the election was over, he was going to see how he could push ahead with Michael's reforms. Without starting another nuclear war with the teachers. And it really was time to do something about this Tory Toff stuff. Ed Miliband had blown it trying to sell his 'One Nation' agenda. But there had definitely been something in it.

That was what he was passionate about. About showing that the plan could work for everyone.

But David Cameron was not one of life's pumpers. He did not pump. This other David Cameron, the guy who liked throwing off his cufflinks and his tie and – what was the line they'd suggested, loved 'taking a punt' – he was into all that. But this David Cameron most certainly was not.

So which David Cameron were they planning on asking people to vote for here? David Cameron the Prime Minister. Or David Cameron the slightly deranged shirt-sleeved pumper.

Maybe it didn't matter. Maybe Craig and Lynton were right. If he just took off his jacket and looked a bit worked up, perhaps the narrative would change. The Bubble Breathers would write how their campaign was back on track. And then The People would properly embrace this other David Cameron. Whoever the hell he was.

The chamber was going crazy. Ed Balls was in hysterics. Someone behind him was laughing so hard they sounded like they were going to be sick. Even Yvette Cooper was having to fight to prevent herself from cracking a smile.

Where had that come from? Harriet had asked him her bog-standard question about numbers of women in the cabinet. So he'd lobbed his bog-standard answer back – better pensions for women, more jobs for women, tax cuts for women, shared parental leave, better childcare, more flexible working. How she should stop trying to score cheap Westminster points.

And then she'd hit him with it. Kicked him straight in the groin with it actually.

'Well, he's reluctant to answer the question [no, he hadn't been], which is unlike him [what's she setting me up for here . . .], because normally when he's asked about numbers of women he's quite forthcoming [oh for Christ's sake . . . not the *GQ* interview . . . here . . . at DPM's questions . . . for fuck's sake Harriet].'

It had been over five years ago. Six. It was six years ago now.

Lena had been quite excited about it. But she'd also warned him – 'It's Piers Morgan. Be careful.'

Well, yes, that was sage advice. It was Piers Morgan. One of the biggest and bubbliest of all the Bubble Breathers. And it was *GQ*. JFK had been photographed for *GQ*.

So he'd thought to himself a little bit about how he wanted to play it. Not too much, because you could overthink these things. But it was a good opportunity, and he wanted to get it right.

It wouldn't be 'soft' – Piers Morgan didn't do soft interviews with politicians any more. Not after the Iraq photo business. But it was an opportunity to cut away from the usual Westminster bullshit.

And he knew what Morgan was after. Nick Clegg the

man, not Nick Clegg the politician. Which was perfect, because that was what he wanted as well. To show he could be a part of this world, whilst at the same time demonstrating how this world was not a part of him. Nick Clegg, a man in Westminster. Not Nick Clegg, a man *of* Westminster.

He knew precisely how he was going to do it too. He was going to tackle Morgan head on. His interviewer would try to either open him up or show him up. Tease out some great new revelation, or paint him as another political hack, squirming and ducking for cover.

Well, he wouldn't squirm. And he wouldn't be delivering any great revelations either. He'd answer him on his own terms. Open himself up. Say what he actually thought.

So Morgan had kicked it off. *Was it true he'd had a conviction for arson?* No. It wasn't true. It had been a caution, not a conviction.

But he had committed arson? Yes. But only as a sixteen-year-old exchange student. He'd burnt some cacti during a party at a German professor's house.

Was he arrested? No. He'd done a short stint of community service.

OK, that opening had possibly sounded a touch more defensive than he'd have liked. But that was what had happened, so he'd answered. He hadn't been convicted, he hadn't been arrested, he'd only been sixteen years old. It had been a cactus he'd set fire to, not a refugee hostel.

Had he ever taken drugs when he was young? He wasn't going to answer that. It wasn't relevant to what he did as a politician today.

Why should politicians be able to duck questions about whether or not they broke the law? Politicians should be able to duck questions that weren't relevant to their jobs as politicians.

Obama didn't duck questions like that. He answered truthfully. That's what people wanted to hear from their politicians these days. Why wouldn't he answer a simple question like that? Was he joking? Did he honestly think a British politician could start submitting themselves for interrogation like that over things they did when they were kids?

Right, that bit had definitely sounded defensive. But again, he'd answered honestly. What wasn't relevant to his job as a politician wasn't anyone else's business. That's what he believed. So that's what he was going to say.

Could a politician run the country if they were an alcoholic? Probably not.

When had he last been drunk? The previous summer.

Paralytic? No, he'd been with his family. Was that OK?

No. It wasn't OK. This was not going well. It wasn't how he'd planned it at all. 'Was that OK' had just sounded petulant. The whole thing had sounded defensive again.

And he wasn't trying to be defensive. He was trying to answer honestly. He was just trying to be Nick Clegg.

But he couldn't find him. Iraq. CCTV. How rich he was. Every time he'd been asked a question he'd said what he actually thought. No spin. No bullshit. And every time it came out sounding like he was trying to hide, or shift position, or backtrack on something he'd already said.

And it was then Morgan had asked him about the women.

Did he think he was good in bed?

That was actually the easiest question he'd had. The simplest one to throw back. *'Do you think you're good in bed?'* Who in their right mind would answer a question like that? Who in their right mind would ask a question like that? Unless they were looking for a smash in the face. He could do it. He could punch Piers Morgan right now, and there wouldn't be a person in the country who wouldn't say, 'good for Nick Clegg.'

But he didn't punch him. Instead he heard someone say hesitantly, then with laughter, 'Um . . . er . . . I don't think I'm particularly brilliant, or particularly bad!'

What a typical Liberal Democrat answer. Sitting on the fence.

'Since the only judge of that is my wife . . .'

Hang on. Who was this guy who had started talking about his wife?

How many women would actually know for a fact if he was good in bed?

'Er . . . not . . . er . . . not a list as long as yours, I'm sure.'

A list? First this guy's talking about Miriam. Then he's swapping lists over other women he's slept with. Who the fuck is this bloke?

How many are we talking. Ten, twenty, thirty?

Thirty women? Whoever he is, this isn't a man who's slept with . . .

No more than thirty.

Oh fuck, no! Please! Morgan says thirty, so you say thirty. If Morgan had said fifty, you'd have said fifty wouldn't you? Whoever you are, Jesus Christ. Take a look at yourself.

So there are thirty women out there who could answer the question?

'It's a lot less than that.'

Too late for false humility now pal. Way too late.

And what would the general consensus be, did he think?

Come on then big guy. What would they say? 'Oh Piers, he was an animal . . .'?

'You'd have to ask them!'

Ever had any complaints?

Any complaints? That's it. That. Is. It. Whoever you are, and whatever you think you're trying to do here, enough.

'Oh God, yes of course.'

Right. So you've not just come here to brag about the number of women you slept with. You've come here to brag about how crap you were while you were doing it. You really are a piece of work my friend.

What would his wife say?

Shit. I don't believe it. I don't believe even *you're* going to answer . . .

And that was when he'd realized. The man who'd sat there for over a minute, bragging on-the-record to one of the nation's most high-profile journalists, in an interview with one of the nation's most high-profile publications, about his extensive list of sexual conquests. It was a man called Nick Clegg.

And a moment later he'd heard Nick Clegg – heard himself – say:

'I think she'd be very content and happy.'

Content. And happy.

'I'll put it to the Right Honourable Gentleman again. And this time I'd like a straight answer to a straight question. What does his wife think when he fucks her?'

'Mr Speaker, I've already answered that question. But let me try and put this in words the leader of the opposition can understand. When I fuck my wife she is very content and very happy.'

That was six years ago. Before any of it. Before Cleggmania. Before the coalition. Before the protests. Before the chants. Before the shit started coming through the letterbox.

Back when he thought he could control it. Or at least manage it. If only he'd known then what he knew now. Knew how politics took you and broke you apart and then put you back together in a way that meant there were times you couldn't even recognize yourself.

But he hadn't. So here he was, with Harriet Harman

peering down over her glasses at him, with her mocking, self-satisfied look. And George Osborne sitting next to him, muttering the odd word of support, whilst trying to keep a straight face himself. And the entire House howling and baying and laughing at his expense.

Or they thought it was at his expense. But it wasn't. Because whoever it was they were laughing at, it wasn't him.

It was a good bash. A very good bash. The inner office was heaving, and out in the corridor, where James Stewart (Labour press officer James Stewart, not the other one) was manning the wine table, they were stretching all the way back down to the double doors.

A very positive sign. Ed Miliband was only too aware you could accurately gauge the state of your political fortunes through the volume of Bubble Breathers at your Christmas party. And the two giant ice buckets of beer by the doors were both almost half-empty, and it had only just gone seven-thirty.

Now, if the ice buckets had still been full by nine, they'd have been staring at a serious political problem. 'Stewart, it's nine o'clock, and I've counted at least fifteen unopened bottles of Becks.' 'Yes, I noticed that too. I think we may need to think about having another review of the Mansion Tax policy.'

But the ice buckets were emptying nicely. And what's more, his party was taking place the day after George Osborne's Christmas party. Canapés. Champagne.

Proximity to real power. The Bubble Breathers would never miss the Chancellor's bash. But they'd still managed to shrug off their hangovers and turn up this evening.

So the party was swinging. And the time had come for Ed Miliband to Vogue.

Up until now he'd just been casually chatting, easily dispensing the trademark Miliband wit and charm. But now he had to go to work.

Bob Roberts moved into position on his right shoulder. Ayesha Hazarika, speechwriter and general fixer who he'd just poached from Harriet Harman, took the post on his left. And they began to move.

Now nothing was casual. Their job was to place him on display. To guide him around the room with measured but elegant precision.

Bob and Ayesha would insert him into a conversation, give him the space to cut a few shapes, then move him on. They knew that left to his own devices he'd have spent the rest of the evening chatting to Emily Maitlis about bank reform. But that's not how a leader Vogues. Leadership Voguing is all about continuous movement. Clean lines. Controlled actions. Meticulous repetition.

He hit the first huddle. Delivered his little introductory joke. Inserted a short but topical self-deprecating anecdote. Accepted, then batted away his single serious political question. Then moved on.

New huddle. New joke. Same anecdote [prefix 'As I was just saying over there']. Bat off question. Move on.

Next huddle. Another joke. Same anecdote [same prefix]. Wait for the serious political question.

'Ed, we were just talking about politicians and their favourite films. Cameron said *Lawrence of Arabia* today. I think I read somewhere yours is *Twelve Angry Men*?'

Twelve Angry Men. Sidney Lumet, 1957. But not really about twelve men. About one man. Henry Fonda. Juror Number Eight.

From the opening scene in the courtroom you could feel it. The heat. That oppressive, claustrophobic blanket lying across downtown Chicago. And there's Juror Number Eight. Immaculate in his cream linen suit. He has a wedding ring on his hand, and an expensive (though not ostentatious) watch on his wrist. And like the other jurors, he's been in courtroom 228 for the best part of a month.

But in all other ways he's unlike the others. There's something that sets him apart. How he holds himself. The way he talks. The way when they first walk into the jury room, he stands alone at the window, lost in thought.

Alone for the moment. Then, meticulously and methodically, he begins to make his case. Or unpick the case as set out by The People.

The knife. He'd been out walking and found the identical knife. A million to one chance the boy's father had been stabbed by the same knife? Yes, but it's possible. And yes, he's well aware he'd broken the law purchasing it.

The passing L train. If you brought two bits of testimony together – the woman who said she'd seen the stabbing through the last two cars, and the old man who said he heard the boy shout, 'I'm going to kill you' – it proved there was no way the old man could have identified the voice. The L had been roaring by *for a full ten seconds* before the killing.

And as he lays out the evidence, he finds he's not alone after all. One by one they start to turn to him. The decorator. The pensioner. The immigrant. The ad executive. The salesman. The banker. Eventually, he wins all of them round. He confronts their bigotry and their vanity and their arrogance and their ignorance and their timidity and their apathy, and he prevails. Juror Number Eight wins them round. And wins their vote too.

So is *Twelve Angry Men* Ed Miliband's favourite film? Hell, it's not his favourite film. It's the blueprint to his life.

'No, Ed's favourite film is *The Usual Suspects*. Googled it this afternoon.' One of the Bubble Breathers cut straight across him.

'Great choice. Brilliant film. Spacey's amazing.' A second Bubble Breather.

'Yeah, great film.' A third BB.

Ed Miliband had been caught mid-Vogue. What exactly was going on here? *The Usual Suspects*? It's a good film, but since when had it been *his* film?

For one thing, it doesn't have an uplifting ending. In fact, it has a nightmarish ending. It ends up with everyone dead, and the evil genius on the loose. It isn't about people coming together for the common good. Everyone comes together for the common bad, and it all goes downhill from there. Yes, there's a brilliant loner who eventually prevails against all the odds. But he turns out to be the Devil.

Then he thought to himself, 'Yes, but quite a cool, contemporary Devil.' And now he's firing off suspicious glances, one in the direction of Bob, and the other in the direction of Ayesha. After which he turns back to the Bubble Breathers.

'No, *Twelve Angry Men* is still my favourite film. At least, I think it is.'

He knew what had happened here. Just another of those moments when politics reaches in, takes a tiny piece of you, and slips away without you even noticing.

Who's Henry Fonda? How many focus group eighteen-to-twenty-five year olds have ever heard of Lee J. Cob? Or E. G. Marshall?

But Spacey? Gabriel Byrne? Benicio del Torro? These guys are box office. Pete Postlethwaite? He was a Labour man. Even appeared in a Labour PPB.

So on that basis *The Usual Suspects* was a good choice. A better choice than *Twelve Angry Men*. And a free choice. What's your favourite film? *Twelve Angry Men* or *The Usual Suspects*? What's your favourite book? *Varieties of Capitalism* or *On Chesil Beach*? What's your favourite band? *A-Ha* or *Oasis*?

It costs you nothing. It's just a microscopic part of you, after all. A memory from childhood. A teenage emotion. A University spring.

And what's any of that when you have an election to win? And a country to run. And a world to recast in your image.

Of course each of these three men knew full well they would have to give. And that politics would take. They'd seen what it did to people. To Gordon. To Major. How it chipped away. You started off clearly defined – at least in your own mind – and then one day you looked up, and your features were ragged and indistinct. The broad outline was still there, but the details – a lot of the things that made you unmistakably you – had gone.

Witnessing this redaction of a soul up close was bad enough. But to fully understand it you had to experience it for yourself.

In David Cameron's office, right next to his desk, was a long rectangular mirror. It was there when he'd moved in, and it had never occurred to him to get rid of it. Every now and then he'd catch a glimpse of himself. Notice how the sharpness of his chin was gradually being erased, and grey flecks were beginning to pebbledash the side of his hair, and the taut waistline was starting to sag.

But that didn't bother him unduly. That was natural. That was just middle-age taking its leisurely toll.

It was those other mirrors that framed his reflection that bothered him. The daily newspaper cuts. The occasional news bulletin. The times (they'd told him he shouldn't do it) he poked his head below the line of some of the comment sites.

That's where he met The Monster. This man who'd had a disabled father and nursed a disabled son of his own, but who now wanted to throw sick and disabled children out on to the streets. And then sell off the hospital wards that were treating them. And then persecute and harass their struggling parents (assuming they were low-paid parents, of course).

This man was an animal. Vote for him? If he ever came face to face with him he'd punch him. But he never would come face to face with him. He couldn't. He didn't exist.

And he'd tried to prove it. Remind people who David Cameron really was. He'd started to work references into his speeches about how much he'd personally relied on the NHS. And how he knew what it was to live with someone with a disability. The League had encouraged him to go further. To spell out in detail what it had meant to him growing up with his father, and raising Ivan.

Because politics was cunning like that. There was a method to the way it would distort and misrepresent you. It knew full well if it initially did so in quite subtle ways, you'd be tempted to reveal a little bit more of yourself. To try and counteract the distortion. And then it could take whatever new fact you revealed, and subtly distort that as well.

So he'd tried to prove he wasn't a monster. And people had listened to the speeches. And they'd read the interviews. And they'd said, 'Look at that David Cameron. He's actually using his dead father and his dead son to try and pretend he isn't a monster. That man's a monster.'

Ed Miliband didn't see a monster, he saw a wimp. The wimp who'd stabbed his brother in the back. The homicidal wimp.

The Salon That Was No Longer a Salon saw it too. They thought about different ways of countering it. One thing they considered was talking down the wimpishness and actually talking up the homicide. 'Ed Miliband had the ruthlessness to knife his own brother. What about that, eh?'

They'd quickly dropped that one. Then they'd considered talking up Syria. 'Ed Miliband was the man who stood up to David Cameron and Barack Obama. Tough enough? Hell, yes.' But they were trying to organize a trip for Ed to the White House. Maybe best to save Syria for the debates.

Then they'd thought about putting out some colour on the *real* Ed. What about the Ed and Ken story, for example?

Now that one definitely had potential. Ken Livingstone had just won the nomination for Mayor. And Ed had stood by him, despite a backlash in the party.

Then it emerged Ken's written a book. Some kiss and tell about his time on the GLC and his dealings with Blair and Brown. And about his kissing and telling about a succession of women who were going to have to bring up the child he'd fathered without him.

So Ed called Ken in to his office for a chat. He'd been loyal to him, as he knew. A lot of people had encouraged him to distance himself from Ken's campaign. He hadn't done that. This book, though. It wasn't going to be helpful.

And Ken just started being Ken. He'd never planned for the book to coincide with the Mayoral election. Things just happened to turn out that way. And the stuff about Blair and Brown was old history – no-one was going to be worried about that. And the stuff with the women? They'd wanted children. And they hadn't been able to find the right man. So he'd obliged. They were all still good friends. It was all very amicable.

And all the while Ken was talking Ed was getting more and more tense. Ken wasn't listening. He was droning on, in that slightly patronizing 'I've been in this game a bit longer than you young man' way of his.

And suddenly Ed snapped. Slammed his hand down on the desk. 'For fuck's sake, Ken!' And Ken almost jumped out of his seat. He was a prince of the Left. A socialist A-lister. No-one had spoken to him like that for years.

There were a couple of members of The Salon Who Were No Longer a Salon in attendance. And they were almost out of their seats too. And now Ed was on *his* feet, laying down the law. And they were thinking, 'Wow. Look at this guy. He's a proper Warrior God. If only the rest of the country could see this.'

But then think about it a bit more. They needed Ken. He was a prince of the Left after all. And unity was Ed's big thing. Pulling the party together after a traumatic defeat, etc. And the Mayoral election was going to be a big test of Ed's leadership. So maybe best to let Ken have his book. They could find another way of showing people Ed Miliband wasn't a homicidal wimp.

When Nick Clegg looked in the mirror he saw nothing. No reflection at all.

It was like over the past five years he'd slowly been becoming invisible. Even the protestors had started to drift away. Like the others, he'd been trying to think up ways of showing who Nick Clegg really is. But it's hard when people can't actually see you.

This was what no one outside of The Cell properly understood. As Deputy Prime Minister it was a daily struggle to even remind people you were there.

Barack Obama comes to visit. There's David Cameron, on the doorstep of Number Ten, smiling for the cameras, cementing the special relationship. And he's sitting just inside. Moments later he's shaking hands with the Great Icon himself. Him, Nick Clegg, chatting one-to-one with the most powerful man on the planet.

And no-one gets to see it. It's David and Barack playing

table tennis. David and Barack flipping burgers for the troops. And he's there. He's standing just off to the side. 'Sorry, Deputy Prime Minister. Can you take a couple of steps back?'

Then someone in The Cell had come up with a solution to the 'visibility problem'. They'd been approached by a guy who wanted to do a documentary. Follow them round. Twenty-four-hour coverage. Up close. Personal. The real Nick Clegg, not the cypher. Clegg Uncut. Clegg On The Wall. I'm a Deputy Prime Minister, Get Me Out Of Here.

It would be perfect. They would show him at work. Show The Cell at work. Committed. Unaffected. Principled.

And independent. That was the most important thing. It would show them pursuing their own agenda. Fighting for their own policies. They would have a distinct identity. Who knows, he might even find Nick Clegg again.

And then David Cameron had vetoed it. Too disruptive. Intrusive. Not conducive to the efficient working of government. Shorthand for 'the rest of the cabinet and the backbenchers would go ape-shit.'

He'd considered ignoring him and going ahead with it anyway. But then there'd be a big row. And what was he supposed to do, threaten to bring down the coalition because he wasn't allowed his own TV show? He'd just look vain and petulant. Another example of politics taking, him trying to give, and politics snatching away.

And anyway, he knew. They all knew. This was what

it was. This was the game. Each of them had placed their own signature on the dotted line. No one forced them into it.

So they carried on. In the hope that at some point politics would stop taking and start to give something back. And every now and then, when they were least expecting it, it did.

The face was fuller and the nose a bit narrower. But the thin, circular glasses he was wearing were quite similar to a pair he used to wear. The eyebrows also had that same curve, just at the point where they started angling up from the brow. And the lips were slightly flared, like his own.

It was hard to tell what colour shirt he was wearing, given the photograph was in black and white. It could be white, but the top half of the photo was relatively distinct, and the shirt didn't look quite crisp enough. Cream perhaps. The jacket was dark – black or blue. It was a little harder to tell with the jacket, because the bottom quarter of the photo was faded with age.

He'd looked for that image amongst the sea of faces above him. But he hadn't been able to spot it. Not that he'd been expecting to. The Hall of Names at Yad Vashem displayed over 600 pictures and Pages of Testimony. Approximately one for every 10,000 victims. But even then, even with that abstraction of the horror, there were too many. The young boys and girls. The old men and women. The husbands and the wives. The

fathers and the mothers. The brothers and the sisters.
There were still too many to register them all.

And then they'd handed him the file. It wasn't a bulky
file, just about the size of an A4 notepad. But it contained what he was looking for.

It gave him a date. January 18, 1945. The Germans
were retreating from the Ardennes. The US First and
Third Armies had just linked up at the Rensiwez bridge.
Russian troops were marching into Warsaw. And that
was the day Dawid Kozak, his grandfather, had died.

The file gave him the place. The camp's name was
Harzungen. Harzungen was a satellite camp of the
Mittelbau-Dora concentration camp, which was itself a
sub-camp of the Buchenwald concentration camp. Harzungen was situated just outside the town of Nordhausen,
in the Thuringia region of central Germany – known as
the country's 'Green Heart'. Today it was a tiny village
of about 200 people, but between 1944 and 1945 around
4,000 inmates had been crammed into its make-shift
'living quarters'. The camp itself was made up of fourteen barracks, ten of which had housed his grandfather
and the other prisoners. It was surrounded by barbed
wire and an electrified fence, beyond which the prisoners could see a local church and a small cluster of
picturesque little houses.

The file had also given him an explanation of how.
Harzungen was a forced labour camp. A series of underground tunnels were being constructed in the area
to create production sites for the Luftwaffe, safe from

allied bombing. The majority of prisoners at the camps were political internees from the Soviet Union, Poland and France, but from May 1944 the Nazis began transporting Jews to the Mittelbau-Dora complex, along with members of the Sinti and Roma populations.

His grandfather had been put to work on constructing a new airfield. Harzungen was a relatively benign facility compared to some of the other camps. There was rudimentary medical support provided by an elderly and sympathetic German physician, and the sicker or weaker inmates were sometimes fortunate enough to be given 'light duties', such as building wooden blocks, or earth removals. On other occasions they were sent out to load the lorries of local businesses in the area. When they did, they were spat on in the street by the villagers.

The camp itself was guarded by soldiers of the Luftwaffe, rather than the SS, which meant that the beatings and exhausting roll calls and summary executions that were regular features of other parts of the Buchenwald complex were rare. Food was provided on a regular basis, and the barracks were generally clean. On the final Christmas day of the war the prisoners were allowed to celebrate mass, officiated by a Belgian priest, and attended by the camp commandant and his officers.

But the work regime itself was harsh. Most of the prisoners were forced on to gangs constructing the underground tunnel network. Accidents involving rock slides and collapsing scaffolding occurred regularly. The air was thick with toxic dust and gases. Cases of tuberculosis, silicosis, pleurisy and blood poisoning were common. So was a condition the prisoners dubbed 'purple lip disease'. First the lips would discolour, then the eyes would become ringed by blue circles. This was a symptom of the gases devouring the blood's haemoglobin. Within seventy-two hours they were dead.

Of the 4,000 prisoners at Harzungen, 556 died. And Ed Miliband now knew his grandfather had been one of them. Dawid Kozak. Born Czestochowa, Poland, 1909. Died Harzungen, Germany, 1945. Murdered in the Shoa.

It was politics that had brought him this understanding. His visit to Israel had been primarily political. The Salon That Was No Longer a Salon had decided it was a good way of filling in the foreign policy gap on his leadership CV. His visit to Jerusalem and meeting with Benjamin Netanyahu would send a signal to members of the Jewish community alarmed by his stance on Gaza and Palestinian recognition. While his trip to Ramallah and meeting with Mahmoud Abbas would reassure Labour activists he remained sympathetic to the Palestinian cause.

But it hadn't been exclusively political. Although he was Jewish, Ed Miliband did not grow up in a Jewish household. His parents had deliberately sat apart from 'the community'. There had been no bar mitzvah, no Shabbat, no Hanukkah. There had not even been much discussion of family history. He had a memory of visiting his grandmother as a boy and seeing a photo of a man with round glasses and a dark jacket and a white shirt (though it might have been a cream shirt). He'd asked who the man was and his grandmother had started to cry, and they hadn't talked about it again.

As he entered politics his Jewishness hadn't even been in the background. It simply wasn't a part of what Ed Miliband saw when he looked at Ed Miliband. And amongst Labour's Jewish supporters the word had already gone round. With David there was maybe some hope. But Ed? Well, everyone knew he was a Goy. During the leadership election one of his press officers had been asked, 'What does Ed Miliband think about being the first Jewish leader of the Labour party.' 'Oh, David's much more Jewish than Ed,' she'd responded.

But then his Jewishness had started to become political. His first speech as leader – in which he'd spoken out about the Gaza flotilla incident – earned him a personal rebuke from the Israeli ambassador. His stance on Palestine sent further ripples across the party's Jewish base. And word went round again. Ed Miliband wasn't his father's son, he was his mother's son. Everyone in the community knew about Marion Kozak. She'd been one of the founding signatories of 'Jews for Justice for Palestinians'. And what's more, she'd signed in her maiden name.

So again, politics had started to reshape him. He'd sat down with Stewart Wood and they'd discussed what to do about the Jewish issue. He had to bring his Jewishness forward a little, they'd decided. Not too much. But just enough so that the people it mattered to would be able to glimpse it.

He started reaching back, casting around for fragments. Some were tiny. His mother had liked Woody Allen. His grandmother had cooked him chicken soup and matzo balls. And some were more substantial. Like the time in his twenties when his mother had taken him back on a visit to Czestochowa. They'd just been leaving the house she grew up in when a man appeared and started shouting, 'The Jews are coming to take back their property.'

But it was all good colour. So the stories began appearing in articles and as lines in his speeches. Political anecdotes presented as personal anecdotes. Ed Miliband has a hinterland.

That was the message they wanted to put out. Some people noticed, and some didn't. But one of the people who did start gazing around this gradually expanding hinterland was Ed Miliband himself.

What had begun as an exercise in personal rebranding was becoming – in part – a personal journey. He'd begun reaching out to the community grandees. Lord Kestenbaum and Lord Mandelson were invited round for 'a chat'. A private dinner with the Jewish Leadership Council was arranged. He approached the actress Maureen Lipman and asked if he could take Shabbat with her and her family.

And The Salon That Was No Longer a Salon nodded its approval. It was working. They were finally making headway with their Jewish problem. Ed Miliband recognized that too. He could see all this was excellent politics.

But he also recognized there were other places he needed to go. Places that had nothing to do with reassuring the swing voters of Finchley and Hendon.

Which was why he was standing there. With the faces looking down at him. Holding that file. Holding his grandfather properly for the first time.

He had the photo now as well. And tomorrow they were going to visit his aunt Sarah and the rest of her family at her kibbutz outside Tel Aviv. This time they would be able to talk about him. They'd be able to talk about all of them.

Just in front of him, on a low table, the staff had opened up the Book of Remembrance. He stepped forward, picked up the pen, then turned to one of the officials. 'How much can I write?' he asked.

So the three men wait. And still the clock ticks down. And each of them knows that whatever happens when the clock stops counting, it won't be Ed Miliband or David Cameron or Nick Clegg standing at the door of Downing Street on Friday morning, waving to the cameras.

Someone will be standing there. But it won't be them.

00.40 . . . 00.39 . . . 00.38 . . . 00.37 . . . 00.36 . . .

11. The Silent Bark of the Big Dogs

It boiled down to this. Should David Cameron stick with the dead cat? Or should he cut the dead cat loose?

He could see the argument for cutting it loose. People were genuinely angry. The MPs had been getting calls. Well, they said they'd been getting calls, but he had his doubts about that. 'I've just seen Michael Fallon's comments about Ed Miliband stabbing his brother in the back. And I'd like to register my strong disapproval.'

For one thing, most people didn't know who Michael Fallon was. For another they all thought Ed Miliband *had* stabbed his brother in the back, and they didn't like it. Plus, no-one phoned MPs any more. Not about things like this. If Michael had just announced a badger cull, or the construction of a new wind farm, perhaps.

But that didn't alter the fact they were getting a lot of bad feedback from the party. Some people thought it was low politics. Which was OK, he could handle them. He knew that sort of criticism was just coming from the usual back-bench troublemakers. The only people who scrabbled towards the moral high-ground in the middle of a general election campaign were people who wanted you to lose that campaign.

But some of the other criticism was more troubling. A

couple of the shadow ministers had phoned to say they thought it made them look rattled. And when people phoned to say something made you look rattled, what it meant was they were starting to get a bit rattled.

It also meant – and this was the thing that was troubling him the most – they weren't grasping the strategy. And by this stage everyone was supposed to understand the strategy.

But they clearly didn't. It wasn't just that they were phoning up being rattled. They were wandering about sounding off about 'Lynton's dead cat bounce'. And it wasn't a dead cat bounce. What Lynton had done was 'throw a dead cat on the table'. They should have known that. Not the MPs, so much. But certainly the members of the cabinet. Each minister should be able to understand the difference between a dead cat that was bouncing and a dead cat that was lying spread-eagled across the table.

This was the theory behind Lynton's dead cat – the one on the table, not the one bouncing around. You're in a room, and you're having an argument. What's more, you're losing the argument. Everyone else in the room is ganging up on you. And you know whatever you say, or whatever you do, or whatever fact you come up with – it isn't going to make the slightest bit of difference.

Which is the moment you reach into your jacket, pull out a dead cat and toss it theatrically on to the middle of the dining room table. Suddenly everyone's shouting, 'Look, a dead cat!!!' and, 'Oh my God, where did he get that cat?!!' and, 'That's terrible! Oh look, that poor cat!!! Who would do that to a cat?!!' And no-one's bothering about your argument any more.

So that's the theory, as explained by Lynton. Though the way he tells it is with a 'Jeez, look, there's a cat on the table.' Or that's the way people who have heard him tell it, tell it. Whenever people tell stories about Lynton they insist on making him sound like an Australian who's just walked off the set of *Prisoner Cell Block H*.

Anyway, that's the theory, and this was the practice. Labour's non-doms policy had struck a nerve. It had given them precisely the sort of definition they wanted (Tory Toff Cameron v People's Champion Miliband), and what's more it was still running. They were getting the issue to roll over, and it looked like it was going to start eating up another news cycle. Time to toss a dead cat on the table.

So they cast around for an issue. Tax, immigration, welfare. Didn't really matter. In the end, they settled on Trident renewal. Trident would do the job because it's one of those big, meaty, security-of-the-nation, transcends-national-politics, sort of issues. Just the sort of issue for a bit of low politics.

Then they quickly banged out an article. Russia. North Korea. Rogue states. Bond villains hiding under dormant volcanoes. Usual scary 'nuclear blackmail' stuff. But then they slipped in the key line. 'Remember: Ed Miliband stabbed his own brother in the back to become Labour leader. Now he is willing to stab the United

Kingdom in the back to become Prime Minister and put our country's security at risk.'

And there was the dead cat. Ed Miliband stabbed his own brother in the back. Give him half a chance and he'd stab you in the back. He'd stab the whole country in the back. Hand Ed Miliband the keys to Downing Street and by Christmas Kim Jong Un would be in Buckingham Palace sipping tea from the Queen's china.

So they had their dead cat, but now they needed someone to throw it. Michael Fallon. He's the man. A rock. A trooper. When the shrapnel is flying, Michael Fallon will catch a piece in his teeth, spit it out and floss with it.

And that's important, because when you throw that dead cat on the table you also need to have someone who's prepared to stand there and keep shouting, 'Look, a cat, a dead cat!!!' just to make sure everyone's seen it. You can't just throw your dead cat on to the table, then quickly whip it off again, in the hope no-one notices.

And Michael was just the man for that. So they whacked the article over to the *Times*, and the next day it appeared, with the perfect headline: '"Back Stabber" Miliband attacked over Trident'. Then Michael went on TV – and with the shot and shrapnel bursting all around him – repeated the charge. 'This is an issue of leadership . . . clearly Ed Miliband wants power . . . he's shown what he's prepared to do to get power . . . the danger for our country is that he could be weak in what he achieves . . . this is an issue of leadership and judgement . . . the British people are entitled to know what sort of man might be the next Prime Minister, and what he is prepared to do to get into Downing Street.' Essentially the old homicidal wimp line. He's stabbed his brother in the back. He'll stab the country in the back. He'll stab you in the back.

But it worked a treat. The Bubble Breathers were going nuts. 'Deeply personal and dishonourable' – the *Guardian*. 'Michael Fallon "should be ashamed" after personal attack on Ed Miliband over Trident renewal' – The *Mirror*. 'Backlash follows Tory attack on "backstabbing Labour leader"' – The *Independent*. Then Ed Miliband responded himself. 'Michael Fallon's a decent man but today he's demeaned himself and demeaned his office. Decent Conservatives across our country will say – come on, we're better than this. David Cameron should be ashamed.' Which made the Bubble Breathers go even more nuts. And now everyone was shouting and screaming and hollering over Michel Fallon's dead cat. And, more importantly, no-one was saying a word about non-doms.

Perfect. Except Isabel Hardman – a sort of Bubble Breather's cross between Carrie Bradshaw and Sherlock Holmes who writes for the *Spectator* – noticed the following paragraph from an article Boris Johnson penned in his *Daily Telegraph* column back in 2013. 'Let us suppose you are losing an argument. The facts are overwhelmingly against you, and the more people focus on the reality the worse it is for you and your case. Your best bet in these circumstances is to perform a man-oeuvre that a great campaigner describes as "throwing a dead cat on the table, mate". That is because there is one thing that is absolutely certain about throwing a dead cat on the dining room table – and I don't mean that people will be outraged, alarmed, disgusted. That is true, but irrelevant. The key point, says my Australian friend, is that everyone will shout, "Jeez, mate, there's a dead cat on the table!" In other words they will be talk-ing about the dead cat, the thing you want them to talk about, and they will not be talking about the issue that has been causing you so much grief.'

Which is a typically baroque bit of Boris writing. But that's not what attracted her. What caught her attention was that before he was working as David Cameron's Big Dog, Lynton Crosby was working as Boris Johnson's Big Dog, on his two successful mayoral campaigns. And unless Boris had lots of friends who were cast members on *Prisoner Cell Block H*, Lynton must have been the 'mate' who told him all about the dead cat strategy. And what she'd just seen, with Michael Fallon and his attack on the homicidal wimp, looked remarkably like a dead cat strategy. Which meant, in fact, it wasn't Michael Fal-lon's dead cat. It was Lynton's dead cat.

And it's this that really lay at the heart of David Cam-eron's current dilemma. Those people calling on him to cut the dead cat loose weren't actually calling on him to cut the dead cat loose. They were calling on him to cut the Big Dog loose.

And he could have. He had a speech that morning, and he could have gone out and said, 'I have serious concerns about Ed Miliband's leadership. But we're going to win this election on the arguments. No-one on any campaign led by me is going to sink to personal abuse, and everyone in my cabinet and on my team is well aware of that.' And then he could have got Craig or someone else to dribble out a line about how he'd called in Lynton and had a little talk with him. 'You have to remember Lynton's from Australia. They do their politics a bit differently down there. The Prime Minister's had a quiet word with him . . . sorry? . . . yes, Lynton still enjoys the Prime Minister's full confidence.'

He could have done all that. But there were a couple of issues with it. The first was that at that point the dead cat would stop becoming a distraction from a problem and become the problem. This narrative the Bubble Breathers were trying to get up and running – 'Tory campaign chaos' – was going to get traction. And when it did, people really were going to start getting rattled.

The other was that if he sent his Big Dog to the kennel he'd be there for the duration. He wouldn't be able to risk bringing him out again, because if he bit someone a second time he'd end up having to put him down. Plus, a Big Dog that's muzzled is no good to anyone.

And there's another major reason why he was reluctant to bring Lynton to heel. Lynton hadn't actually done anything wrong. Quite the opposite, in fact.

The problem here wasn't Lynton's dead cat strategy. It

was the way Boris felt the need to boast publicly about Lynton's dead cat strategy. He loved Boris. Well, he got on with Boris. But Boris just couldn't help showing off about his Big Dog.

Yes, you want them exerting their influence. Otherwise what's the point in getting yourself a Big Dog in the first place? And you want it to be known they're exerting their influence. That's important too. It gives your message and your strategy extra potency. 'Look at that stunt with Fallon. Classic Lynton.' The imprimatur of the Big Dog gets you extra column inches and added air-time.

But at the precise moment they're exerting their influence they mustn't be in sight. Because if they are, then at that point the messenger becomes the message. Suddenly it isn't about Ed Miliband stabbing his brother in the back. Or even about Michael Fallon stabbing Ed Miliband in the back for stabbing his brother in the back. It becomes about how Lynton Crosby's just told Michael Fallon to stab Ed Miliband in the back for stabbing his brother in the back.

And that's not necessarily a bad thing. If people are screaming 'There's a dead cat on the table!!!' or they're screaming, 'Lynton Crosby's just thrown a dead cat on the table!!!' there's no major difference. They're all still concentrating on the dead cat.

But tomorrow you're going to be unveiling your new tax cut. Or revealing your plan for £8 billion of extra spending on the NHS. And when you do you can't afford to have people shouting, 'Look, another of Lynton Crosby's dead cats!!!'

Which is what you have to understand about the Big Dogs. They can be seen, but not heard. Or heard, but not seen. Seen and heard. But just not at the same time.

That's what people should notice. The silent bark of the Big Dogs.

David Cameron knew all this. And he knew it because Lynton Crosby had explained it to him. Lynton had this showman's reputation. But that was mainly because people sit at dinner parties explaining how they know life's showmen, not life's programme sellers. When you meet him he's quite understated (not just for an Australian), and is happiest just sitting there chatting about his wife Dawn and the kids. His opponents – very few of whom *have* actually met him – imagine this hard-drinking, hard-swearing, Antipodean Malcolm Tucker. But he actually looks like he's rector of a good old-fashioned grey-brick Scottish university, who's just reached the mid-point of his tenure. He looks settled.

And he hated the idea of anyone catching him when he was barking. Though he didn't quite phrase it like that. The way he put it to Cameron and Craig and the rest of The League of Extraordinary Advisors, was, 'Whatever we do, we don't let them see the wiring.'

He was obsessed by it. Time and again the Bubble Breathers would be on the phone to Craig banging on about 'process'. They needed 'process stories'. Not what the Government was doing, but how it was doing it.

What's behind this announcement? Who's behind it? How's it going to be spun? Why's it going to be like that? Who's been squared off on the announcement? How have they been squared off? Who was digging in against the announcement? Why were they digging in against it?

And that was just in peacetime. Now, during the election, there were no big announcements. The whole thing was one giant exercise in 'process'.

But Lynton was adamant. 'Don't show them the wiring.' Don't let them see the Big Dog bark.

And David Cameron liked that. Everyone in politics was always fighting for the limelight. Trying to get themselves inserted at the end of some Bubble Breather's copy as a 'senior source'. It didn't seem all that long ago he was fighting for the limelight himself.

So he picked up his pen and jotted down a few lines. 'Labour are playing fast and loose with our security . . . is Ed Miliband really committed to the Trident deterrent . . . Michael Fallon was right to raise this, and he was right to raise it in a pretty frank way.'

He was fighting for a different sort of limelight now. And his Big Dog was going to help him get it.

Of course the thing about the Big Dogs – the thing that the politicians, or the Bubble Breathers or the Big Dogs themselves never let on – is that they're primarily show dogs. Yes, they know their stuff. And your average political Big Dog will have more clever political tradecraft

rattling around in his head than a dozen ordinary political Little Dog advisors. But each of the campaigns has
hundreds of advisors. So if you were to get all your Little
Dogs together, you'd be able to generate the Big Dog's
bark in the end.

But that's not what the three men were looking for.
They wanted a strong, sinewed beast at their side. A dog
they could take out for a strut.

So take Lynton's dead cat story. When anyone heard it
for the first time they'd say to themselves, 'The dead cat.
The table. Brilliant! That's why we pay Lynton the big
bucks.'

But basically, every PR man or ad man or person
who's ever watched an episode of *Mad Men* knows
that story. Only to them it's not a story, just a simple
line. 'If you don't like what's being said, change the
conversation.'

But who wants to hear the same, tired old line? When
they can get to hear the silent bark of the Big Dog.

The members of Ed Miliband's shadow cabinet would
never tire of telling the story of the first time he took his
Big Dog for a walk. David Axelrod. Best in show. The
man who won the White House for Obama. And then
won it again.

A proper hire. £300,000 worth of hire, to be precise.
Douglas Alexander flew over to the States and brokered
the deal. That's the phrasing people were using. 'Brokered the deal.'

Although, what the actual deal was seemed a little vague. Axelrod wouldn't be doing any spinning. He'd be giving 'strategic communications advice'. Precisely what sort of strategic advice was also a little vague. Some of The Salon That Was No Longer a Salon seemed to think it would be advice on messaging. Others said it would be to give guidance on Ed's image and presentation. Axelrod himself was reported to have expressed fears about how the Tories would spend the last few days of the campaign 'playing the politics of fear'. So he'd told Douglas he thought that's when his services would best be of use. Those final crucial few weeks. Or final crucial few days. So he and his key lieutenant Larry Grisolano would be monitoring the campaign closely from their office in the States. And then he planned to fly in for these last crucial days. If Douglas could just make out the check to AKPD Message and Media.

Understandably, Douglas was excited by the deal he'd 'brokered'. And as soon as the news broke that Labour had got itself a real Big Dog, everyone else started getting excited as well.

Or nearly everyone. There were a few siren voices raised. No one doubted David Axelrod was highly skilled. But three hundred grand? PLP Chair Dave Watts told Ed, 'That's quite a lot of money for a comfort blanket for Douglas.' Which Ed thought was rather unfair.

But Ed also recognized there could be some muttering if no-one ever got to run around with this Big Dog of his. So slap bang in the middle of Easter recess the shadow cabinet received an urgent email. A special meeting had been organized to introduce all shadow cabinet members to David Axelrod. Attendance was expected.

And so children were put down and wives and husbands dragged out of work, and from the four corners of the nation the weary shadow ministers dragged themselves back to Westminster. They shuffled into the meeting room at Brewer's Green and arranged themselves around the table. At which point they were dragged back out of their chairs and placed in a delicately arranged seating pattern. The likes of Chuka Umunna and Tristram Hunt were ushered to the front of the room and the likes of Jon Cruddas, Michael Dugher and Jon Trickett were shooed politely to the back.

Then the door opened and in walked Stefan Rosseau, the PA photographer. And people were looking at each other. They couldn't remember having a photographer at shadow cabinet since Ed's first shadow cabinet, way back in 2010.

And then the door opened again and in walked Ed and Douglas and David Axelrod. Douglas, in the view of one of his colleagues, was looking like 'a schoolboy who was about to wet himself'. Ed – dressed in a dark suit, white shirt and purple tie – looked like he'd just been awarded first prize in a clarinet competition. David Axelrod – also dressed in a dark suit, white shirt and purple tie – looked like a middle-aged tech geek who'd just been taken to the office of some giant multi-national who wanted to buy his on-line start-up.

Then there was a pause, as Stefan started grabbing some photos. Which went a little bit awkwardly because Harriet Harman wasn't sure whether she should be talking to Ed, who was on her left, or Larry Grisolano, who was on her right. And Larry Grisolano – who looked a bit like he was the last person to see Jimmy Hoffa alive – was unsure about whether he was supposed to be talking to Harriet, who was on his left, or Yvette Cooper, who was on his right. And Ed wanted to talk to David, but he wasn't sure whether he was supposed to be leading the conversation with David, or listening to David. So he ended up sitting there with this slightly peculiar smile on his face, like a guy on a blind date who thinks it's going quite well, but isn't entirely sure if his date thinks it's going well. And the rest of the shadow cabinet – who weren't even in shot – didn't have a clue what they were supposed to be doing, and were sitting there feeling like wedding guests who have turned up to the church, to find they've only actually been invited to the evening reception.

Then mercifully Stefan got his final shot, the door closed and Ed Miliband bid welcome to their new guests. But the welcome fell a bit flat after he announced, 'David's on a very tight schedule, and we've only got him here for forty minutes, so when it comes to the discussion if you could all keep your questions and comments brief.' At which point everyone in the room suddenly started staring straight ahead of themselves, because they knew if they dared look to either side they were going to catch a glimpse of the person next to them. And that glimpse would turn into a knowing look. And that knowing look would become a silently mouthed 'What. The. Fuck. It's Easter, I've had to leave the kids with the grandparents, and the wife's giving me the ice treatment, and I've spent four hours on the M6, and when I finally get here I get shoved half a mile below the salt, and have to sit for fifteen minutes watching someone papping Larry The Icepick talking to Harriet about her plans for her pink battle bus, and Douglas looking like he's the little Dutch kid with his finger in the dyke, only to get told not to bother the Big Dog with too many questions because he's on a tight schedule, and all while we're paying him £300,000, which at the moment is working out at a rate of *seven and a half thousand pounds a minute.*'

And then David Axelrod rose and started to say a few words. And it was strange. He was talking, and what he was saying was quite interesting. Despite their cynicism everyone in the room was actually quite impressed. He had clearly been well briefed. He obviously knew the British political scene quite well. When he said the words 'Tories' and 'David Cameron' in that low, deliberate, Stuy Town accent of his it sounded a bit strange, like a child speaking French for the first time. But he was talking, and Ed was nodding sagely, and Douglas was looking as if he was about to burst. Then he finished and they went round the room, and people asked him some questions. So he answered them in that low, deliberate, Stuy Town voice. And again, everyone was thinking, 'OK, fair play. This guy knows his stuff.'

Then before you know it, forty minutes was up. So Ed stood and David stood, and Douglas just about managed to stand, and with a nod of thanks they walked out of the room. There was a brief little bit of after-chat, then all the members of the shadow cabinet picked up their papers and went their separate ways.

A few hours later the weary MPs were walking back through their front doors, retrieving kids from their grandparents and trying to make conciliatory noises to frosty spouses. 'How did it go?' they were asked. 'What's he like?' They took off their coats, started making themselves a cup of tea and explained how it was all quite interesting, and how David Axelrod seemed to be quite a switched-on guy. 'So what sort of things was he saying?' the curious wives and husbands and grandparents enquired.

They poured the water, then stirred in the milk and dropped the teabag in the bin. And it was really funny. Now they came to think of it, they couldn't remember a single thing David Axelrod actually said.

There is one thing about a show dog, though. When people look at it, they can't tell it's a show dog. All they see is a big dog. They've no way of knowing it's a proper Big Dog.

It looks well trained. Passive enough. Trotting along dutifully by its owner's side. But how can they tell? Get too close and who knows what may happen? They could hear its bark from halfway down the street. Didn't see it barking. But they could certainly hear it. Best to give it a wide birth. Let sleeping Big Dogs lie, and all that.

Ryan Coetzee, Nick Clegg's Big Dog, looked passive enough. He's quite short and cuddly looking, with a slightly mischievous glint in his eye. Like the comic lead in a moderately successful romcom.

But like the other Big Dogs, when he talked about politics, he exuded understated authority. His thoughts always seemed to be running ten seconds ahead of the thoughts of everyone else in the room.

Though that's not what Nick Clegg needed him for. What Nick Clegg needed his Big Dog to do was keep people at a safe distance whilst he did the things that needed to be done.

Not that he realized that's what he needed him for when he first hired him. What he was looking for was a strategist and an organizer. The Cell was focused inward. On creating space inside the government. He needed someone to look outward. Someone who could pull together a strategy for making sure they stayed in government after the election.

But that was before he fully realized what that strategy would entail. Before his Big Dog sat him down and explained exactly what he'd have to do to keep his party alive.

The problem, Ryan explained to him, was that they were spread too thin. They currently held fifty-seven seats. The private polling they'd done and the national polling they were looking at showed them the most they could hope to hold on to was thirty to thirty-five seats. The Cell was doing a great job in starting to shift public perceptions. But there was no point pretending. He was unpopular, his party was unpopular, and there was no prospect of reversing that unpopularity by May 2015.

Nick Clegg listened to all this. And a bit of him wanted to argue, but he didn't. Partly because it would have looked unseemly for him to say, 'I'm not that unpopular you know.' Partly because Ryan was explaining all this in that compelling – if slightly chilling – matter-of-fact way of his. And partly because it was true, and although it was unpalatable, everyone knew it was true. Though not as unpalatable as what his Big Dog had to say to him next.

They were going to have to let people go. They didn't have the bodies, they didn't have the money and they didn't have the other resources to defend fifty-seven seats. Lorely Burt in Solihull. Majority of 175. She's gone. Bradford East. David Ward. Majority of 365. He's gone. Wells. Tessa Munt. Majority of 800. She's gone.

Ryan was calmly going through his list, drawing a red line through people's careers and lives. And these were Nick Clegg's colleagues. Friends. He'd known them for years. Decades, in some cases.

And he asked him, 'So that's it? We're just going to

tell them it's over?' And Ryan looked up at him and shook his head. 'Oh no. We're not just going to cut them like that.'

Nick Clegg inwardly let out a sigh of relief.

'We're going to give them all six months. We're going to give them fundraising targets and recruitment targets and canvassing targets. And the ones that meet those targets, we're going to fight for. It's the ones who don't who we're going to cut.'

And Nick Clegg thought to himself, 'Jesus. I'm basically going to be triaging the parliamentary party. They're never going to stand for this. There's going to be an uproar.'

Then he looked at Ryan. And Ryan was looking back at him, with that look in his eye. And he knew. They would stand for it. Because it wouldn't be him giving each of his MPs the thumbs up or thumbs down. It would be Ryan doing it.

And what were the MPs going to do? Risk trying to get past the Big Dog? Take on the Big Dog?

Good luck with that. Some people said he was just a show dog. That Nick didn't naturally warm to his focus-group-driven brand of machine politics. That it was still Jonny Oates who had his ear. You could go round him to Nick. Nick would listen.

But what if they were wrong. What if Ryan wasn't just a show dog? There were other people who said Nick was listening to Ryan more than he was listening to any other member of The Cell. And they also said Ryan could be pretty ruthless if he wanted to be. What if you tried to go round him, and the Big Dog woke up? What if he woke up and his bite turned out to be even worse than his bark?

And that's one of the other reasons why Nick Clegg got himself a Big Dog. One of the reasons all three of these men had their Big Dogs. Their bark may have been worse than their bite. Or their bite may have been worse than their bark. But it was only the Big Dogs and their owners who knew for sure.

And the clock continues to tick down. David Cameron is in the Manor House. Nick Clegg is in the flat. Ed Miliband is in his Lego House. And the wives and the spinners and the body-men and the speechwriters and the bullet-catchers and the gurus are all milling around.

But not the Big Dogs. The Big Dogs have fallen silent now. And tomorrow, whatever happens, they will begin the search for a new master.

00.35 . . . 00.34 . . . 00.33 . . . 00.32 . . . 00.31 . . .

12. The Morality of Self Interest

The lights of the passing car swept the ceiling in a narrow arc, then vanished. The room was black again. Though not to his eyes. They'd long since adjusted to the darkness.

It had been the right thing to do. He had no doubt about that. It was the right thing to do for the country, and for the party. And ultimately – although looking at the carnage unfolding on the news bulletins it was hard to visualize at the moment – it was the right thing for Syria, and the region.

It was true that Rosie and Douglas had both told him they would have trouble holding the MPs in line. They hadn't been sure of the numbers. Maybe as low as forty. Perhaps as high as seventy. And that would have damaged him. There was no point denying it. A big part of what they'd been doing was to demonstrate how he'd managed to bring the party together after the election. A lot of people had warned it could all split apart. Well it hadn't. He'd held things together. Which had been important for him. And important for the party, obviously.

And it wasn't just the MPs. The members were getting very concerned. The anti-war lobby was beginning to rev the engine again. People like Dianne Abbott and

Jeremy Corbyn were rummaging through their ward-robes, looking for their bloodied Iraq War shirts.

Actually, that was too harsh. A lot of people had a lot of serious concerns. And he'd told Cameron that. When he'd sat there in his study (it was still strange going in there. A bit like going back to dinner at your old house a couple of years after you'd sold it), he'd explained it all to him. It was vital, he'd said, that people could be reassured about the legality of the war. Failing to comprehensively interrogate the legality of the con-flict was what had led to the Iraq catastrophe. Another issue was the intelligence. They couldn't afford another dodgy dossier. The available intelligence would have to be presented in a transparent way. Then there was the UN. They had to have international support. It couldn't look like it was another piece of British and US adven-turism. The weapons inspectors' report would also be hugely important. There didn't seem much doubt it had been Assad who had deployed chemical weapons. But the inspectors had to be given time to properly investi-gate and present their findings. And parliament had to have the final say. They would only be able to carry the country if parliament had given a firm stamp of approval to their plan of action.

And to be fair, David Cameron had listened politely, and engaged courteously. He'd been in 'statesman mode', which involved pulling himself up a little higher in his chair, and ... talking ... slightly ... more ... deliberately.

Anyway, he'd set out his bottom lines, and over the course of the next forty-eight hours Cameron had responded. The legal advice would be published. As would – taking into account the usual national security considerations – the intelligence assessment. He would also be submitting a motion to the UN for approval by the P5. He could also guarantee no military action would be undertaken until the inspectors had reported. And he would allow not one but two commons votes – an 'in principle' authorization of the proposed intervention, and a second vote before any strikes were actually carried out.

And that had all been good, and very helpful. But there were still serious problems. Rosie and Douglas had told him the rebellion was growing. And Hilary Benn had also begun identifying troubling issues with the military and diplomatic strategy.

OK, some people were questioning why his Shadow Communities Secretary was advising him on matters like this. But Hilary had a sharp mind and solid judgement. And his name still carried a certain cache with the Left of the movement. Which was useful. Jim Murphy and Ivan Lewis were his defence and development spokesmen. And he'd listened to what they'd had to say. But they had a tendency to be a little bit too hot on this stuff. These were sensitive issues. Matters of war and peace.

Emily Thornberry had also been invaluable. Not everyone liked Emily. She could be a little on the arrogant side. But as Shadow Attorney General she brought a legal perspective to the debate. And, he'd started to realize, she was articulating a number of his own concerns about the government's strategy.

If the attack against Syria did go ahead, what was the objective, she'd asked? The removal of Assad's chemical weapons? The removal of Assad himself? The end of the Syria conflict?

Which may have been a little bit outside her brief. But David Cameron hadn't really answered any of those questions. Perhaps he could have pressed him a little harder on those things when they'd met. But David Cameron was the Prime Minister, not him. It hadn't been his responsibility to put together the plan of attack. It had been his job to critique it, and – if he thought it was in the national interest – back it.

And it had become increasingly apparent that David Cameron was having enough trouble convincing his own ministers and backbenchers to support the plan. The whips were picking up increasingly frantic activity from their Tory opposite numbers. The Bubble Breathers were reporting the rebellion on the Tory side was also building. Which wouldn't matter if he decided to throw his weight behind Cameron. Nick Clegg was just about managing to hold his MPs in line. So together they'd have the votes.

But his own doubts had begun to increase by the hour. Obviously he had to address the issue on its merits. But if David Cameron was defeated, it would be a staggering blow to his authority. And if Cameron wasn't able to keep his own party together on the issue, he could hardly expect him to split his own apart to save the Prime Minister's skin.

And then they'd seen the motion. Hilary Benn had been on to it straight away. Picked up a pen and began scribbling out a possible amendment. He knew the best way to defeat the government. And by doing so, stop the rush to war. They wouldn't rule out military action, but they would demand a number of safeguards. And the crucial one would be 'That such action must have regard to the potential consequences in the region, and must therefore be legal, proportionate, time-limited and have precise and achievable objectives designed to deter the future use of prohibited chemical weapons in Syria.' No-one could accuse them of ignoring Assad's atrocities. But they were demanding sensible and legitimate safeguards to ensure no repeat of the catastrophe of 2003.

He hadn't started in that position. He was prepared to admit that to himself. His instinct had been to back the government in the same way he'd done on Libya in 2010.

But the more he'd thought about it, the more he'd come to the conclusion that this wasn't just the best course of action, it was the only course of action. Yes, there was an element of self interest. Defeating David Cameron in such a dramatic way, on such a vital issue, could have untold political consequences for the government. But it was also the right thing to do. The country had been about to go to war. And he'd stopped that war. It had been the right thing to do and the morally correct thing to do. One of those rare occasions in politics when morality and self interest align.

Another yellow arc swept across the ceiling, and then vanished. It wouldn't be until the first shafts of daylight began inching across the ceiling that Ed Miliband finally managed to fall asleep.

The water was so cold it felt hot on his skin. He swept his arms forward and lowered his head downwards. For a second his world became dark and silent. Then his head broke the surface again, and everything was sharp and bright. Off to his right the mid-afternoon sun glanced off the tops of the trees, and went skidding out across the water.

He twisted his body around, so he was looking back at the house. Whenever he saw Chevening, with its rolling lawn, its willows and redwoods and lily-garlanded lake, there was a moment when he allowed himself to believe. Convince himself it was over.

The travelling. The running. He could rest now. He'd reached his destination at last.

But he knew he hadn't. In fact, in some ways, the grand house and surroundings generated their own anxieties. It was almost as if the house was standing there, taunting him. 'So this is what's become of the great Nick Clegg. Remember all the things you were going to do? All the things you were going to become? And here you are. Splashing around in your grace and favour lake, in the shade of your grace and favour trees, in the grounds of your grace and favour mansion.'

He lowered his head back into the darkness.

None of it had been about himself. None of this had been for him. Channel 4 had recently made a play about the coalition negotiations. There'd been a moment when the David Cameron character had offered him the title of Deputy Prime Minister, and the guy portraying him had played it like he was a child who had just set eyes on his first-ever Christmas present.

He lifted his head up and it broke back into the sunlight.

It hadn't been like that. One thing nobody realized was how tired he'd been. How tired they'd all been. Everyone was exhausted. Unless you'd fought an election, you couldn't understand what it felt like. The campaign emptied you. By the last week, half the team had been on the brink of collapse. Excitement and adrenalin can only carry you so far. And for them the adrenalin had kicked in too soon. The whole Cleggmania thing had sent an electric charge through the campaign. No-one had been prepared for it. There had been a moment when they'd actually been ahead in the polls. When some people had started to believe they were really heading for government. Not as a junior partner, but an actual Liberal Democrat-led administration.

And they just weren't equipped to deal with that. They didn't have the circuit breakers in place to cope.

So by the end, when they saw it had all been a mirage –
that they had actually lost seats – people couldn't handle
it. They'd just gone down. And then they'd suddenly
been told they had to drag themselves up off the floor
and get ready to negotiate their entry into government.

He kicked his legs outwards, and began propelling
himself away from the house.

And they had been prepared. Before the campaign
had started they'd done all the work. They had all the
position papers and all the policy papers, and they knew
all their bottom lines.

But you can't really prepare. If you're a small party,
and you've been out of power for the best part of a century, there's no way to prepare for your first opportunity
of power.

He wasn't into football much, though the boys were.
But he remembered reading or hearing something once
about how the England football team didn't prac-
tise penalties. They'd been getting pilloried for it because
they'd just gone out of another tournament that way.
And he'd seen whoever the hapless manager was at the
time trying to explain that there was no point in practis-
ing penalties, because taking a penalty wasn't a technical
issue, it was a mental one. There was no way you could
possibly hope to recreate the pressure of a big match
situation on the training ground.

And that's how it had been for them. There was no
way of preparing yourself for coalition negotiations
where one false move, or one careless turn of phrase, or

one sloppily worded paragraph could cost you the chance of governing your country for the first time in a century.

He kicked out again, and spread his arms wide. High above a plane's vapour trail was cutting a thin groove into the sky.

Take tuition fees. The only issue anyone ever remembered, and was ever likely to remember. During the election he'd signed the pledge, Vince had signed the pledge, Danny had signed the pledge, they'd all signed the damn pledge. OK, so they promised they'd scrap tuition fees. But no-one had decided what they'd actually replace the bloody tuition fees with.

So there they were, a week after the election, going eyeball to eyeball with George Osborne and William Hague and Ed Llewellyn (who doesn't look like he's blinked in his entire adult life). And people were almost on the floor again, because the latest post-election, pre-coalition adrenalin rush was starting to wear off. And the cabinet secretary Gus O'Donnell was beginning to drum his fingers on his desk and warn that any further delay to the formation of a government was likely to start having a serious impact on the financial markets. He'd been passed the word that if the talks dragged out much longer the party might start wobbling again over doing a deal with the Tories. And that's when they came to him and said, 'Nick, they're digging in on tuition fees.

We could go back and try and hammer something out, but that's going to take more time. Or we can just see if we can get them to kick it into the long grass, and work something out later.'

And at that moment he wasn't thinking about titles. Or ministerial cars. Or grace and favour mansions. All he was thinking about was, 'I need to get some sleep.'

So they kicked the issue long. They'd all finally managed to get some sleep. And a couple of months passed. They were fit, and they were perky, and they were starting to quite warm to this being-in-government thing. So one warm afternoon he sat down with The Cell and they started to go through the position paper they'd drawn up on tuition fees. There were several options – lifting the cap (suicidal), simply raising the income level at which loans were paid back (dangerous), a lower cap (less dangerous, but expensive), a graduate tax (complex), a new system of loans and means-tested grants that was simply branded a graduate tax (dangerous and complex).

His own preference was for going with the new system of loans and means-tested grants, and just calling the whole thing a graduate tax. If people got behind the back of the policy and managed to paint it as tuition fees by another name, they were in trouble. But it was probably the simplest way to resolve the whole issue. So they batted it around a bit. But they weren't really looking at things all that politically. That's the way they used to do things. They needed to look at this issue on its merits now. This was a major policy decision. And that's what serious people in government do. They make calm, measured decisions. So they agreed to kick it around some more. And with that, Nick Clegg waved them goodbye. He was off for a trip to his new grace and favour residence down at Chevening.

A few months later they were back again. Not so fit and perky now. They realized they had a serious political problem. And they'd just learnt the hard way you can't just switch off the political radar because you're worried it might interfere with the business of making serious decisions in government.

The Tories weren't budging. George Osborne had basically been chasing Vince round his office telling him it was time to man up and come in behind their fees policy. Nothing was in the manifesto agreement, so there was no cover for them there. And it was being framed as the first big test of the coalition since the government was formed. So what were they supposed to do? Bring the whole government crashing down after just seven months?

He knew what he had to do. And he knew what he couldn't do. The kids were already rioting in the streets. If he tried to slide it past them now they'd spot it a mile off. They didn't have any options left. They had to just go with the higher repayment threshold, explain this was the price of doing business in coalition, and take the hit.

So he signed it off. The MPs were going to go postal. The members were going to go postal. But at least he could justify it to himself. He'd known this was what government was going to be. Compromises. Hard choices. He'd done what he'd done in the best interests of the country. In the long run – the very long run – people would recognize that.

Nick Clegg stopped paddling. Despite the sunshine the water in the lake was especially cold today. He was going to have to get out soon.

He pushed his head downwards, and the darkness and the silence enveloped him for one last time. It would have been nice to stay under there. There was no way they could get to him here, where it was so quiet and black.

And then he broke the surface, and everything was bright and clear again. In front of him was that grand stately home, with its immaculately manicured lawn, its trees arcing around in their geometrically perfect semi-circle, and its beautiful hedgerows that appeared to have been shaped at the hand of a master sculptor. And Nick Clegg knew. It wasn't over. It was never going to be over. The travelling. The running. He was never going to rest.

Or if he was, it wouldn't be here. Wherever his final destination was, this wasn't it.

*

He held the magazine in his hand. It was perfect. The whole thing was perfect. The League of Extraordinary Gentlemen were doing cartwheels.

There was Sam smiling out from the cover. She looked incredible. Like a model. No, better than a model. She was leaning casually against the sofa, with her head slightly tilting to one side, and her phone resting in her hand. If you'd got a model to pose for that shot it would seem precisely that – posed.

But Sam just looked natural. Like someone had just come in and caught her chatting to one of her girlfriends.

Three and a half million people read 'You' magazine, the main *Mail on Sunday* supplement. Or that's how many normally read it. As soon as people saw that photo of his wife, he knew they were going to be fighting each other for copies.

And obviously there was the headline too. 'We were at breaking point.' Which had taken him aback a little when he first saw it. He knew it was true, obviously. But when you saw it spelled out like that . . . well, it did stop you for a moment.

But that was what they'd agreed. It would help them. Yes, it would help in a political sense. The *Mail on Sunday* was the best-selling mid-market in the country. And the demography of its readers perfectly overlapped their key seat target demographic. Plus it was a woman's magazine. And everyone knew they had a bit of a woman problem.

But it would help both of them. People would get to see who they were. Or they'd get to see who Samantha was, and then through seeing her, they'd see a bit more of him. The real him.

It hadn't been easy to arrange though. And he was glad of that. There were some political wives (and husbands) he knew who would bite your hand off for the chance of a *Mail on Sunday* feature. Samantha wasn't one of those wives.

They talked about it several times. How 'the guys' had wondered if she'd be interested in doing a little bit more press? Obviously, she already had her charity work. But they'd been thinking maybe she could do something around the local elections. Perhaps follow her about on the campaign trail.

And she'd agreed. In her own way. 'I'm happy to,' she'd told them, 'but if I do you have to understand I'm going to be saying what I want to say, not necessarily what you want me to say. So if that's OK with you, fine.'

So they'd set that one aside for a while. But 'the guys' kept coming back to it. They had figures that showed Samantha added an extra two points to their national poll rating, they said. They didn't have anything of the kind, of course. But it was a nice line, so they started floating it out there anyway. And they kept coming back to the woman issue. Labour were overhyping it, yes. But there was something there. The idea that women found him a bit slick and phony. This could be a way of counteracting that.

And, of course, there was the NHS issue. They called it the NHS issue. They said it would be helpful if they could 'flesh out' his stance on the NHS. Another phrase they used was 'humanize' his position.

What they meant was, he should sit down and talk about the death of his son. And that Samantha should sit down and talk about the death of her son.

Ask any politician, and they'd tell you protecting the family was the hardest part of politics. And they'd tell you in exactly that way, in precisely those terms. The imperative to protect.

But it wasn't true. The hardest part of being a politician wasn't working out how to protect your family. It was about working out how to use your family.

That was what made it so complicated. If you really wanted to protect the family, you could do. Obviously you couldn't insulate them from the abuse you received. But you could at least keep them safe. You just said they were out of bounds. No photos. No news footage. You didn't take them to any political events. You didn't use them in any PPBs. You didn't have them on your election material, or on your Christmas cards.

And that would be it. The Bubble Breathers would moan, but they'd respect the no-fly zone. The family would be out of harm's way. People would literally not know what they looked like.

And the Bubble Breathers and the spinners and the pollsters would all say, 'This is not helping X's image. People want to know their politicians have proper lives.'

But it was rubbish. Because people do have proper lives. Lives that don't extend to worrying about what Joe Bloggs Politician's kids look like.

So when he heard politicians saying, 'The hardest thing is to protect the family,' he knew it wasn't true. Even when he heard himself saying it.

Politicians used their families because they thought it would give them an edge. And that was what he had to wrestle with. How much of an edge did he want? How much of an edge did he need? How much of an edge could he manufacture, and still look at himself in that long mirror by his desk?

There were different ways of managing it. One was that you hid behind the team. So there would be the ritual like they'd gone through with Samantha and the local elections.

Craig and a couple of other people from The League would sit down with him and explain how they needed more of the family. And he'd say no. Which they knew he'd say. And then they'd hand him a list of all the things they wanted from Sam and the kids. And he'd say absolutely not. Which they also knew he'd say. Then they'd say, 'Well look, what about this little thing at the bottom of the list. Can we at least try that?' And he'd say, 'OK. I'll try. I'll have a chat with Sam. But I'm telling you, she isn't going to go for it.' Sometimes she would. Sometimes she wouldn't. But they'd tried. He'd tried.

The other thing was to mentally picture yourself in the midst of a sort of spousal arms race. So someone from The League would come to him and say, 'The word around the lobby is the *Mirrror*'s going to be doing a feature with Ed's wife. They're going to be talking her up as "Miliband's secret weapon". Just thought you ought to know.'

And then someone else would come up to him and casually say, 'Have you seen Miliband's Christmas card? Got Justine and the boys on it. Looks quite nice actually.'

Gradually they were ratcheting it up. And he was thinking, 'OK, I know what me and Sam agreed. But if he's going to be putting the wife and kids out there, it's going to start to look quite odd if I don't do it.'

One problem with this approach was Nick Clegg. Nick – and this was a very 'Nick thing', though he did admire him for it – wouldn't go there at all. Zero access to the boys. The odd photo or interview with Miriam maybe. But nothing with Miguel and Antonio and Alberto. Sam knew this as well.

But eventually they'd worn him down. As they always knew they would, and he always knew they would.

The BBC were going to be doing features on each of the leaders. And they needed family access. Ed was giving them Justine and the kids. Even Nick was giving up his mother. They had to have something *intimate*.

And so he'd begun the negotiations. With his own wife. And with himself. OK, not the flat. They could have the house in Oxfordshire. It would at least show the world they don't live in some palatial mansion. And they could film the children. But no direct interaction with the children. And the children could only be shot from behind. And they could have a question or two with her. But only general stuff. Nothing about Ivan. They were his red lines. And he was also going to tell the BBC what they'd agreed. That this was his last election. Then they'd be done with it all. Forever.

And that was how you justified it to yourself. You had a camera crew in your kitchen, filming your kids as they were eating their dinner. But you'd only allowed them to film the backs of their heads. Which meant you were still being a good father and husband. You were still protecting them.

And then The League had come back one last time. They'd had bids from the *Mail* and the *Sun* for a big election interview with Samantha. The *Mail on Sunday* was offering 'You' magazine. Ten pages and the cover. And he'd thought, 'They want ten pages with me?' But then they'd explained it. And he'd looked at them hard, because he knew what it meant. And they knew what it meant.

So he'd explained it to her. How they'd want the flat. And the kids. And most of all, how they wanted her.

And how they'd want to talk to her about Ivan.

She never talked about Ivan. Not to anyone. She couldn't. He'd tried to explain it to The League. But there was no way they could properly understand. Thank God they couldn't understand.

But the two of them had sat down, and they'd talked

about it. Run through what the *Mail* wanted. And how this would be the last one. Even though he knew he'd said it before. But this really was it.

And she'd agreed.

Partly for the reasons he always trotted out when he was asked about this stuff. Because they loved each other, and this was a joint journey they were both on, and she wanted them to see the real David Cameron, and she was prepared to do anything she could to help him succeed.

And partly because he'd failed. All the walls had crumbled now. The red lines, all the things he'd promised her, all the things he'd promised himself. One by one they'd disappeared. He'd tried to protect them all, as much as he could. But in the end he hadn't been able to.

So they'd discussed the final red line. Across one wall of the flat was a giant picture of Ivan. No one outside had ever seen it. Whenever they'd had anyone filming in there – even when people like Michelle Obama had been up there – no one had been allowed to show that picture. And that was the one thing they still wouldn't give up. They wouldn't let them have Ivan's photo.

The interview had been with the *Mail on Sunday*'s editor Geordie Greig. And he'd done a great job, actually. He could easily have overwritten it. There was a line about her reaching for the handkerchiefs. And another about a momentary crack in her voice. And how he'd offered to pause for a while, but she'd insisted they carry on. But that was it. And Sam had come across staggeringly well. 'It takes a long time before you see sunlight poking through the dark fog but never does the pain go as it's so connected to love.'

He put down the magazine. They basically had everything now. The house. The flat. The children. Samantha. Him. There was nothing left. He'd handed over everything.

Except Ivan's picture. That was one thing he had done. He'd at least managed to protect his son.

David Cameron reached forward, gathered together his papers and settled himself down on the sofa by the low coffee table in the corner. He would still be able to look at himself in the mirror. Just not today.

The clock is still counting. And Ed Miliband has this momentary flash of a child huddling in the corner of a rubble-strewn building, with tears running down her dusty cheeks. Nick Clegg has this feeling of ice-cold water swirling around his body. David Cameron can feel Ivan's breath on his cheek.

And each man looks at the clock. And he says to his God, 'Make it happen. Make sure this hasn't all been for nothing.'

00.30 . . . 00.29 . . . 00.28 . . . 00.27 . . . 00.26 . . .

13. Dave and Nick

Nick Clegg could see where David Cameron was going wrong. He was trying to screw it in, with the screwdriver. But that's not what you did. It wasn't an ordinary screw, it was a cam lock. Cam lock. There was a joke in that somewhere.

Anyway, you didn't screw your cam lock into the wood in the conventional way. You just pushed it in, and turned, and that locked the panel into place.

He put down the briefing note. 'No, you don't screw it in. You push it in, then turn.'

'What?' He was still on all fours, trying to get the screwdriver to fit into the bloody screw head. But every time he managed and started trying to twist it, the damn thing kept spinning round, and the screwdriver would pop out again.

'Don't use the screwdriver. Push it in with your thumb. Then when it's settled into the hole, that's when you use the screwdriver. One turn should do it. You should be able to feel it tightening.'

He put down the screwdriver and gently pressed the circular silver lock forward. It clicked into place.

'That's it. Now use the screwdriver.'

He picked up the screwdriver again and started to twist the lock.

'No, not that hard. You're not screwing it in, you're just locking it into place.'

He twisted the screwdriver in the other direction and heard a second, louder click.

'OK, that should have done it. How's it feel.'

Laying down the screwdriver he leant forward and pulled against the two sides of the cupboard.

'Solid. Thanks.'

When he'd signed up to the coalition agreement this wasn't exactly how Nick Clegg had envisaged their policy discussions taking place. But they were still feeling their way with each other, and he thought he should probably take it as a compliment that he'd been invited up to the flat to witness this slightly clumsy attempt at prime ministerial DIY.

He'd been tempted to suggest they save it for another day, and leave David to his labours. But then he'd recognized there was something quite comical about this moment. Perhaps in the midst of their discussions they would inadvertently make some sort of decision that would echo down the ages. Like Churchill and Lord Halifax's walk in the Downing Street Rose Garden. Or Blair and Brown's dinner at Granita.

At this time and on this date, the Ikea Accord was struck. The baby cabinet they were working on can still be viewed today in the British museum. If you look closely, you can even see the mark where the Prime Minister turned his Philips screwdriver the wrong way.

'Bloody hell. Why won't this fit in now . . .'

He was trying to manoeuvre the second panel into position, but it was obvious the screws and holes weren't aligning.

'Here, throw me over the manual.'

Without turning he reached for the thin white booklet, picked it up and tossed it in the general direction of the sofa. He wasn't entirely sure this was appropriate. He was the Prime Minister, after all. Nick was meant to be his deputy. By rights it should be Nick down here on the floor struggling away, and him sitting on the sofa calmly issuing instructions.

Plus, it was a little bit embarrassing. You shouldn't really have to ask another man for help in putting together your own daughter's playroom cabinet. Men were meant to be programmed to instinctively know this sort of stuff. Putting together flatpack IKEA furniture had become the twenty-first-century equivalent of making fire and hunting wild boar.

Nick Clegg opened the manual, flicked past the dire warning in Arabic script of the dangers of mis-assembly, and came to the section he was looking for. The Incomprehensible Assembly Diagram. Experienced eyes skimmed across the page. He'd grappled with this type of IAD before.

'Ah, that's it. I see what the problem is. You've got it the wrong way round.'

'How do you mean?'

'The panel. You've got it the wrong way round.'

'What? You mean I need to . . .' He started to flip the panel horizontally.

'No, not like that. You need to flip it over longways, not sideways. So the cam screws align properly with the holes.'

He twisted round and looked at him with a frown. Cam screws? Was he taking the piss now?

'Seriously. That's what they're called. Cam screws, or cam dowels, or something.'

He turned his attention back to the panel and began to lift it so he was effectively twisting it back to front. Despite his frustrations he had to admit there was something quite funny about all this. And maybe something quite important.

He certainly couldn't imagine kneeling down here with Gordon Brown issuing the instructions. 'No David. No, no, no. That's not how you do it. For God's sake you're doing it all wrong. See, that's what I told them. This is no time for a novice.'

He eased the right-hand side of the cabinet forward, and with a final bit of pushing and tugging, slid it into place.

'That's got it.' He eased himself back from the half-assembled cabinet and twisted round so he was facing the sofa.

'I haven't got a clue about this sort of stuff. I did manage to put up a shed once. But Sam's the expert, really.'

He was about to ask him why he hadn't just got one of

the Downing Street maintenance guys to put it up for him. But he knew why. You needed to keep hold of something from before. Even if it was just one of the little things, like putting a cupboard together by yourself.

'Do you want to run through that paper now? I can finish this off later.'

No. They may as well finish off the cabinet now. The paper could wait. And if they could successfully put an IKEA cabinet together, there was nothing they couldn't achieve.

In the first months of the coalition it was the question David Cameron and Nick Clegg got asked more than any other. How did they get on? Were they really close? Were they actually friends?

Of course, most of the people asking weren't asking in a neutral way. The Bubble Breathers were hoping to uncover splits between them. 'Coalition begins to crumble after only [a week, a fortnight, a month – delete as appropriate],' was the story they all wanted to write.

Some of their colleagues – especially their back-benchers – were questioning them in a tone bordering on disbelief. 'OK Prime Minister, I know we have to do business with him. But do you really find Nick Clegg a decent and honourable man to work with? Honestly?'

The activists would ask with a genuine feeling of desperation in their voices. 'Nick, please. Tell me you don't really get on with that man. You can't. He's just too awful for words.'

And naturally, they'd tailor their answer to their audience. 'We're working very well together on confronting the difficult challenges facing the country.' 'Listen, you don't have to worry. I know precisely how to manage Nick Clegg.' 'Heh, look, it's me. Nick. What do you think? But we've all got to make this work now.'

But they were all asking the wrong question, in the wrong way. All the questions had as their genesis the same premise. These are two men from different political parties, from entirely different backgrounds, with entirely different political outlooks. How can they possibly get on?

But really, people should have reversed it. The question should have been, 'Why wouldn't they get on?'

Nick Clegg and David Cameron weren't from different backgrounds. Yes, they'd been born to different mothers, and they had different fathers, and they'd lived in different parts of the country, and they'd never really known each other til politics threw them together.

But in many other ways they were very similar. They had both grown up in stable, comfortable homes, they'd both gone to good schools, they had both done well in their chosen careers, they both had beautiful wives who were successful in their own right, and beautiful children who they loved, and who loved them back. They'd managed to secure the package. Both of them.

Yet still people insisted on treating them like they

were members of two entirely separate, exotic tribes, who had been brought together as part of some strange sociological experiment.

Like the time they'd all had dinner together. They'd agreed it would be an informal private thing up in the flat. Just Dave and Nick and Sam and Miriam. No photos, no briefing, nothing. And the next morning both of them turned up to their respective meetings, and everyone was sitting there on the edge of their seats. How did it go? How did they got on? What did they all talk about?

And they both felt like saying, 'It was a disaster. Miriam punched Sam, and then Nick threw wine in Sam's face, and then Sam and then David got Miriam in a headlock and started rolling around on the floor . . .'

It went fine. Of course it did. They were two well-educated, well-brought-up, middle-class couples. They knew how to get on with people socially. They'd talked about current affairs and politics and family and food and holidays. And then they'd kissed each other farewell, and gone home and gone to bed.

This is what neither man could quite get their head round. The presumption others had of either great tension and distance between them, or great empathy and intimacy.

They had a good relationship. That was it. It was in both of their interests to have a good relationship. The country and the government needed it, obviously. And they needed it too. They'd invested a lot of political capital convincing each of their parties to sign up to the coalition arrangement. And also, it was easier. Who wanted to spend their time working alongside someone who they didn't get on with? They could both do without that.

So they worked on it. They started playing tennis together occasionally. Friendly matches. Though these were two middle-aged men, so there was obviously a little competitive edge there.

Nick Clegg was probably the more naturally gifted player. He had a bit more power, and he was more agile around the court. But David Cameron was wily. He'd stay back on the baseline, and just keep returning. Return, return, return. Not attempt to play a dramatic passing shot, or hit a flamboyant winner. Just return, return, return. And eventually Nick would get impatient, and whack one into the net, or smash it long.

Which in some ways was a reflection of their characters. Or a reflection of how they viewed each other's character. David quite liked Nick. But he could be a bit urgent. And Nick had quite warmed to David. But there was a complacency about him that grated occasionally.

It didn't matter though. Their relationship was good. And it was in both of their interests that it was good. So they carried on having the odd game of tennis. And they agreed to have another dinner with the wives soon.

It had all gone fine. Though he didn't really enjoy these events that much. They'd corral a load of workers into the canteen or out on to the shop floor. And then they'd scatter the bosses around the audience just to keep an eye on everybody. Then he and David would walk out, and there'd be a little buzz of excitement. It was the Prime Minister and the Deputy Prime Minister, after all. They didn't wander in every day. And there were a few cameras, and a lot of people in smart suits, and a couple of them had those funny ear pieces.

So David would get up and say a few words, and then he'd get up and say a few words. And it was all a little bit stilted. But the audience would listen attentively enough, and then they'd start taking a few questions. But soon the novelty of the moment would begin to wear off, and people would start to get a bit bored, and the camera lights would go out because they'd got all the footage they needed. And there'd be a bit of an unreal and fake feel to the whole thing.

But it was symbolically important. Both of them, side by side, showing the coalition was working smoothly.

They'd certainly been side by side today. There'd been half a dozen questions and – with the exception of the AV referendum where it was written into the coalition agreement they could agree to disagree – they'd backed each other up on everything. Libya, Syria, even the cut in fuel duty that had got a lot of his own activists very exercised.

But he'd got through it with what he thought was commendable self-discipline. So David had thanked all the Boots factory workers for their time, and there'd been a round of polite – if relieved – applause, and they both began to walk off. And they'd been heading out the back, and walking past a row of factory trolleys piled high with bottles of water, which meant they were out of view of the audience, and he turned to David and said, 'If we keep doing this we won't find anything to bloody disagree on in the bloody TV debates.'

And David laughed. Then he half-turned and saw Lena urgently gesturing at him. She seemed to be pointing at something in the centre of his chest. So he looked down. And his heart sank.

His TV microphone was still attached to his lapel.

Things had changed after Boots. There'd been a predictable reaction in the press. 'Clegg in "too close to Tories for comfort" gaffe.' Which wasn't what he'd actually said. But there was nothing the Bubble Breathers relished more than an unscripted microphone moment.

There'd also been a fairly predictable reaction from inside the party – both parties in fact. The comment had crystallized a lot of concerns. Or provided the excuse for people who had been desperate to find a reason to be concerned.

So express them they did. The members were angry when they'd read about the comments. The backbenchers were angry. Even some of the ministers were angry. OK, they knew they had to work together for the good of the country. They all accepted that. But why did they have to go around acting as if they really did *like each other*?

Which they both thought was a pretty silly reaction. But they also recognized something was different now. At the beginning it had been in both their interests to project an image of unity. A year later? Not so much.

They'd had to show the country they could provide stability. And they'd done that. There wasn't any danger of the cash tills running out, or the banks locking their doors any more. And so when people saw them both standing there telling them how they needn't worry, David and Nick had everything in hand, it didn't reassure them any more. It just got on their nerves.

In fact, their demonstrations of unity were now starting to create precisely the reverse effect of what they intended. The more they were seen together, the more negative the reaction. And the worse the reaction within their parties, the more cracks were starting to appear in the plasterwork of the government. In other words, it was their shows of unity that were now creating the divisions.

So very subtly, and without any fuss, they began to move apart. Being members of the British middle classes, nothing was said. There were no pained conversations or unpleasant scenes. But the date they had pencilled in the diary for their next tennis match was allowed to drift past. And the joint factory tour programme was quietly shelved. And neither of them could quite manage to find the time to arrange a new dinner with the wives.

But when they saw each other in meetings their

relationship was still good. They got on just fine. Why wouldn't they?

Lynton Crosby pointed at the map. 'Here. This is where we win it. This is where the majority comes from.'

For a moment it looked like his finger was pointing to the Isle of Wight. But then he began to rotate it in a circular motion around the entire south-west coast.

Which made sense. That was where they'd decided to target the Lib Dems. In previous strategy meetings there had been talk of picking up as many as seven or eight seats off them.

'How many are we aiming for?' he asked. 'All of them,' Lynton replied.

Everyone in the room let out a laugh, including him. But then they saw Lynton was just sitting there with this inscrutable expression on his face. At which point everyone stopped laughing.

Was he being serious? All of them?

Yes. He was being serious.

'You really think we can win every Lib Dem seat on our target list? All twelve?' someone asked incredulously.

Seats like North Devon had a majority of 6,000, someone else interjected. Cheltenham had a majority of almost 5,000. When he said 'win all of them' he didn't actually mean them as well, did he?

The Big Dog shook his head. No. When he said 'all of them' he didn't mean all of the seats on their current target list. He meant all of the seats in the region, period. Every single one.

There was an awkward silence. Sometimes people forgot Lynton was Australian. Perhaps he didn't actually understand what the political make-up of the south west was. Yes, the Lib Dems were in serious trouble. But some of these seats remained bandit country for anyone not wearing a yellow rosette. David Laws in Yeovil had a 13,000 majority. In Bath they were sitting on a 12,000 majority. He wasn't seriously suggesting they targeted those was he?

Lynton just shrugged his shoulders. If they wanted to win a majority, that was how it was going to have to happen.

There was another moment of silence as people allowed what he'd said to sink in. So if they were going to target every single Lib Dem seat in the south west, how was he proposing they go about it?

Two ways, he explained. Through strength. And through stealth.

First, they had to swamp the area with resources. The election spending cap would kick in from December. So they had to start carpet bombing the region now. Leaflets, direct mailshots, the works. They also had to expand out of their current forty-forty target list. They needed to get as many bodies as they could spare, and start sending them west, across the river Avon.

The second thing was they had to maintain the element of surprise. The Lib Dems couldn't know they were coming, or they'd pull everything they had back there. There could be no briefing of the plan. As far as anyone was to know, they were realistically targeting ten seats, maximum. They should also try a bit of serious misinformation as well. Get someone to start passing the word around they were struggling down there. 'Just between you and me, we're finding the south west a pretty tough nut to crack,' that sort of thing. And they should also target some of the Lib Dems' remaining names. Vince Cable. Norman Baker. That would distract them and make them divert resources away from the key battleground.

Everyone looked at each other. It was a high-risk strategy. Some might say a reckless strategy. Every activist and every pound they deployed trying to knock over seats like Bath and Yeovil and Twickenham represented a resource they wouldn't be able to deploy defending their own marginal seats from Labour. If they didn't sweep the board in the south west, and then Ed Miliband managed to break through their own defences, it would cost them the election. Every seat the Lib Dems held made it harder for them to win a majority, but at least it left open the possibility of another coalition. Every seat Labour won brought the removal vans a block closer to Downing Street.

David Cameron leant back in his chair. So essentially this was the choice he was being presented with. Play safe, hold off Labour, and prepare for a second coalition. Or take Lynton's gamble and go all out for the majority. But if he went for the majority, there was only one way to get it.

He'd have to completely destroy the Liberal Democrats. And he'd have to completely destroy Nick Clegg.

They still got on fine face to face. Although they didn't really have all that many face-to-face meetings now. Their first-term programme was virtually finished. The Commons was like a ghost town. They were struggling to find enough legislation to fill the timetable. The whips had started sending people back home on Wednesday evenings.

When they did meet up the conversation occasionally turned to what might happen afterwards. Though it was all quite general stuff. Nick had indicated his own personal preference would be for a continuation of the coalition. But he'd made it clear he wasn't sure he could deliver his party on that, unless the numbers made a deal with Labour impossible.

David had hinted that would be his preference too. And also subtly let it be known he thought a hung parliament was the most likely outcome. What had they decided? 'We can't let them know we're coming.'

But their political estrangement was basically complete. MPs from both parties were calling it 'conscious uncoupling'. The Bubble Breathers were describing it as open warfare.

David had given the green light to The League to brief that he was considering a minority administration – rather than a new coalition – if parliament was hung after the election. He put his name to a personal email to Tory MPs lambasting their coalition partners for being 'all over the place, unable to decide whether they want to stick to the plan, or veer off it.' Nick had given an interview to *The Times* in which he declaimed, 'I have been in coalition with a party who have mutated almost out of recognition. We went in with partners who told us they were green, but they are not. They told me they weren't going to bang on about Europe, but it's all they bang on about. They said they believed in civil liberties and they want to trash them.'

He'd started to let it be known that if there was a new coalition he would no longer be prepared to sit next to David at Prime Minister's Questions. There would be no more Downing Street photo calls. No more joint appearances.

At the final coalition cabinet meeting before parliament dissolved both of them had handed out mementoes to mark the occasion. David had arranged for special bottles of 'Co-Ale-Ition' beer from a local Oxfordshire brewery. Nick had passed around tubs of Yorkshire crisps made by a company in his constituency. Someone suggested they pose for an official photograph to mark the occasion. Both men had said no.

So now it was just Silvio Berlusconi they were waiting for. Nick Clegg looked up at the clock. Thirteen minutes past. Pretty par for the course for Silvio.

He would never admit it to anyone, but he actually liked these mini-summits. It was an environment he understood. Yes, there were times they could be intensely frustrating, and others when they could be tediously boring. But it was a world he knew. He could easily recognize and navigate the myriad procedures and protocols and diplomatic niceties. And because of that, if the situation required it, he could sometimes find a way to discreetly subvert them.

Despite the cynicism of the Bubble Breathers, not to mention a large swathe of the political class, he also found this was a forum where you could get things done. Perhaps that was because these lower-level international gatherings tended to take place away from the Bubble Breathers' prying eyes. They had no interest in the various clauses and sub-clauses of obscure pan-European treaties.

But if you took the time to properly examine those sub-clauses then you could actually achieve quite a lot. Nothing that would move mountains or reshape continents. But you could cut through a bit of red tape here. Or secure agreement for a new regulation there. And somewhere in Europe, somebody's life would become just that little bit easier.

Plus, in here, he was his own man. Obviously he had to operate within certain parameters. He was technically representing the Prime Minister. But so long as he didn't do anything crazy, like sign up to the Eurozone or threaten to march on Moscow, he had a relatively free hand. For all practical purposes he wasn't representing the British Prime Minister, he *was* the British Prime Minister.

And that was how the other people in the room

treated him. Some of them were heads of state in their own right. But they engaged with him as an equal. And there was no point pretending – he quite liked that.

At the beginning, just before they'd signed up to the coalition agreement, there'd been some discussion internally about whether he should ask for his own department and cabinet position. Foreign secretary was the one that had been mentioned most frequently. In the end he'd rejected the idea. It would have involved relatively long periods when he'd be out of the country, and he felt – they all felt – he had to have a role where he could sit across everything. If he didn't it would be too easy for the Tories to marginalize them.

On balance he still thought he'd made the correct decision. But when he was in these meetings, there were times when he did start to wonder . . .

'Sorry, sorry, sorry!!!!'

Silvio was finally making his entrance. It was always quite something to see. He would explode into the room and then freeze. He'd be standing there, framed in the doorway, his entourage arrayed around him, as if posing for a photograph. And then he would plunge forward again, grasping shoulders, kissing foreheads, issuing profuse and totally insincere apologies.

He'd met him a couple of times before at summits and other diplomatic events. 'Neeek!' he would cry, whenever he saw him, and then go rushing past.

There was a brief pause in the frantic glad-handing as he circled the table, his interpreter on his shoulder, searching for his chair. Then eventually he came to a halt, directly opposite him.

The predictable shout of 'Neeek!' echoed around the room. His arms shot forward in greeting.

'Neeek, let me say this. I read that your Cameron has had thirty women. Tell him that is nothing. Tell him Silvio says I've had sixty women!!!'

There was a moment of silence and Nick Clegg could feel the eyes of two dozen assembled leaders and diplomats swivelling towards him. How would the Deputy Prime Minister of the United Kingdom respond to this bizarre intervention?

And he knew there was only one way he could respond. He threw back his head and let out a roar of laughter. And Silvio Berlusconi threw his arms in the air and started laughing. And soon everyone in the room – the prime ministers and the foreign ministers and the ambassadors and the foreign policy aides and the interpreters and the bag carriers – they were all laughing.

And Nick Clegg was sitting there, laughing along. And he was thinking to himself, 'Fucking Berlusconi. They're not David Cameron's women. They're mine.'

David Cameron had one last decision to make. What were they going to do about Sheffield Hallam?

Nick Clegg's majority was 15,000. But Labour were reported to be throwing everything they had at it. A lot of students had digs there. And the latest polling showed there was a real possibility he could lose the seat.

They could approach it in two ways. Treat it like a normal campaign and push hard. Nicola Bates had come second for them in 2010. Or step back and quietly encourage local Tory voters to come behind Nick.

There was an obvious rationale for helping him out. If they were going to try and form a new coalition, they needed Nick Clegg. If he lost, then Vince Cable or Tim Farron would take over, and there was no way either of them would sign up for a deal. They'd as good as said it was Labour or nothing.

But given their new strategy, there was also a case for making Nick Clegg fight for every vote. The Lib Dems would have to divert even more resources there. It would pull his personal attention and the campaign's attention away from the south west. And it would send an important signal to the MPs and the activists – when David Cameron says he's going all out for a Conservative majority he really means it.

So he thought about it. And then he passed the word back. Let's go easy up there.

The clock is still counting. And in Westminster, in the upstairs flat in Number Eleven Downing Street, Florence Cameron is fast asleep. Beside her, her toys and books are piled neatly in the cabinet that sits by her bed. The low, white cabinet her daddy and his friend Nick had made for her.

00.25 . . . 00.24 . . . 00.23 . . . 00.22 . . . 00.21 . . .

14. Waiting for Nicola and Nigel

The water below looked ugly and grey. So did the sky above. Dirty-looking clouds hung down in thick bunches, and the rain they were depositing was being smeared around the windscreen by the taxi's ineffectual wiper.

He felt tired. The heater was turned up full blast, and he'd had to get up early to write his copy. He knew he wouldn't be getting back to his hotel til late that evening, and they needed to have his column by four.

Ahead of him the traffic was making its long, slow procession across the bridge. It was down to a single lane, which meant they'd been held at the entry slip road for the best part of half an hour.

'What time's your meeting?' The cab driver had three fingers of his right hand balancing gently against the steering wheel, and the heel of his left palm resting casually on the gearstick. One sudden gust and they'd be over the edge and into the Firth of Forth.

'Not til ten. I've left plenty of time. No need to rush.'

He glanced over to the cabbie. He had long shoulder-length hair and what looked like the accumulation of four, possibly five, days of stubble. He was wearing a light-blue rain mac with a dark stain on the sleeve. The zip appeared to be missing. His jeans were black, but the bottoms seemed to be flecked with white paint. A pair of thick-soled white trainers rested against the pedals, and he was wearing odd socks. One was red and the other had a strange sort of interwoven yellow and green pattern.

'And it's the SNP office you're after?'

'Yes, that's right.'

Two of the remaining three fingers detached themselves from the steering wheel.

'Is our Nicola going to be there then?'

No. His Nicola wasn't going to be there. He'd been trying to catch up with her for the last four days, without success. Someone had said she'd been in Kirkcaldy last week. And there was a rumour she may be putting in another appearance. But that's all they seemed to be. Whispers. 'Have you heard? They say Nicola is coming.' But she never did. At least not when he was there.

'No. Afraid not. I'm just meeting the local candidate.'

He nodded. 'Ah, Roger Mullin. Good man.'

'Oh. So you know him?'

'Aye. I'm an SNP member.' The last of the red cones disappeared behind them. He flicked the indicator and the car began to accelerate forward.

'So do you think you're going to do well round here?'

'Oh yes. Everyone round here will be voting SNP.'

The bridge's flared stanchions fell away to the side. He could see the road ahead was channelling them through a narrow cut. Just beyond, partially obscured by the rain, a series of wide fields were starting to prise open the landscape.

'What makes you think the SNP will do so well here?' He reached into his jacket and slipped out his notebook.

The cabbie eased the gearstick back, then lifted his hand and gestured around him.

'Look about. There's nothing here. Used to be mines. Last one closed in the mid-eighties. Was a time there were eight, nine thousand guys underground in this part of the world. That's all gone now.'

The rain was getting heavier. He lifted his hand once more, and the methodical beat of the wipers quickened. To little discernible effect.

'All right, the bridge was good for us. Right enough it was. Created a few hundred jobs. Good jobs. Good pay. But they only lasted a couple of years. Then when the bridge was finished most of the guys were on their way again.'

A peal of thunder drifted across the horizon.

'I was on the bridge for a few years. One of the lucky ones. Got kept on after it was completed. They kept a few of us.'

The journalist's pen began to slide across the notebook.

'But you don't work on the bridge any more? You just drive this cab now? Sorry, I don't mean "just" but . . .'

He nodded.

'Just the cab now. I left the bridge four years ago.'

'And what made you leave? If the money was OK, and there's not much other . . .'

'Number of things. The hours. There was a lot of night work. People. I had a few friends there at the beginning, and they all moved on. And the jumpers. The jumpers were hard.'

His pen paused on the page.

'The jumpers? The things . . .'

He gave a thin smile.

'No. Not the things you wear. The jumpers. The suicides.'

'Oh. I see. Sorry.'

'They'd pick them up on CCTV. Then they'd get me on the radio and I'd climb into the van and drive out to them.'

They were passing through open country now. He sensed that if it wasn't for the weather it would actually look quite picturesque.

'I always remember this one guy. A kid he was, only seventeen or eighteen. I'd spotted him myself. Normally they'd radio me, but this one I spotted straight away. The bus had stopped on the far side of the bridge and I could see him turn round and start walking back. And when you see them walking back, you know. So I ran out to the van and jumped straight in, and went tearing out to the middle. It's strange, quite a few wait til they're right out in the middle before they do it. Like it's going to make any difference at that height.

So I get out there, and it's cold and really windy, and I

can see this kid. He's standing there, no coat on, just jeans and a T-shirt. And he's standing right at the edge, with his back to me. And I shout over to him, "You all right, pal?" And there's nothing. No reaction. It's like he doesn't know I'm there. So I say to him again, "Are you all right . . ." And he's vanished. Just like that. One second he's there, and the next he's gone.'

The road had narrowed down to a single lane. On either side a carpet of yellow and green oilseed rape was swaying and glistening in the rain.

'But this kid's lucky. It's really windy you see, and the wind is tearing at the water, stirring it up. So the guys on the boat – in the end there were so many going over they put a permanent rescue boat down there – see him come down and hit the water feet first. Now, if it's calm, you hit the water like concrete and it's over. But the water's cresting and troughing, and he lands right in the middle of one of the troughs. So they drag him out, and the guys in the boat can't believe it. He's got a couple of broken legs, and his arm's all banged up, but he's alive.'

A small bead of sweat had appeared at the side of his brow, and was beginning to slide slowly down his left cheek. He wiped it away, then reached over and twisted the heater control anti-clockwise.

'So a few days later the police are by his bed interviewing him. And they ask him, "Why did you do it, son?" And you know what he tells them? He tells them he's got his exams coming up. And he's so scared of mucking up his exams, and so scared if he mucks up his exams he's going to muck up his life, he just wanted to finish it all.'

He shook his head. Outside, a fresh rumble of thunder rolled over the roof of the car, and away across the fields.

'But here's the strangest thing of all. About a year later we get a phone call. It's the kid. And he says it's coming up to the first anniversary of the day he went over. And he wants to come back. He wants to walk out on the bridge and just stand there for a moment. Right at the exact spot. And we say, "OK, if you think it might help you." I mean, if he's planning on trying to end it again he's not going to call us up and let us know, is he? But we tell him someone will have to go out with him, just to make sure everything's on the level. And he says that's fine. So about three weeks later, on exactly the same day it happened, I pick him up in the van, and we drive out on to the bridge. And as we're heading out there I say to him, "I was out here with you that afternoon. I spoke to you. Did you hear me talking to you?" And he looks at me and he shakes his head. He says he doesn't remember a thing about it. Last thing he has is walking out of his house and getting on the bus. And then the next thing he knows, he's waking up in hospital. So we go out, and I stay in the van, and he walks over to the edge and he just stands there looking out. He's not there for long, just three or four minutes. And then he gets back in and I drive him back. And every year for the next three years he'd ring us up. And we'd take him out, and he'd stand at exactly the same spot. And then he'd get back in the van and we'd drive him away. Then one year he just never rang. And we didn't ever see or hear from him again.'

The journalist put down his pen. The wipers were losing their uneven battle with the downpour. He turned to his left and gazed out of the rain-flecked passenger window. The yellow and green carpet of oilseed rape had gone. They were just passing empty fields now. Empty and lifeless.

'Aye, if you see Nicola you can tell her from me. She's going to do very well around here. She's going to do very well indeed.'

The tension was building. The current speaker was ploughing gamely on, but it was a thankless task. Like he was addressing an audience of thousands of excited crickets. Everyone was turning to their right and their left, passing the word. As if they were all worried that if they didn't communicate it out loud, it wouldn't happen.

Nigel was coming.

There had been all sorts of rumours circulating throughout the day. The first, and most alarming, had been that his flight had been cancelled. Fog in Washington. He wasn't going to make it. Then they'd been told he'd flown over in a private jet, had landed, and was on his way down to Margate in a helicopter that belonged to one of the party's donors. Then there'd been a story that he'd missed the flight and wasn't going to arrive til the evening. Then it had emerged it wasn't him that had missed the plane, but one of his aides. Everything was OK. He was driving down from London and due to arrive at any moment.

Soon, Nigel would be here.

Everyone appeared to be sporting their Sunday best for the occasion. For the men that meant a smart, dark blazer, red or light-grey trousers, bow tie and a purple rosette. For the ladies, floral print, a modest heel and pearls were the order of the day.

Most of the delegates agreed the Winter Gardens had seen better days. The hall was hot and stuffy, it was impossible to get a pint of decent beer, and they had never heard of any of the acts that were being advertised in the foyer. Who were 'The Dreamboys'?

They were also feeling a little tired. These conferences could drag on. That man Patrick Flynn had been quite good. And they'd liked that nice boy Stephen who had talked about immigration. Seemed to have a good head on his shoulders, that young man. But some of the others did seem to like the sound of their own voices a bit too much.

But none of that would matter. When Nigel came.

It was true that things had got a bit harder for them in the last year. There had been a time when everywhere you went, people were Ukip. When they'd been out working in the European elections they would drive by and honk their horns. Come up to you and shake your hand in the street.

And there was still a lot of that. Well, a bit of that. But there was no denying, things had got tougher. Obviously there were the leftists who were out there bullying people and causing trouble and spreading the most wicked lies about them. And they'd try and put people right. But if you threw enough mud, eventually some of it would stick, wouldn't it?

And some of the things the papers printed. Shameful. Absolutely shameful. All it needed was someone to say some stupid thing on the interweb, and there they'd be all over the front pages. Every political party had a few rotten apples. But did you ever hear anything about the idiots in Labour or the Tories? No, you did not.

So it had got harder. They saw it when they were in the Legion, or down at the bingo. People were still quite supportive. But there was just something about the way they'd talk to you now. There was a lot of, 'I agree with plenty of what he says. Don't get me wrong. He talks a lot of sense. Especially about the Poles, and all those benefit tourists and such. And he's right. Things can't go on like they have been. We're full up as it is. But I don't know. I'm not saying he won't get my vote. I'm definitely thinking about it. But I can't quite put my finger on it. Sometimes he's a little hot. That's it. He can come over a bit too hot now and again.'

And that's why this conference had come just at the right time. They needed a bit of a pick-me-up. And they were going to get one!

When Nigel came.

The thing they had to get across to people – and perhaps they hadn't been as good at explaining this as they should have been – was that they weren't racialist. Or extremist. Or what was it David Cameron had called them? A bunch of fruitcakes and loonies.

What a terrible thing for a Prime Minister to say. Really. A man in his position should have known better.

They were good people. The cared about their country. They cared about their communities. And they could see them changing. Being changed right in front of their eyes.

You only had to pick up a paper to see what was happening. Those gangs that had been doing all those terrible things to those children. And no one had raised a finger to stop them. The waiting list at the doctors' surgeries. It could take over a week just to get an appointment now. And there were times you'd go into the post office or the bank, and some of the people in there could hardly speak a word of English. All you were trying to do was buy a book of stamps, and the person opposite couldn't understand you.

That's what everyone needed to understand. Something had to be done. Someone had to stand up and say, 'Enough is enough.'

And they would. When Nigel came.

Finally it looked like something was starting to happen. A line of about a dozen people in suits had walked into the hall and sat down in the seats right in the centre, at the front. Someone else was standing off to the side and gesturing to the current speaker. They seemed to be running their hand across their throat in a sort of chopping motion. And to the far right of the stage a crowd of photographers and people with TV cameras were beginning to cluster together.

They couldn't say this enough times. They were good people. They were friendly people. If only the men with the cameras would take a proper walk around this conference. There were old people, there were young people, they were people from the north and from Scotland and from Wales. There were even some people who had flown all the way from Spain to be there.

And there were people of all different colours as well. If you looked around this hall you'd see that nice Nigerian lady, and an Asian lady, and even a man with a turban. The man with the turban. Was *he* a racialist?

Yes, they were passionate. And now and then people might mistake their passion for something worse. But that was because they cared.

And you needed something to care about these days. That's what the country needed, some of that old Blitz spirit. Their parents had got through an entire world war without any social workers, or handouts, or any of these so-called 'food banks'. But that was because everyone looked out for everyone else back then.

Now? Now it was everyone for themselves. A sense of community. Knowing who your neighbours were. Being able to rely on your family to look after you when things started to get a bit harder. When they'd been growing up, these were the sort of things people just took for granted.

But not any more. That was one thing you had to say for the immigrants. They understood the importance of family. But now everyone was so – how did they say it – 'mobile'. The children would move out. Then they'd move away. And you might see them and the grandchildren at Christmas, and maybe another couple of times through the year. And then your old friends would move away too, to try and be a bit closer to their children and their grandchildren. And you might bump into someone you knew in the library, or down at your local pub. But they were shutting all the libraries now. And the pubs were so noisy, they were just trying to attract the kids. Expensive too. And you had to be careful as well, out on your own. You didn't want to risk being out alone too long after dark these days.

It was scary. It really was. They didn't mind admitting it. The way everything was changing. It was hard to watch. If only someone could just make it all stop and turn back all the clocks. Back to a time when everyone took the time to say hello to everyone else in the morning. And you could leave your front door off the latch. A time when everything felt *safe*.

Of course you couldn't just put the clock back. They knew that. Things would never be exactly the same as they were. But somebody had to do something.

And they would. When Nigel came.

*

First and foremost these three men saw a political problem. David Cameron knew that if the polls were right, Nigel Farage was on course for half a dozen seats. The shift in votes from Tories to Ukip would probably hand Labour another ten to twenty seats. In other words, the former commodities trader from Kent could well cost him the election.

Ed Miliband knew if the polls were right he was facing wipe-out in Scotland. Labour were set to lose forty seats north of the border. If that happened there was no way he could win a majority. And that was just in Scotland. Since January the Tories had been hammering the line that a vote for him would hand Nicola Sturgeon the keys to the back door of Downing Street, and it was starting to gain traction. In other words, the former solicitor from Glasgow could well cost him the election.

Nick Clegg knew if the polls were right he was facing wipe-out everywhere. In Scotland the SNP were threatening some of his safest seats. Even Charles Kennedy, who was sitting on a 13,000 majority up in Skye, was facing a serious challenge. He was supposed to be leader of the third party, the natural home for people of protest. And now he was in danger of becoming leader of the fourth party, or even the fifth party of British politics. The people of protest were suddenly taking their votes elsewhere. In other words, the former commodities trader and the former solicitor could kick him and his party out of government for good.

So they'd called everyone together. The Cell, and The

League of Extraordinary Gentlemen, and The Salon That Was No Longer a Salon. And the Big Dogs. They'd all sat in on it too. And they'd tried to come up with a plan.

But they were all a bit stumped. Where had all this come from? Where was it all going? How had Nigel Farage and Nicola Sturgeon managed to get themselves on the grid?

David Cameron's problem was he was getting conflicting advice. They needed to move towards Ukip and neutralize them. They should be much tougher on immigration. They needed to adopt a more aggressive stance on Europe and spell out their red lines for the referendum.

Or that's what some members of The League were telling him. There were others telling him he had to take Nigel Farage on. Farage kept making mistakes. His statement that people should be scared of Romanians moving in next door. His interview when he'd heaped praise on Putin. They should be hitting him hard on this sort of stuff.

And then there were some people who were telling him he shouldn't really be doing anything. Don't move towards Ukip. Don't move to attack Ukip. Don't move anywhere. Just stick to the original plan.

Which was the advice he most wanted to hear, of course. So for now they were sticking with the plan. Or blithely and foolishly ignoring the Ukip threat. It depended on your perspective.

*

Ed Miliband didn't have a Ukip problem. He would have a Ukip problem if he listened to some of the more excitable members of his shadow cabinet. Especially those from predominantly working-class, northern constituencies, who were warning him the people's army was starting to make inroads into their base. But his private polling was showing Nigel Farage was hurting the Tories, not them. That was why The Salon That Was No Longer a Salon had started talking about the 'thirty-five per cent strategy'. If they managed to get their vote share up to thirty-five per cent, Ukip would drag the Tories down to a level where he should just about be able to scramble over the line.

The SNP were a different matter. They'd only become a serious problem after the referendum. Though again, they'd have become a problem a lot earlier if he'd listened to people in the shadow cabinet.

And some others. Gordon Brown had apparently been wandering around a good eighteen months before the referendum warning that Labour were going to lose seats in Scotland. A lot of seats, potentially. But he'd just dismissed that as Gordon being Gordon.

Some worries had also been expressed by Iain McNicol, and by some of the Brownite shadow cabinet members who were still close to Gordon. But again, he hadn't taken too much notice. People were always worrying about something.

Then he'd seen some of the figures they were starting to get from the referendum polling. And although he hadn't exactly panicked, he'd certainly reappraised his thinking a little.

So he'd asked Douglas to take a look at it. And Douglas had reassured him and the rest of the shadow cabinet that everything was in hand. Which had caused some friction with a few members of the shadow cabinet, especially those who still had Gordon bending their ear. There'd been a bit of a bust up. A couple of people had confronted Douglas – who had now been appointed general election coordinator – on his SNP and Ukip strategies. And Douglas had pushed back. And someone had said something about out-of-touch people living in north London. Which was where Douglas lived. And Douglas had said something about English racists. It was all a little bit unfortunate.

But then the referendum had happened. And at that point he and Douglas and the shadow cabinet and Mrs Turner at Number 37 Queensferry Road and everyone else knew that Labour had an SNP problem. But now the formal start of the long general election campaign was about twelve weeks away. So really, they'd left it fairly late in the day to do anything about it.

Nick Clegg had even less idea what to do. Up in Scotland there was basically nothing he *could* do. They didn't have the resources, they didn't have a base to rest on in the Scottish Assembly, and their poll ratings were just as dire as they were south of the border.

With Ukip it was slightly different. Where Ed Miliband

and David Cameron saw a threat, he'd sensed an opportunity. The other two party leaders were running scared of Nigel Farage. But there were a lot of capital and small 'l' liberals who were desperate to see someone confronting him and his saloon-bar populism directly.

Which is when they'd come up with the idea of a debate. Nigel Farage was the man of the moment. But debating was Nick Clegg's forte. Farage had never participated in a major, prime-time political shoot-out before. He had, and he'd emerged with three notches on his gunbelt. It would give him profile, it would let him showcase his platform, and it would give him the opportunity to expose Farage's bluff and bluster in front of a national television audience.

So they'd thrown down the gauntlet, and Nigel Farage had accepted, and everything had gone like clockwork. Placed back in the debating studio he was in his element. It was like 2010 all over again. He'd started a little bit tentatively, but then he'd got into his stride, and Farage had started to crumble. He'd looked hot and shifty under the TV lights, and as the debate had gone on he'd become more agitated and aggressive, and by the end he was reduced to just ranting at him and the audience and Nick Ferrari the moderator.

And then they'd got the result of the post-debate viewers' poll. Farage had won by more than twenty points. Which was troubling. Because the debate had been their one good idea.

*

But it wasn't just political with these three men. It was also personal.

They had spent their lives preparing for this. Every hour of every day of every month of every year of their adult lives spent working towards this moment. *Their moment.*

And what had Nigel Farage done? He'd flitted about the Tories, then he'd flitted over to Ukip, then he'd flitted away from Ukip, then he'd flitted back to Ukip. Where was the Big Plan? Where was his League of Extraordinary Advisors? Where was his Big Dog? It wasn't supposed to be happening like this. It wasn't supposed to be how things worked. *Where did Nigel Farage fit into the natural order of things?*

And who was Nicola Sturgeon? She'd only been leader of her party since November. Where was her vision? Alex Salmond was supposed to be the one with the vision. What did she know about life in The Bubble? What sacrifices had she been forced to make? Had she ever had to push her family and her children out in front of the cameras? *Did she even have a family and children?*

And this was what they hated the most. What these years of pitiless toil and crippling self-doubt and soul-shredding compromises would not – could not – let them accept.

Nigel Farage and Nicola Sturgeon were *Naturals.* Everyone was saying it.

They were calling them authentic. Unspun. Neither was part of the political establishment. Each was challenging the Westminster elite. Both were leaders of a movement, not just a political party. In their differing ways they were bringing people hope. In the face of their challenge the two-party system was crumbling. Together they were going to break the mould of British politics.

It was bullshit. Every last word of it.

A Natural? Had any of these people actually seen Nigel Farage? After lunch? After one of his famous 'five bottlers'?

Authentic? Unspun? Did anyone understand how the SNP operated? Nicola Sturgeon hadn't diverted from her party's line-to-take since she joined as a sixteen year old.

Not part of the establishment? Nigel Farage had been an MEP for a decade and a half. Challenging the elite? As Scottish First Minister, Nicola Sturgeon took home more than David Cameron.

Leaders of movements? They were leaders of cults. Quasi-religious sects. Look at how Douglas Carswell had been marginalized for challenging the glorious leader's world-view. Or the vitriol directed at anyone who'd tried to make a stand against independence during the referendum campaign.

Hope? Sturgeon was literally peddling the language of division. She was an avowed nationalist. She didn't want to bring people together, she wanted to see the Union broken up. Nigel Farage was an old-fashioned populist. What had Russell Brand called him? 'A pound-shop Enoch Powell'. That's exactly what he was. He might as well slap 'no dogs, no Romanians, no HIV sufferers' on his election posters and be done with it.

Why couldn't people see any of this? How was it they were falling for these false prophets?

If only they could see them up close. Smell the cigarette smoke on his clothes. See the coldness in her eyes. Then they'd know.

They'd know these people weren't *Naturals*. If you were in a room and Nicola Sturgeon suddenly walked in, did anyone think the atmosphere would change? That you'd feel an electricity in the air?

If Nicola Sturgeon walked into a room she'd disappear. She'd vanish into a crowd of two. Nigel Farage would turn up, laugh at his own jokes and spill wine down the front of the host. Neither of them had *The Thing*. They couldn't. It took years to cultivate. And even then, it had to already be there. Within you.

It wasn't within Nigel Farage or Nicola Sturgeon. They were political dilettantes. Two frauds. And people would recognize it. The People would recognize it. When it came to the moment of decision, they would look at them. And then they would finally see them. And at the point when The People saw, the natural order would be restored once again.

In her modest semi-detached Swanley bungalow the middle-aged woman removes her pearl necklace and places it carefully by the large mirror that occupies the left-hand side of the dressing table. Reaching for the small pot of Vaseline, she dips in a finger and guides it gently around her lips. Then she pulls back her hair with one hand, places her other hand across the base of her chin, and stares wistfully at the reflection of the twenty-two-year-old girl gazing back at her.

In a clean and spartan flat in north Queensferry, the man flicks at the TV remote, pushes himself back on to the brown sofa and begins to remove his thick white training shoes. For some reason the first one is a struggle, and he has to push and pull at it a few times before working it free. Then, holding it in his left hand, he tips it upside down and shakes it – he feels sure there's something rattling around in there. He runs his fingers around inside the sole. Nothing. He looks down at the grey carpet. Nothing.

Up on the wall, in the corner of the image on the flat-screen TV, is the image of a clock.

00.20 . . . 00.19 . . . 00.18 . . . 00.17 . . . 00.16 . . .

15. It's About the Politics

David Miliband looked distracted. Which didn't unduly bother them. Everyone knew distraction was his social default position.

He hadn't come out with anything that really constituted a story. And that was starting to bother them a bit. But there was still time. The coffee hadn't been served yet.

If they'd been working for a broadsheet the stuff he'd been saying about a political economy might have merited a few lines. But it would be a struggle to turn what he'd said into something for their readers. To be honest, there were a few bits of what he'd said that even they were struggling with.

These lunchtime meetings with leadership candidates were the worst. For a start, they never came on their own. Lisa Tremble, his press officer, was very good. And you could have a laugh with her. But when the hired guns were around the principals never properly relaxed. It was like having a bodyguard sitting there. A constant reminder that people were out to get you, and if you let your guard down once you might never get the opportunity to let it down again.

Plus, you could never get a candidate to drink in the

middle of a campaign. One of the first tips any young political journalist was taught was how to drink at lunch. How you fill the mark's glass to the brim, but yours only halfway. That way when you raised it to your lips you could fake taking a sip and put the glass back down without it being so obvious you hadn't drunk anything. It also gave you an excuse to top up your glass, and then top up theirs. That way the mark was drinking at twice the rate you were.

But David Miliband knew how the game was played. He was sticking studiously to the water.

The other problem was they were lunching with the bookies' favourite. There were some rumours circulating that his brother was actually doing better than people were reporting, and that some of David's backers had been laying off a few four-figure bets to artificially protect his price and maintain momentum. But if it was true the race was tightening, he wasn't showing any sign of it. He was still trotting out the same crushing platitudes about not taking anything for granted, and never wanting to second guess Labour party members.

People could say what they liked about Ed Balls, but you could at least have a decent lunch with him. He'd always bring a story, and a couple of decent Gordon anecdotes with him. But then Ed Balls wasn't going to win. So he could afford to.

'You're sure we can't tempt you with a small aperitif, David.'

'Sorry?' His attention was focused on the door, where a woman in dark sun-glasses and a baseball cap was making an ostentatiously discreet exit. From the back it could have been Madonna, but from the angle they were sat at it was impossible to tell.

'Aperitif?'

'Oh. No, thank you. I'm fine with water.'

Lisa Tremble looked at both of them with a sympathetic smile. If they were going to get anything they were going to have to do it the hard way.

'And what about your mother? I know you say she's staying out of all this, but she'll be glad when it's all over, won't she?'

He reached for his glass and took a short sip of his water. They could see his radar robotically beginning to sweep the horizon for hostiles.

'Yes, I think she will. But she's proud of both of us. And she's not taking sides.'

'Of course. But it must be hard to see her two sons in the middle of something like this. Look at the briefing that's starting to come out against you from Ed's camp. That's got to hurt. Both her and you.'

He picked up the glass again. It was a longer sip this time.

'Briefing?'

'Yes. That stuff we were all getting last week. David's just Peter Mandelson's pawn. If he won, it would be him and Blair pulling the strings. He's not strong enough to stand up to them. Look at the time he bottled it when he was supposed to make the move against Gordon. He's too indecisive to lead. He hasn't got the killer instinct.'

His hand still rested on the glass.

'Well, wherever you're getting that from, it won't be coming from Ed, and it won't be coming from anyone close to Ed. We've both been very clear about how this contest is going to be run.'

They both smiled. You had to hand it to the guy. He knew how to hold a line.

'OK. But seriously, I mean, this is your own brother you're talking about. It's not like it's just coming from the Tories, or some junior shadow cabinet minister you don't get on with. Your own brother.'

He turned to Lisa. She gave a slight shake of the head.

'I know Ed and his people would not be behind anything like this.' As he said the words his hand tightened on the glass. They could both see the tips of the fingers starting to turn white.

Jesus fucking Christ. The man didn't know. It wasn't a line. He genuinely had no idea.

'David, they're briefing against you. It's not just us. Everyone's getting it. They're ringing round. Senior people in his team. His shadow cabinet supporters. They're really going for you.'

He removed his hand from the glass and placed it flat on the table. His face was perfectly still.

'I know Ed wouldn't be behind anything like this. We've talked about it.'

As he spoke, his gaze travelled back to the doorway.

Both of the journalists swivelled in their chairs to see who it was he was looking at this time.

But there was nobody there.

The trouble was, it wasn't true. The story The Salon That Was No Longer a Salon had been putting out about the big heart-to-heart between the two of them. The late-night dash. 'I don't want to be the reason you don't stand. I think you should do it.' It hadn't happened.

The Salon had been hoping this would put The Brother Thing to bed. But two of the *New Statesman*'s top Bubble Breathers, Mehdi Hasan and James Macintyre, had done some digging around the story for a book they were writing on Ed.

And David and his people swore blind Ed had never even set foot in his house that week. The day some of Ed's people claimed the meeting had taken place was the day David had publicly declared he was running for the leadership himself. And the alternative day some of the members of The Salon had claimed it had happened, he'd been out campaigning in Worcester. According to David and *his* guys the first they knew about it was when Ed phoned him up and just told him he was going to run. David might have said he wouldn't stand in his way, they couldn't quite remember. But it wouldn't have made any difference what he'd said, because Ed had decided to run against him anyway.

And so when the book came out – they actually ended up calling it *Ed* – The Salon That Was No Longer a Salon's tale of what happened had collapsed. There was no way that was going to lay to rest The Brother Thing. But even worse, it had created a massive new mystery. If that wasn't the true story of what had happened between the two brothers, what was?

And so, like Victorian explorers hunting the source of the Nile, a posse of Bubble Breathers began fanning out as far afield as north London and Leeds and Boston, Massachusetts, to try and uncover the solution to British politics' most perplexing conundrum. Just why *had* Ed Miliband stabbed his brother in the back?

One theory centred around The Incident. Everything that had transpired between Ed Miliband and David Miliband could be boiled down to a single event. David had nearly pushed Ed under a car when he was four years old. Ed had smashed one of David's cherished toys when he was seven. One of them had stolen away the other's love when they were in their early teens.

So the explorers hunted high and low. And found nothing. No near-death experience. No toy. No girl.

But it was there. If only they'd known where to look for it. When he was twelve years old, Ed Miliband's father Ralph had been given the opportunity to take up a teaching post in Boston. His mother had been reluctant to leave her own job, and David, who was by then seventeen, wanted to stay in London. So it was decided that Ed would go out and stay with him, while his mother and brother remained in the UK.

Later, when he talked about that time, Ed Miliband would describe it as one of the happiest of his life. He was alone with his father, and they bonded as a father and son should. They went to baseball games. They went bowling. They went to eat at McDonalds. He no longer had a father, he had a dad.

But soon, too soon, he had to return to London. And shortly after he returned, David went out to stay with his father himself. Older, and already a seasoned Labour party activist, he signed on to work for the campaign of Boston mayoral candidate Mel King. King, a black community activist, was taking on Ray Flynn, a pro-life scion of the Boston Irish democratic machine. One day, whilst handing out leaflets, David was set upon by a posse of racists. Whether the attack was motivated purely by prejudice, or sponsored by King's political opponents, wasn't clear. David escaped without serious injury. But King immediately called a press conference to condemn the attack, and David found himself a minor Boston celebrity, an urban political folk hero, and the pride of his radical Marxist father.

It didn't take much imagination to understand how this news was greeted by the young Ed Miliband. His elder brother had usurped him. Again. Dad and Boston were supposed to be *his*. David had university. What was he doing taking a stupid gap year in the first place? He'd wanted to be in London, hanging out with his friends, when Dad had stayed in the States. It was Ed who'd gone out to be with him. And David knew what it was like. They all knew. The dark places Dad could drift to when he was on his own. And then David had gone over there – on a whim – and managed to wangle his way on to the campaign of some great black political hope, and managed to get himself shoved around a little bit. And now look. He was on TV, and in the papers, and the apple of Dad's eye. *It wasn't fair. Boston was supposed to be his. And it had been his. And now David had stolen that from him as well.*

It was there all along. Right under their very noses. Hidden in some obscure book by Michael Newman. *Ralph Miliband and the politics of the New Left*. A treasure map tucked away on page 258. The map that led its reader directly to The Incident.

Except that it didn't. The Incident was a convenient theory. A narrative abstraction. In reality, Ed Miliband and David Miliband were composites. In the same way everyone was a composite. The product of hundreds and thousands of people and places and thoughts and moments. The reason no-one hunting for the truth behind the truth behind The Brother Thing had uncovered David Miliband's Boston fracas wasn't because it was hidden, but because it wasn't relevant. Or no more or less relevant than any of their other thousands of life experiences. David never talked about it. Ed never talked about. *Because they were burying it deep in their subconscious, perhaps?* No. because they'd just forgotten about it.

So the explorers finally realized there probably wasn't anything to The Incident theory. If they were going to find the source of The Brother Thing they would have to start to cast their net a bit wider.

Then people started to come up with the Freudian Theory. This theory held that it was all about the father. The battle for the Labour leadership had in fact been a proxy battle. A fight over a father's love, and a father's legacy.

It was why Ed had run his leadership campaign from the Left. It was why he had defined himself against Tony Blair and New Labour. Everyone knew Ralph Miliband detested Blair and his 'Project'. Oh yes, he was immensely proud of his boys. But he didn't grasp their infatuation with Labour party centrism. And so when Ed began shifting his party leftwards, it wasn't a political shift, but an emotional shift. He wasn't primarily trying to bring his party closer to power. He was trying to bring himself closer to his dead father.

Unfortunately, this theory was wrong as well. Ed Miliband's positioning was entirely political. He had recognized, correctly, that the only way to win the leadership election was by positioning himself to the Left. That was, he judged, the way the party was moving. And even if it wasn't, there was no way he could compete with David for votes on the right of the party. He had the endorsements of the Blairite wing sewn up.

So Ed's move to the Left did not represent a homage to his dad. It just represented smart politics. In time, when he calculated that moving his party back to the centre would be an unnecessarily laborious and counter-productive task, there were odd occasions when he rationalized his approach by evoking his father's memory. The Willy Wonka speech was a case in point. But his actions weren't Freudian. They were Keynesian.

Which meant the explorers were stumped again. Then someone came up with a brilliant new theory – the Oedipus Theory. The leadership contest hadn't been a proxy battle for the love of a father. It had been a proxy battle for the love of a mother!

It was really Marion Kozak who sat at the heart of this filial struggle. Friends of Ed had confirmed to the explorers that in reality he had always felt closer to his mother than his father. He had after all spent more of his formative years at her side than at his dad's. They confirmed that she was also highly motivated politically – supporting the striking miners and campaigning robustly for the cause of a free Palestine. And, if anything, she was more able to understand Ed and David's engagement with the Labour party. Unlike her husband, she had consistently viewed Labour as a legitimate – if flawed – vehicle for the delivery of meaningful social change.

And so, the Oedipus Theory held, both sons were actually battling to be true heir to their mother's legacy. And what's more, it would be a living legacy. They would be able to look at her and say, 'Mum, I'm leader of the Labour party now. And I might even be on my way to being Prime Minister.' And they would actually be able to see the pride, and the love, in her eyes.

But again, the theory was flawed. For the same reason the Freudian Theory had been flawed. Ed's moves had been political. To believe the Oedipus Theory it required you to believe that deep down Ed Miliband truly believed his mother would be overjoyed if her youngest son secured the Labour leadership, but dismayed if her eldest son seized the crown. Which in turn meant you basically had to believe Ed Miliband was a sociopath.

So, by now, the explorers were well and truly stumped. They'd looked high and low for the source of The Brother Thing. And they'd come up with nothing. And so they set down the packs, lit their camp fires and started to pore again over their parched and stained maps of this dark, mysterious political continent. And little did they know the solution to the mystery had been in front of their eyes from the very beginning.

The preparation for Ed Miliband's first speech as Labour leader had been a chaotic affair. It was being written by what could best be described as a shift system. Various Labour worthies – including several members of what at that time was the still embryonic Salon – were mingling around in the bar of the Midland Hotel, waiting for their slot. Everyone had been given a pre-arranged window – 18.00, 18.30, 19.00 – where they would be ushered up in their twos and threes to see Ed and Stewart and Mark and a few other members of the team. And they would bat around some ideas, throw in a couple of lines, and then they would be ushered out and another little group of the great and the good would be ushered in.

Not surprisingly, this format made for great stake-holder management, but slightly less great speechwriting. People would turn up late, or people would barge in early, or people would arrive in the wrong group, or people would linger too long and overrun their slot. As a result various drafts were produced, different ideas were inserted and rejected, and numerous pages added and then deleted.

In the midst of this chaos – being tossed around like a leaf snatched up by a ferocious gale – was a sentence that provided the answer to the whole mystery. A sentence that was currently leading a charmed existence. It was in, then it was out, then it was in again. It was pushed to the back of the speech, then to the middle of the speech, then it wasn't in the speech at all. And then, miraculously, it was right up at the very front of the speech. Which is where it stayed.

Although very few people noticed it. Most attention centred around the section claiming a new political generation had been born. 'Generation Ed' they'd called it – for a mercifully brief moment. That and the passage where he'd said Iraq had been wrong. And David had been caught on camera testily turning to an applauding Harriet Harman and snapping, 'You voted for it. Why are you clapping?'

But if they had noticed it and thought about it, and then placed it in the context of what had gone before – and indeed, what was about to follow – people would have understood. Or if they hadn't understood at that moment, it would have at least set them on the path to understanding. A path that would have eventually led them to the source of The Brother Thing.

This is what Ed Miliband said.

'The gifts my parents gave to me and David are the things I want for every child in this country. A secure and loving home. Encouragement and the aspiration to succeed.

'In those ways my family was just like every other. But in some ways it was different.

'I suppose not everyone has a dad who wrote a book saying he didn't believe in the Parliamentary road to socialism.

'But you know, it wasn't a cold house.

'It was warm, full of the spirit of argument and conviction, the conviction that leads me to stand before you today, the conviction that people of courage and principle can make a huge difference to their world.'

It wasn't a cold house. The line was just sitting there, all alone, in the middle of the text. To the trained eye, it looked like some form of 'pre-buttal', a word the politicians used for the refutation of a charge not yet made.

But few trained eyes did spot it. So it just hung there. A line in the wind.

One person who did spot it was Philip Collins. And the only reason he'd spotted it was he'd seen it before.

Of all the people who had been drafted in to help with the speech, his involvement was the most surprising. Philip wasn't a member of The Salon. Nor was he destined to become a member of The Salon That Was No Longer a Salon. He was a member of The Salon That Would Never Be a Salon. He was David Miliband's speechwriter.

Just before the speech was due to be 'locked' – or as close to being locked as anything ever was in Ed Miliband's team – he'd received a call from his friend Greg Beales. Given the circumstances, Greg would entirely understand it if he told him to just fuck off. But was there any chance he could look over the final draft of Ed's speech and give him some feedback?

And because they were friends – and because he'd just spent the best part of a month labouring over David Miliband's utterly redundant leader's speech, and was curious – he said yes. So he read it, and immediately realized it was just as big a mess as he'd expected it to be. At which point he went back to Greg and diplomatically – though not too diplomatically – told him he thought it needed some work. Or words to that effect.

A couple of hours later Greg phoned back. Given the circumstances he would entirely understand if this time he really did tell him to fuck off. But was there any chance he could come over and maybe help him talk Ed through some amends to the speech?

And because they were friends – and because he didn't really have anything much to do now his own beautifully crafted leader's address was pushing up the daisies – he said yes, in principle. But he'd have to check with David first.

So he spoke to David, and explained to him how, given the circumstances, if he told him to fuck off he'd quite understand, etc, etc. And David thought about it for a little bit and then told him he could do it, so long as he didn't put any of the stuff that had been in his speech in Ed's speech. There was no way he was going to have his words coming out of his brother's mouth. Or words that Phil had put into his mouth coming out of his brother's mouth.

So Philip had gone over to Ed's suite, and it had been a little bit awkward at first. But he knew Ed from way back, and Ed knew him from way back, and neither of them felt especially warm towards each other, but what the hell. So Phil began talking to him about the structure of the speech, and how he should take the personal stuff and use it as the spine around which he could construct his political philosophy. And then when he'd done that he could build some hard policy around the philosophy and just build out from there.

So Ed and Greg and a couple of Salon members who were in attendance said, 'Great.' And they started passing him the bits of the speech that contain personal stuff. He saw the line, 'It wasn't a cold house,' which he thought was a bit odd. In David's speech they'd accentuated the positive, describing how it was 'a warm house'. And he saw a couple of other bits. He asked where the rest of it was. 'The rest of what?' they responded.

And that's when he realized. This was all the personal stuff they had. But it contained nothing. No colour, no detail. If you heard this, Ed Miliband had been living his life in bland monochrome. So, for example, the bits in David's speech about his father had all been fleshed out. He didn't just 'serve in the navy'. He joined at eighteen and was at D-Day. He didn't like hammocks so he slept on the table.

When he'd left his last ship just before the 1945 election, his commanding officer's last words to him had been, 'Goodbye Miliband, don't vote Labour.'

And he knew he'd promised David not to use any of this stuff. But this was Ed's stuff too. It was his family history just as much as it was David's. So he asked him, 'Why haven't you put any of this in yourself? The hammock. The voting Labour line.'

And Ed was looking at him. And The Salon were looking at him. And it was at that moment that Philip Collins properly understood. He hadn't used it because he didn't know it. This wasn't his history. And he said to himself, 'Jesus. I know more about Ed Miliband's father than Ed Miliband does.'

It wasn't a cold house, he'd said. But it had been, in truth.

Or maybe not a cold house. Cold wasn't right. As David Miliband said – or was going to say in his own speech – it could frequently be a rich and stimulating and lively house.

Not a cold house. A political house. That was it. A political house. That was the source.

The whole Brother Thing. It was just a politics thing. Everything in Ed Miliband's house had been a politics thing. Everything in his life had been a politics thing.

That's why there had been no great incident. How could there be? The only thing that had real resonance within their young lives was politics. Girls. Toys. They were there, in the background. But they weren't going to fight over them. Because at the end of the day it was only politics that mattered.

And yes, Ed Miliband had realized at a young age that politics was the route through to his father. And his mother. But politics was his route to everything. It was his route to his father. It was his route to his mother. It was his route to his brother. It was his route to university. It was his route to his career. It was his route to his friends. It was the route to the books he read. It was the route to the films he saw. It was the route to everything. It was the road map to his life.

And so the question, 'How could Ed Miliband have

done that to his brother?' should really have been reversed. Why wouldn't he do that to his brother?

It's just what you did in politics. It *was* politics. You set yourself your goal. You convinced yourself your goal was just and pure and – crucially – that only you could achieve it. So you set your course, unflinching and unyielding. You came across an obstacle. You removed the obstacle. Sometimes subtly, at other times brutally. And then you rationalized your brutality. It was unfortunate, but it had to be done. The morality of self-interest. And then, just to make your passage slightly easier, you constructed a narrative around your journey. To make it clear where you'd been, and where you were going. At times the narrative charted your route faithfully. Occasionally it played a trick or two. Like the visit to see your brother in the middle of the night to tell him you were going to challenge him for the prize he'd coveted all his life.

And then you secured your goal. And it was all worth it. All the sacrifices. All the compromises. You had prevailed. What better proof could there be that your decision to embark on your journey had been the right one? And you stood on that stage, with the cheers of the crowd still ringing in your ears – slightly muted cheers in the judgement of some. But the bulbs were flashing, the Bubble Breathers were scribbling and the cameras were rolling. And you knew that back at home your mother was watching. And that was the moment you were able to look out into the crowd, find your brother and fix your gaze on him and say, 'David, I love you.'

And as you did so, you knew you meant every single word of it.

She looked older since the last time he'd seen her. It was strange the way it happened. You could meet someone on and off for years and they'd be exactly the same. And then one day you'd bump into them, and age had pounced.

But the fire was still there. It was still alive.

He felt nervous when he first walked into the flat. Partly because she retained the ability to dominate the space around her. And partly because he hadn't been sure how she'd react to what he had to say.

But he had to come. He couldn't bear to sit back and just watch it all unfold.

So they sat there. Two old Jews. Looking at each other the way old Jews do.

At first she didn't want to engage directly. It was hard. She admitted that. It was quite hard on her.

Precisely. It was hard for everyone. For her. For the people who cared about her. It would be hard for both of them. And the wives. And the grandchildren. Everyone was going to lose from this.

And she listened. He could see she was listening. And she heard. She was absorbing it, and processing it.

But that was what worried him. He'd seen Marion Kozak do this before. The way she would use other people's arguments to energize herself. She was not a great original thinker like Ralph had been. But she was strong. She'd grow. When the men were tiring and starting to look at their watches, she'd be there. Seemingly getting stronger by the hour.

And he could see it starting to happen again. They weren't boys now. They were men. They had their own paths to follow.

Yes. But she was still their mother. They both loved her and they both listened to her.

She smiled and nodded. Of course she loved them. They both had. Ralph had surprised himself with how much he loved the boys, given the ambivalence he'd felt when she'd first become pregnant. But they had expressed their love by teaching each of them to think for themselves. To question. Always to question.

But this was different. Surely she could see that? They weren't fighting some corporate monolith or totalitarian regime. They were fighting each other. And unless someone stepped in, they were going to hurt one another.

Perhaps. Perhaps not. But they had gone into this with their eyes wide open. And they hadn't just stumbled into this. David was a former foreign secretary and Edward was a former environment secretary. Titles didn't really impress her all that much. But neither of the boys had got where they were by accident.

He knew he was losing. He could see her steeling herself. Like the old days. She was growing stronger by the minute. He didn't have much time left.

'But Marion, you're talking about politics. I'm talking about family. At the end of the day, that's the most important thing. It's always got to be about the family.'

She paused and looked away. And for an instant, for a split second, he thought he'd landed a blow. For the first time since he'd arrived he felt her starting to weaken.

Then she looked up at him. And he could see it. It was back again. The fire had reached her eyes.

'No. It's about the politics. Always about the politics.'

Ed Miliband sits there looking at the clock. It's nearly time now. Less than a minute and it will be done. Everything that has happened, it's all about to be swept away.

It had happened for a reason. He knows it. He doesn't have a God. Not a God in the classical, biblical sense. But he knows this was all meant to be. It's going to be like it was in Manchester. There were moments back then when some of them thought they'd lost. But he knew. He'd always been able to feel it.

He could feel it again. How it would soon be over. How it would mark the end. The decision to stand, the decision to challenge David. His victory would bring all that to a close. No-one would ever ask again 'why did Ed Miliband stab his brother in the back.'

He looks at the clock again. Then he looks at everyone in the room.

'OK, I'd like to just go to everyone in turn. And I'd like you each to tell me, in a few brief words, what you think we should say if we lose.'

00.15 . . . 00.14 . . . 00.13 . . . 00.12 . . . 00.11 . . .

16. The Last Gunfight

David Cameron had Ed Miliband cornered.

'You see, I've given you the opportunity to answer, and you won't. And you know why you won't? Because you can't? And you know why you can't? Because it's true. If the result of this election were to be a hung parliament, then Nicola Sturgeon would be sitting at the head of the Cabinet table and you'd be pushing a trolley round, passing out the tea. So I'll ask you again, will you refuse to do any deals with the SNP? Yes or no?'

The camera swivelled round and began zooming in, dragging his image forwards so it was filling the screen. The shot was so tight it was possible to see the veins around his temples pulsating.

'I'm not going to start trying to predict the result of the election a month from polling day. You're asking me about deals. I'm not going to begin opening negotiations with anyone before a single vote has been counted. If I were . . .'

'Oh! So you've admitted it. You are preparing to do a deal with Nicola Sturgeon. You're just not prepared to let anyone know what it is yet.'

'Oh, why don't you just fuck off. David . . .'

The room descended into laughter.

'I think you may have just lost the election there, Ed.'

He had to laugh at that one himself. And he had to admit, Tom Hamilton was an excellent David Cameron.

Though the young advisor wasn't really getting the plaudits he deserved for his David Cameron. That's because Alistair Campbell was the front-of-house David Cameron. The one who popped up in all the Bubble Breathers' write-throughs of his debate prep. Tom was a sort of stunt Cameron.

It was always a tricky thing to know what was the best thing to do with Alistair. He was resolutely loyal. And he had a genuine love for the party. But he just couldn't walk away. Every election there he'd be, floating around the campaign headquarters. In 2010 he'd managed to wangle his own desk, which was almost totally empty, save for a copy of his latest book. Nobody really knew what he was doing, or quite what his role was supposed to be. But they didn't have the heart to say, 'Alistair, what are you actually doing here?' So they'd left him to it.

And he was a quite good Cameron as well. He managed to capture his arrogance. The swagger. Alistair was quite physically imposing too. Which could make a difference if he found himself standing next to Cameron when the positions were drawn.

But Tom really knew how to keep pushing him. He kept driving in at him. Which was what he needed. He had to be tested now. It had been almost five years since the leadership hustings. There'd been the Paxman interview and audience Q&A, which had gone fantastically well. And obviously he had the weekly PMQs sessions. But Thursday's debate would be very different.

Actually, it wouldn't be a debate, it would be more like a wild-west shootout. He wasn't quite sure how they'd ended up here, but there were going to be seven of them taking part. Him, Cameron, Clegg, Farage, Sturgeon, Leanne Wood from Plaid, and Natalie Bennett from the Greens. No-one had ever seen a debate format like that before, and for all their planning and strategizing no-one in The Salon That Was No Longer a Salon knew how it was going to work out.

The one thing they did know was this was going to be the main showdown. It was the one debate that everyone in the country would watch. Well, maybe not everyone in the country. But anyone who was minded to spend an evening watching seven politicians shouting at one another would be watching this one.

And it represented his first and last opportunity to take David Cameron out. For five years he'd had him in his sights. He'd managed to wing him a few times at PMQs. But it was desperately hard to draw a proper bead on him. Cameron was always ducking and dodging. He almost never answered the question and was always falling back on his prepared lines. And whenever it looked like he might be in real trouble he'd just retreat behind the wall of noise being thrown up by his backbenchers.

But there wouldn't be anywhere for him to hide this time. There'd be a neutral moderator pressing him to answer, and a neutral audience on hand to give their instantaneous reaction. If Cameron tried to run from him on Thursday, he wouldn't get far. This time he'd have to stand and fight.

And of course, everyone knew David Cameron didn't want to be having this fight at all. He'd spent a year trying to back out of the debates. Putting all sorts of obstacles in the broadcasters' way. But they'd finally managed to back him into a corner.

OK, the format wasn't perfect from their perspective. Having the Greens and Plaid Cymru and the SNP on the platform wasn't what they really wanted. All three parties were trying to win votes from the left, so he knew he'd be as much of a target for Wood and Bennett and Sturgeon as Cameron would. Farage was also talking a big game about making inroads into Labour's heartlands, so he knew he'd have to watch him as well.

But he knew what his main job was. He had to take David Cameron down. A single exchange, a single memorable line would do it. And if he did, if he finally managed to bring him to his knees in front of a shocked but awe-struck nation, then it would basically be over. The Tories' entire campaign was built around him. How he was weak, how he was weird, how he was a wimp. And if the weak, weird wimp managed to cut their champion down on live national television that campaign would crumble. There'd be a new sheriff in town.

'OK, Ed, can we go again, but with you and Nicola Sturgeon now.'

Tom Hamilton stepped back, and Ayesha Hazarika

stepped forward. He wasn't sure about that. He'd need to manage Sturgeon, but Cameron was the main target. And Tom had been properly testing him. The adrenalin was pumping now.

'Ed, why aren't you prepared to talk to us? Yes, we have our differences. But we need to be prepared to put those differences aside for the good of the country. This is an historic opportunity. Don't let David Cameron bully you out of doing what's right. Don't let him bully you, Ed!'

That was one of the other reasons why he was keener to stick with the Cameron line of questioning. Tom was tough, but focused. Ayesha was very nice, but she could be a bit shrill.

'It's not a question of being bullied, Nicola. It's a question, like you say, of doing what's best for the country. And I'm not sure that involves cutting a deal with a party that wants to break up the Union. Now . . .'

'But Ed, that's just letting the Tories off the hook. Look at what they're doing to our health service, our welfare system, our economy. And we can lock them out. We have a once-in-a-lifetime opportunity to come together and shut the Tories out of Downing Street for good. Don't let David Cameron bully you Ed!'

OK, OK. He knew Ayesha was trying to push him. That was good. But again, she was coming across as a bit yappy.

Anyway, he knew how to manage Nicola Sturgeon. David Cameron was the target. They were the only two people who were going to be on that stage who could be the next Prime Minister. That was the fight that mattered.

Because this was his time. You didn't actually manage campaigns, you just had to sit back and let them swirl around you. Going where you were told, meeting who you were told, saying what you were told. But this debate would be his opportunity to show them. To show all of them. They thought he was weak? They'd written him off as a wimp? Well, they were about to get a shock.

The cameraman began to zoom back in close. On the TV monitor Ed Miliband's face again filled the screen. The jaw was locked with steely determination. It was a warrior's face.

Craig Oliver stood in the empty front row and looked up at the stage. Everything was set. It was perfect.

Even the draw had worked in their favour. The PM was on the far right of the stage. He wouldn't have to keep pivoting to face his opponents. It would be harder for people to gang up on him. And he had Leanne Wood and Nicola Sturgeon between him and Miliband and Farage. That prevented the 'comparison shot', the image of him and his two main challengers standing side by side.

He allowed himself a little nod of satisfaction. This whole thing had been a year in the planning. From their first offer to the broadcasters, to their acceptance of the final agreement – the entire plan had taken twelve tortuous months to put together. It had been one of the trickiest things he'd ever tried to pull off. It was like being involved in a vast, never-ending, poker match. One false card, one obvious tell and it would all have been over. The plan would have collapsed.

And now here they were just hours away from watching the whole thing coming to fruition. Something could still go wrong, obviously. At the back of his mind he had this tiny, irrational nightmare that something was going to happen, that the whole thing would have to be called off at the last minute, and another new frantic round of negotiations would have to open up.

Or maybe the PM could have an off day. Some people thought he'd started the campaign looking a bit tense. And he'd been a little below par in the Paxman interview.

But this was an entirely different format. And the PM was too experienced. He'd been in too many of these high-pressure situations to drop the ball now. All David had to do was get on and off that stage relatively unscathed. And everything else would simply take care of itself.

It hadn't been like that at the beginning. Back then nothing had been taken care of. Everyone was drifting blindly along, assuming there was just going to be a repeat of 2010. Three debates, three leaders (possibly with Farage thrown in), and that would be it.

So when he'd first stepped forward and said the PM would only be prepared to do one five-way debate, and possibly another two-way debate with Ed Miliband, there'd been uproar. The broadcasters had immediately come back with a counter proposal – one head-to-head debate, one three-way debate and one four-way debate, involving Farage. And that was where Labour had made their first big mistake. They accepted the broadcasters' offer. What's more, Douglas Alexander had sat in the first negotiating meeting and given him and everyone else around the table a lecture on the importance of letting well-respected independent broadcasters decide the format.

Which meant he was already holding an ace in his hand. By simply signing up to the broadcasters' first offer, Labour had immediately undermined their own negotiating position. It was now David Cameron, and David Cameron alone, the broadcasters would have to bargain with. What's more, by ceding the principle of the broadcasters choosing the format, Douglas Alexander had established a huge hostage to fortune.

So he'd dug in. The Prime Minister would go with that format, or nothing, he'd said. Which wasn't true. But what he wanted was for the broadcasters to overplay their hand. And in the third week of January they obliged. He had been sitting in his office in Downing Street when the phone rang. On the other end was a senior executive from ITV. 'Just to let you know, in ten minutes we're putting out a statement about the debates.' 'OK, thanks,' he'd responded. 'Hang on, don't you want to know what it is?' the executive had queried. 'No, I don't. Because all you want to do is be able to claim you'd fully discussed the issue with Downing Street before you issued it.'

The new proposal was for two seven-way debates and

a third head-to-head debate. But crucially, the broad-casters had warned that if the Prime Minister didn't appear he would be 'empty chaired'. And at that moment he knew he'd just been dealt his second ace.

Up until that point the 'debate about the debates' had been framed as a cowardly Prime Minister ducking and weaving to avoid proper scrutiny from the electorate. But now he'd been handed the opportunity to turn it into an issue of whether or not the broadcasters had the right to intervene in a partisan way in the midst of what was shaping up to be the closest election campaign in living memory. Ofcom began to issue some subtle reminders about the obligation for impartiality. Former BBC head Lord Grade penned an article for *The Times* asking 'who do the broadcasters think they are . . . in the run up to the general election, broadcasters are, for the first time, unequivocally playing politics.' And the word started to filter back that senior executives within the BBC were becoming nervous of the corporation's stance.

So negotiations had re-opened. With the broadcast-ers now on the back foot, and knowing they would have to come up with some sort of compromise that would mean they wouldn't need to carry through their threat of empty chair. And it was in the course of those nego-tiations that he'd been handed – and subsequently played – his third ace.

The final proposal was for only one main seven-way debate. In addition there would be a 'challengers' debate' involving Labour, Ukip and the three other minor parties, plus two audience-led Q&A-style discussions with the three main party leaders at the start and the end of the campaign. Which was a potentially disastrous format for Labour. There would not be the head-to-head confrontation between the PM and Ed Miliband they were desperate for. It would maximize the exposure of the minor left-of-centre parties that were scrapping with Labour for votes. And it would tie up Ed Miliband in the middle of the campaign with lengthy preparation for a debate no-one in the country would watch.

Douglas Alexander, belatedly recognizing the danger, had attempted to argue against the plan. At which point he'd casually leant forward and said, 'But hang on a minute, Douglas. I thought you'd told us all it was up to the broadcasters to decide?'

He began to move along the front row until he was standing on the far left side of the stage. From there he could check the sightlines of the cameras, and see what sort of angle the left-hand long shot would be capturing of the PM.

It all looked good. Ed Miliband thought he was coming to a debate that evening. In reality, he was walking into a trap.

Nick Clegg always went for a walk just before a big debate. It was what he'd tried to do in 2010, primarily to clear his head, and now it had become a bit of a ritual. And it was quite peaceful along here by the canal. There were a few people about, but if he wasn't in his suit and he kept to a relatively brisk pace no-one would recognize him. Or if they did, they didn't bother him.

It had been a bit hard before the second 2010 debate, which had fallen slap bang in the middle of Cleggmania. But it was different now. Everything was different now.

It was quite a cool afternoon and he paused to pull his zipper up to the top of his jacket collar. It may just be his imagination, but he seemed to be noticing chilly weather more these days. He couldn't decide if that meant they were experiencing more chilly days, or if he was just feeling them more.

Really he should have been starting to feel the first kick of excitement by now. His first big national debate of the campaign. Actually, his only big national debate of the campaign.

The Cell were certainly excited about it. They saw this as an opportunity to alter the dynamic of the election. A stand-out performance here, and they would force themselves back into the race. If he did well, given the amount of coverage the debate was going to receive, there would be no way the broadcasters could continue to stick with their two-party script. A big evening, and it would reset the entire contest for them.

And he was capable of it. He knew he could do it, because he'd done it once already. All the tricks he'd been taught back then – stand with his hand in his pocket when the others were speaking (makes you looked relaxed, confident and untroubled by what they're saying) – were second nature to him now.

Obviously they all knew it wasn't going to be another 2010. They'd already put the briefing round damping down expectations. 'Nick Clegg: I Will Not Win Leaders' Debate', had been the headline in Tuesday's *Telegraph*.

But for him it hadn't just been expectation management. He knew he didn't have it any more.

Oh, he had some arguments. Good arguments. The idea that people were looking for a party with a combination of Labour's compassion and the Tories' competence was a winning one. All their private polling backed that up. And now he had a record to lean on, too. He'd been the new kid on the block in 2010 and that had been useful to him. But he was also very inexperienced. He hadn't been able to lean forward and tell portentous anecdotes about his discussions on climate change with Barack Obama.

So he had the ammunition. He had the bullets to fire. That wasn't the problem. The problem was he no longer had the edge. The fingers on his gun hand were too stiff. His reactions had become too slow.

He'd realized in the debates with Farage. He thought he'd taken him in their first head-to-head. When they'd told him about the poll he couldn't believe it. But it was the second debate where he'd finally understood. He'd been poor, by his standards. No-one had needed to show him any polling figures to tell him he'd lost that one.

A teenage boy with a fluorescent hoodie went flying by on a bicycle. Another half a foot to the left and they'd both have been swimming for it.

The problem was, you couldn't force a connection. Yes, you could come up with clever answers and short sharp phrases people would remember and pass off in the pub as their own. And yes, you could shoot down your opponents and their own arguments. But it wouldn't mean anything if you couldn't make that connection with the people at home.

And he couldn't. Some of them might still vote for him. But they simply didn't want to connect with him any more.

So he hadn't done anything like the preparation he'd done in 2010. He hadn't even done that much preparation compared to the work they'd put in planning for Farage. It would have been a waste of time. His heart, and his brain, just wouldn't have been in it.

A middle-aged woman wearing a blue cagoule suddenly stopped in front of him. 'Excuse me are you . . .' He began preparing a smile of acknowledgment. 'Oh, no, I'm so sorry. My mistake. I thought you were someone I used to be at school with. I feel such a fool.' He smiled anyway, and she hurried on her way.

Still, it was only one debate. And given the format, it wasn't going to have anything like the impact of that first debate in 2010. It was an odd arrangement. He couldn't really work out why Labour had signed up to it.

Over to his right he could see the Beetham Tower rising out of the city centre, like a giant mobile phone. Manchester was changing too. Everything, everywhere was changing.

Thinking back, it was like it had all happened to somebody else. There was very little he could remember from the night of that first debate. He could remember feelings – the sense of excitement when he'd first walked out on to that stage. But he couldn't really remember anything much that he'd said, or that either Gordon or David had said. Famously, there'd been a lot of 'I agree with Nick' going on, and he had this distant recollection of thinking, 'Why do they keep agreeing with me so much? How's that helping them?' But that was it. And after that it had all got a bit silly.

He looked down at his watch. It was probably time for him to start getting back.

He began to turn, and it occurred to him that this was the last time. The last time in his entire life he'd go for one of these pre-debate, clear-your-mind walks. He felt a bit like an ageing gunfighter, heading into town for his final showdown.

Instinctively, he reached down and slipped his hand into his right-hand trouser pocket. As he did so he noticed his fingers felt slightly stiff and cold.

It had been a trap. The whole thing had been a set-up.

They'd ganged up on him. Nicola Sturgeon. Leanne Wood. Even Natalie Bennett, who everyone had told him wouldn't be able to get her words out in a coherent sentence. They'd just kept hitting him again and again.

He hadn't been able to land a blow on David Cameron. OK, David Cameron hadn't landed too many on him. But he hadn't had to. He'd just been able to stand back and watch the three women pumping bullets into him.

There'd been a moment when he'd looked across and he could actually see him smiling. Bennett and Sturgeon were hitting him again and he'd looked over and seen this huge self-satisfied grin on David Cameron's face.

Nick Clegg had hardly been present. Nigel Farage had looked terrible, with sweat pouring down his face. But even he'd managed to trip him up. Farage had issued some sick dog-whistle about HIV sufferers and health tourism. And Leanne Wood had nailed him. Said he should be ashamed of himself. And Sturgeon had nailed him too. And then it had been his turn, and he'd fumbled it. He'd been trying not to hype the moment up, and give Farage the headline he was looking for. So he hadn't really responded. They'd had to put out a tweet from him after the debate was over. He'd been standing next to the guy for two hours, and they had to put out a damn tweet.

No-one needed any polls to tell them how it had gone. The Tories were wandering around the spin room with these massive grins on their faces. Tom Baldwin had nearly had a fight with Craig Oliver, telling him it had all been a fucking stitch-up. Then the first actual poll had come out – and he'd come fourth. Sturgeon then Farage then Cameron. Then him. Fourth.

And that was only half of it. Sturgeon had topped the poll. Which was disastrous in itself. The SNP were already twenty points ahead up in Scotland. Which was going to put rocket boosters on their campaign. But it was only the beginning. He'd committed to that ludicrous 'challengers' debate' in two weeks' time. Cameron and Clegg wouldn't even be there. It would be open season on him. And the Tories were already whacking posters up around the country of him dancing around as Alex Salmond's puppet. Now it would be him dancing around as Nicola Sturgeon's puppet. And how did they respond to it? If he ruled out a deal with the SNP, Labour's support in Scotland would collapse. But if he even hinted at a deal there was a possibility it would start to hit their support in England.

And now he was going to have to waste another week prepping properly for Sturgeon and Bennett and Wood. Plus, people would be queuing up to see him taking another kicking from the sisterhood. Which meant the debate would get more coverage. Which in turn would suck more oxygen out of his campaign.

What the hell had happened here? This was supposed to be *his* moment. Not Nicola Sturgeon's moment. Not Leanne Wood's moment. Not Natalie Bennett's moment.

Cameron had managed to do it again. He'd had him. He'd finally got him cornered. And he'd slipped away.

And he knew what they would say. Would say? They were already saying it. 'Did you see Ed Miliband being beaten up by those women? So weak.' 'Did you see Ed Miliband tweeting about Farage *after* he'd got off stage? What a wimp.'

In front of him on the make-up table were his hand-scribbled debate notes. He leant forward, and picked them up. 'Happy warrior', 'Calm never agitated', 'Negative – Positive'.

He tossed them aside. Happy warrior? This was supposed to have been the night he won the general election. And now it was hard to see how it could have gone much worse.

The leaders' debate in Manchester was the only occasion these three men were together during the course of the election campaign. Even then, they were only in personal contact for the time it took to shake a hand. Ed Miliband had walked over and placed his left arm on Dave Cameron's right arm, just like they'd told him too. 'Looks assertive, like you're in control.' Nick Clegg had shaken Cameron's hand in a perfunctory manner, with the minimum of eye contact. 'Don't make it look like you're mates.'

And then they'd gone their separate ways. The next time they saw each other it would be over. They would be standing shoulder by shoulder at the Cenotaph on the Friday morning after the election, marking the seventieth anniversary of VE Day. Paying tribute to men who had sacrificed everything for their country.

And the clock still ticked down. But it was nearly time now.

00.10 . . . 00.09 . . . 00.08 . . . 00.07 . . . 00.06 . . .

17. Democracy's Grim Reaper

All that was left for them to do was walk to the car, and that was it. He had one more speech to the faithful later that evening, but this had been the final proper campaign event. The last time he'd be out on the road. The end of the road.

He looked at Samantha, and then he looked at Senders, and he looked at the other members of The League of Extraordinary Advisors who were standing around just preparing the final details. And he thought to himself, 'So this is how it finishes. Standing in the kitchen of a show home in Lancaster, whilst a dozen people work out the best way to get me a hundred yards to my car.'

And then he had another thought. 'Is this really how we make the choice?' We make a man put on a hard hat and a high visibility jacket and a pair of oversize work boots. And we walk him through to the back of a half-built housing estate, on to a building site. And we ask him to bring his wife along, because she's attractive, and if she's in the photo people may actually pause a second to read a couple of words about what he's been doing, rather than turning to the football. And then we line up a lot of photographers and journalists behind an imaginary line, and then we wheel that man out. And we get him to walk around the site, talking earnestly to the site manager and pointing occasionally at random things – like a nearby cement mixer. And then after five minutes we walk him back to a show home, where he takes off his hard hat and his high visibility jacket and his oversize work boots. And then he leaves.'

Which is how we make the choice. We look at a photo of a man in his helmet, and we look at a photo of another man standing talking intently to a pretty but slightly weary-looking nurse. And we decide which of these two men we think is best suited to sit down opposite Vladimir Putin and stop World War Three.

So maybe that's what David Cameron should have been thinking. But he wasn't of course. He'd come too far. Much too far to start questioning the process, thinking about what it all meant and asking himself why he was doing all this. The process was the process. Part of the natural order.

And now everything was ready. The car was in position, the snappers and the Bubble Breathers were back behind their imaginary invisible line and the nice couple from the real house next door were lined up ready to say goodbye. And out they came. A few words with nice couple, a laugh, a wave goodbye. And then they were walking. Him on the left, Samantha on his right, holding hands. He had a determined, confident expression on his face. The car was ninety yards away, eighty, seventy. The bullet-catcher pulled open the door. Sixty yards, fifty yards, forty.

And then it happened. Just for an instant, the expression changed. The mask of confidence faltered and then fell away, and you could see him beginning to bite down on his lower lip. His left hand, the hand that wasn't holding Samantha's, started clenching up into a tight little ball. Then he was at the car, sliding across the near-side back seat, and Samantha was ushered by the bullet-catcher into the far-side back seat, and they were gliding away.

David Cameron was driving away. And for the first time in his life he didn't know where he was going.

Nick Clegg was moving again. The best part of a thousand miles in twenty-four hours – from Land's End to John O'Groats. The last big push.

The Salon had done a fantastic job. The backdrop was sensational. The rugged Cornish coastline, the clouds lowering, the wind sweeping across the imposing cliffs. They'd even managed to adapt the famous sign. 'New York 3147', 'John O'Groats 874', 'Lib Dems Winning Here 2015'.

He looked great as well. Standing tall, hair blowing in the breeze, 'Just like Poldark,' as one Bubble Breather had remarked.

He could relax now. It was almost over. That was certainly what The Salon saw. He was cheerful. Chatty. 'Nick's demob happy,' was the word going around the camp.

And he was. Kind of. There was certainly a sense of relief the election was reaching its climax. Only a masochist would want the madness of the last six weeks extended indefinitely.

But there was something else there too. The TV cameramen peering through their lenses might have noticed it, if they'd been really looking for it. So might the Bubble Breathers, who were stood just a few yards away, scribbling down his final words of the campaign. But it was cold, and they'd been up since four-thirty, and they had a long twenty-four hours stretching ahead of them too.

There was a slight desperation in his words. It was cloaked in politics. But it was there. If people voted for David Cameron they wouldn't get a Conservative government. They had to understand that. They'd get a minority administration that would be dancing to the tune of Ukip and the DUP and the right-wingers on David Cameron's back benches. And if they voted Labour it would be Nicola Sturgeon, with her honeyed nationalism, that would be calling the shots. 'That's not fair!' he cried. If you believed in decency and fairness then the only thing to do, the only thing, was to vote Liberal Democrat instead.

The reason there was desperation there was that he recognized this was the final chance. His only chance.

Not to win seats. Or in this case save seats. Not to win an endorsement from the British people – it was clear their endorsement was going elsewhere.

What Nick Clegg needed – all he needed – was forgiveness. He needed the voters to say, 'OK, we understand. You made a mistake. Don't worry. We're moving on. You can move on too.'

Because in truth, that was what his campaign had been about. Not seeking an endorsement of tax cuts for the low paid, or cheers for the creation of a green investment bank, or a pat on the back for pupil premiums. He hadn't been seeking validation. He'd been searching for redemption.

And there was nowhere else he could find it. This was it. If they turned away from him now, for this one last time, then he would never find what he was looking for. What he'd done over these past five years – what he'd been – would define him. The lecture circuit, some private sector consulting, a cosy European sinecure. That wasn't who Nick Clegg was. But it would be all he would have.

And that would mark the end of Nick Clegg's journey. Here he was, standing on this cliff top, effectively pleading with the people of Britain to grant him absolution. And if they didn't, if they rejected his pleas, then he would never leave this place. He would be trapped here for ever. Imprisoned by the knowledge that he had never been able to make them understand. He'd never been able to make them appreciate what he was trying to do. He'd never been able to make them see who Nick Clegg really was.

So he looked into the camera's lens for a final time.

And his words said, 'Vote for me.' But his eyes said, 'Please forgive me.'

Ed Miliband looked out over the crowd. The auditorium of Leeds City Museum was packed to overflowing. They'd been queuing round the block for the best part of two hours. Although that may in part have been a result of some last-minute sleight of hand from The Salon That Was No Longer a Salon. The Bubble Breathers present noted the venue seemed a bit on the small side.

He'd made quite a low-key start to his speech. The introduction had contained only a perfunctory acknowledgment of his surroundings, 'It is great to be in Leeds.' Which seemed to slightly disappoint and surprise his audience, given he used to live in the town himself.

But they weren't there to be disappointed. They were there to be enthused. They were there to see the next Prime Minister.

And now he began moving through the gears. Britain could be better than this. A country for the many, not just a privileged few. A country that faced down the tax evaders and the hedge funds and the Tory donors.

They liked that. That was exactly what they'd come to hear their next Prime Minister say.

Then he'd begun to work his way through the Tory charge sheet. Food banks spreading across the country. Five years of falling wages for working people. Five years of rising bills for millions of families. Five years of an epidemic of zero hours contracts. Five years of the dream of home ownership shrinking out of sight. They may as well call it what it was. Five years of unfairness.

And they did. They did call it what it was. And they applauded each line. Which was odd, if you thought about it. Applauding the spreading of food banks and rising bills. But they weren't thinking about it. They were feeling it. They were feeling the excitement. They were feeling what it was like to be there in the same room as the next Prime Minister.

Although to those who had been following him throughout the campaign, the next Prime Minister looked ever-so-slightly below par. His delivery was a bit laboured. And he wasn't hitting his applause lines with his usual vigour.

But he was at the end of a long campaign. This was his last speech. And the crowd understood. They would carry him home.

His right hand gripped the lectern. And they sensed it. They sensed something special was coming.

He was going to rescue their NHS. He was going to create a health service that had time to care again. It would be there for their children and their grandchildren as it had been there for them. Three thousand more midwives. Five thousand more careworkers. Eight thousand more doctors. Twenty thousand more nurses. And it would all be paid for by a new tax on mansions, and a new tax on the tobacco companies.

He paused. For a split second they paused. And then

their applause started rolling across the auditorium in waves, as they roared their approval.

And as it did, the next Prime Minister left the room. He closed his eyes and everything around him vanished.

He could still hear the cheers. But all he could see was darkness. And then through the darkness he could start to make out an image. A boy, sitting in a room, watching a group of men arguing. He couldn't quite make out what it was they were arguing about. But from their expressions, it looked like it must be the most important thing in their lives. Then the image faded and he saw a new image. A teenager with an unflattering pudding bowl haircut and an ugly grey jumper, talking to a TV reporter about a university rent strike. The image faded again, and now he was looking at a young man, quite tall, with glasses, walking into a room that he recognized as the Chancellor's office in the old Treasury building. The young man with glasses had a slightly awestruck look on his face. And that image faded, and it was replaced by the image of a middle-aged man standing in front of a large audience. An audience not unlike the one the next Prime Minister had just been addressing himself. And this man was looking out into the crowd. And then he stopped and said, 'David, I love you.'

The image faded, and the next Prime Minster opened his eyes. The applause was still cascading towards him. The audience were all still looking up at him. And he could see it in their faces. Hope. Expectation. Anticipation.

And he closed his eyes again. To see if he could conjure a fresh image. And there was something there. He could just make it out. It was the doorway. That famous, black, shiny door. There was a crowd of people and a crowd of cameras facing it. He could see a figure, quite a tall figure, walking towards the door. He peered deeper, trying to make out who it was. But the figure was blurred. All he could see was an outline. And then the image faded and all he could see was darkness.

The next Prime Minister opened his eyes again. They were still applauding. Some of them had started cheering. And as his gaze traversed the room he could still see it. It was everywhere his eyes settled. That same blood-chilling, oppressive, unyielding look. The look that said, 'We believe in you. We trust you. We know you won't let us down.'

It was done. It was all done. These three men had reached the end. The end of the campaign. And for whoever failed to secure the endorsement of The People, the end of their lives.

Because someone was going to die the next day. Life, as they knew it, would end. Every dream, every thought, every action, every reaction, every hope, every fear, every decision, every twist of fate, everything that had made them who they were and who they wanted to be – from the moment of their political awakening – would be gone. One second they would be the Prime Minister or the next Prime Minister or the Deputy Prime Minister. Then nothing. Only the void. A sea of unending, unpitying blackness.

People said that all political careers end in failure. They were wrong. All political careers end in death. Not just the death of a dream but the death of an existence. And tomorrow the grim reaper they called democracy was coming to claim someone.

In Oxfordshire and Doncaster and Sheffield the windows are shut and the doors are locked. But that won't keep him out. Because on the screen, the clock has finally stopped ticking.

00.05 . . . 00.04 . . . 00.03 . . . 00.02 . . . 00.01 . . .

18. One Man

Big Ben struck ten. David Dimbleby turned, and an image of a smiling David Cameron appeared on the screen in the studio, alongside the words 'Conservatives largest party'. In the Manor in Oxfordshire there was a huge cheer. In the flat in Sheffield, and in the Doncaster Lego house, there was no immediate reaction. The idea the Tories would emerge as the largest party had already been factored in.

Big Ben chimed for a second time and then a third. Craig Oliver leapt to his feet. 'They're going to bottle it!' he shouted. 'They're not going to show the full fucking figures!!!'

At that moment David Dimbleby's voice emerged over the graphic. 'And now here are the figures for each party.' The graphic of David Cameron disappeared, to be replaced by a hologram of him. He was standing on a pedestal, looking directly at the camera, wearing the dark suit, white shirt and blue tie that had become his uniform throughout the campaign. On the pedestal below him were the numbers three-one-six.

'Quite remarkable, this exit poll,' David Dimbleby commented. He was back on screen now, gesturing towards a second hologram of Ed Miliband. His was slightly smaller than David Cameron's, and he appeared to be looking off at a slight angle. Below him his pedestal contained the numbers two-three-nine.

The computer-animated representations of David Cameron and Ed Miliband disappeared, to be replaced by three new holograms of Nicola Sturgeon, Nick Clegg and Nigel Farage. The numbers on the side of their pedestals were fifty-eight, ten and two respectively.

The manor house exploded. Craig Oliver was shouting, David Cameron was on his feet punching the air, Samantha Cameron was screaming. Then everyone lurched forward, grabbed each other and started wheeling around the room in a chaotic, rolling jig. Moments later the phone at the side of the room burst into life. Someone hit the speaker button and a fresh roar came bursting down the line. 'Yeahhhhhh!!!!,' George Osborne shouted down the phone. More screaming and expletives filled the air, and a new voice, an Australian voice, could be heard bellowing, 'Will everyone just shut the fuck up!!! That exit poll could be wrong!!!' 'It isn't wrong!!!,' Craig screamed back, 'I helped set that thing up! It's too sophisticated! There's no way they can get it wrong!!!!'

In Sheffield Nick Clegg stared at the screen. And for the first time in a very, very long time he felt calm. The exit poll could be wrong, of course. But the shit through the letterbox. The figures of him being burnt in effigy. The car with the armour-plated doors. They all made sense to him now.

He reached behind him, prized opened the packet of Marlboro Lights, slipped a cigarette into his mouth and placed the tip over the flame of his lighter. Then he lifted it to his lips, drew a deep breath and leant back.

He could stop running now. It was finally over. The People had moved on. They just hadn't been prepared to take him with them.

In Doncaster Ed Miliband sat alone in an empty room. The walls around him were pristine white. There wasn't a mark on them, never mind a photograph or a painting. There were no chairs, no sofas, no carpets, no furniture of any kind.

There were no other people in the room. Justine, Greg, Stewart and Bob had all disappeared.

There was a window to his left, but it didn't have any curtains or any lattice work or even a frame. There was just a clear piece of glass. Beyond it everything was dark. It was night time of course. But it wasn't that sort of darkness. It was an emptiness. And he knew that if he got up and went to the window and looked out, the cameras and the vans and the policeman and the small crowd of onlookers would be gone. There'd be nothing there.

The only thing that was there was the television. Just sitting in the middle of the floor. And there, in the centre of the screen, was a hologram. A hologram of himself. How odd that this was how it ended. With you sat alone staring at your image, whilst your image sat there staring back at you.

Craig Oliver had been right. The exit poll was too sophisticated to be wrong. In fact it had slightly underestimated the level of Conservative support. The numbers on the base of the BBC's holograms should really have read David Cameron 330, Ed Miliband 232, Nicola Sturgeon 55, Nick Clegg 8, Nigel Farage 1.

Lynton Crosby's plan had worked. The Liberal Democrats were completely wiped out in the South-West of England. And the gains the Conservatives made there were enough to give them a majority of twelve.

Ed Miliband never escaped from the trap set for him in Manchester. Two weeks later, Nicola Sturgeon had destroyed him in the closing moments of their 'challengers' debate', persistently demanding to know why he wouldn't join with her and lock David Cameron out of Downing Street. And at that moment 'Sturgeonmania' was born. Most assessments of the result agreed that the fear of the SNP holding the balance of power had been a decisive factor in swaying wavering English voters over to the Tory fold.

Despite the faith of his supporters, Nigel Farage failed to turn up in South Thanet. He was spotted in a pub with three hours still left til the close of the polls, debating whether to jack in the whole thing and go back to London. He ended up losing by over 2,500 votes, resigned the Ukip leadership, then spectacularly un-resigned several weeks later.

Lynton Crosby won the battle of the Big Dogs, being widely credited with the strategy that secured the Tories their victory. Craig Oliver later told friends that if the campaign had lasted a week longer he'd probably have had to kill him. By the end they'd had to throw a jacket over his monitor to prevent him hurling expletives at people criticizing his strategy on Twitter.

David Axelrod put in an appearance in the closing stages of the campaign, and genuinely impressed people with his advice. 'The thing you have to understand, Ed,' he'd told his client, 'is that the key to politics is authenticity. So when the Tories tell people something they don't want to hear, like a new round of cuts, people don't like them, but they respect them. You should bear that in mind.' And Ed Miliband had nodded, and then forgotten all about it. Axelrod also took the time to inscribe a book to Ayesha Hazarika which read, 'If Nicola Sturgeon is half as good at debating Ed as you are, we're in trouble.'

Ryan Coetzee acknowledged he never really saw the Tories coming in the south west. But he consoled himself with the fact that even if he had done, there would have been nothing he could have done about it. And almost everyone in the Liberal Democrats conceded he'd put in place the best strategy he could. In the end, he'd been overly sentimental in his assessment of how many MPs he could save.

Vikki with two 'K's lost by 10,000 votes and Mike

O'Brien lost by 3,000. Though in the end he didn't vote Conservative. Andrew Mitchell lost his libel action and did not secure a return to the cabinet. But he increased his vote share, a result which he said represented vindication in the eyes of the only jury that mattered to him, his constituents.

In Chester, where Ed Miliband had met his hen party, Labour sneaked home by ninety-three votes. Over in Bolton West, where Lucy Howarth had upstaged David Cameron, Tory candidate Chris Green managed to edge in by 801.

Philip Hammond, the current Foreign Secretary, now has sole use of Chevening. But he doesn't swim in the lake. Ivan Cameron's photograph remains on the wall of the Downing Street flat, and there are currently no plans for any major media appearances by Samantha Cameron or the children. A month after the election the Ministry of Defence confirmed that British military personnel embedded with US and other foreign forces had participated in air strikes within Syria. According to the Syrian Observatory For Human Rights, the death toll from the conflict by then exceeded 200,000 people, over half of them civilians.

On the Friday afternoon after polling day the main parties' leaders assembled for the VE day commemoration. Although he hadn't slept in over twenty-four hours, David Cameron was buzzing as he walked into the holding room. Nick Clegg arrived a few minutes later, looking tired but surprisingly cheerful. Ed Miliband, perhaps understandably, looked slightly shell-shocked. As, for different reasons, did Nicola Sturgeon, who arrived and immediately went and stood by herself in a far corner. The politicians acknowledged each other politely, but spent most of their time talking to members of the royal family and other dignitaries.

A few hours earlier Nick Clegg had resigned as leader of the Liberal Democrats. With the emotions of five years finally catching up with him, he told his assembled activists he had found the result 'immeasurably more crushing and unkind than I could ever have feared'. He announced he would be stepping back from the political front line for the foreseeable future, and had no wish to be considered for a front bench position under the new Liberal Democrat leader. But aware that if he resigned his seat it would force a by-election his party would inevitably lose, he had agreed to stay on as the MP for Sheffield Hallam. The election defeat had trapped him in Westminster.

Shortly afterwards Ed Miliband had also announced he was stepping down as Labour leader. 'I joined this party aged seventeen,' he said. 'I never dreamed I would lead it. It has been an incredible force for progress from workers' rights to the NHS to the minimum wage . . . it will be a force for progress and change once again.' Two days later he flew off to Ibiza for a break with his family. But members of his staff continued to receive regular phone calls, urging them to 'protect the legacy'. Friends who spoke to him immediately after his return all listened to the same analysis. The media had traduced his message. The SNP surge – which no-one could have predicted – had made victory impossible this time. He was planning to set up a new think tank committed to tackling social injustice and promoting the agenda they had developed during his time as Labour leader. Asked about the election result in a CNN interview, David Miliband said Labour had gone 'backwards, rather than turn the page forwards' under his brother's leadership.

David Cameron was said to be 'jumping' around Downing Street in the weeks immediately following the result. But soon everyone had settled back into the old routines. There was a mini reshuffle amongst The League of Extraordinary Advisors, but many of the old hands stayed in place. One of the exceptions was Alan Sendorek who moved, with his moccasins, to a new communications role at his beloved Queen's Park Rangers. Most of the senior cabinet positions remained the same too, with a few new entrants filling the spaces left by the defeated Liberal Democrats. Conservative special advisors moved into the big white room and James McGrory's old office. There were no more shots of prime ministerial shirt sleeves.

The natural order, restored.

He leant forward with his chin resting on his hands, and the warm Shropshire sun on his face. He would never tire of listening to his mother telling this story.

They'd used everything they could get their hands on. Bricks, paving stones. Some of the women had thrown chamber pots and the children had even tossed their marbles under the hooves of the police horses.

They'd parked a truck right across the road and people had piled on the back and were crammed into the cab, jamming the pavement all around it.

The sound of the drums was what they heard first. The Blackshirts had a band out in front, with drums and trumpets. Then the sound of the drums had given way to the sound of galloping horses. Seconds later the sound of galloping horses had been replaced with the sound of screams.

But they hadn't faltered. The police had moved forward in a long line. On those narrow streets it was like a tide rising up towards you. But not a single person had turned or run. Orthodox Jews and Irish Labourers and north London academics stood together. All around her people were stood with their fists in the air. 'No pasarán!' they'd shouted. 'No pasarán!'

And none had. Not a single fascist had passed that day.

She looked down at her son and smiled. 'Now, Jeremy Corbyn, I think it's time for a nice cup of tea.'

The balding man with glasses stored at her. She shouldn't be foolish about all this. Much better if they just took the kids away now, without any fuss.

The young woman glared back at him, with thinly controlled fury. What right did he have to take her kids away from her.

His face betrayed no emotion. He couldn't even be bothered to raise himself to contempt. No-one cared about her now. It was only the children they were concerned with.

Tim Farron gazed at the screen transfixed. You didn't see many black-and-white films any more, and he thought this one would be boring. But he hadn't been able to take his eyes off it. They were going to take her children away from her. How was that right? They were her children. Imagine if someone had just turned up from the council one day when he was their age and snatched him away from his mother!

He felt an anger rising up inside him. It was the sort of feeling he normally got when Blackburn weren't awarded a penalty they should obviously have had. Only this anger was different. It was deeper.

How could they just take Cathy's children away? How could they take him away? It was wrong. It was so wrong.

He stopped. What if she reacted badly? She could. It had been her first gift to him after all. Her and Dad's.

But it didn't fit. It just wasn't him. Well, it was him. Gideon was an old, rich-sounding name, and he came from an old, rich-sounding family.

But that's not where he wanted to come from. OK, it was where he was going to come from so there wasn't any point in worrying about it. And yes, all his friends called him 'Giddy'. But that didn't really bother him any more. It had once, but he'd developed a thick enough skin now.

His mother turned and saw him standing there. 'Yes, Gideon?'

'I don't want to be called Gideon any more. I want to change my name.'

'You want to change your name?'

'Yes, I'm sorry. It's not a criticism of you, or Dad. But it isn't me. I'm not a Gideon. I want to change it properly. By deed poll and everything.'

He wasn't sure this was going well. She was looking at him as if he had walked into the room wearing a pink dress.

'And what do you want to change your name to?'

'Er . . . George. I'd thought about George.'

'George?'

'Yes. I really don't like Gideon.'

She nodded.

'Nor do I. George Osborne is fine.'

They are men now, these three boys. With families of their own. Children who hang on their every word. Who look to them for reassurance that the world around them works. That it's a good world, in which they can feel safe and secure.

But soon that world is going to begin to change. Everything around them will change, and they will change. They will ask themselves, 'Have I got what it takes?' And a thousand voices will shout, 'NO'. So they will reach out to the voices that whispered, 'Yes'. And they will say to them, 'Help me. Show me what it takes. Give me what it takes.' And the voices will reach back. And they will put together a plan. And it will be a good plan. Or at least, it will be a good-looking plan. Then they will start to implement their plan, and as they do so that's when their world will start to change. Incrementally at first, but then rapidly. And they will begin to feel as if they are in a bubble. They will be surrounded by people they can see, but not touch. So they will try to attract that their attention. Occasionally someone will turn and look at them. But most of the time they will scurry on by. Some of the voices that once appeared so friendly will start to sound frustrated. Then angry. It will become difficult to know which voices can be trusted and which can't. Slowly they will notice. Small differences about themselves. About the way others see them. And they will begin to have doubts. They will begin to ask themselves, 'Is this really for me? Is this me?' Then, just when they are starting to convince themselves, 'No, this is not for you,' they will suddenly find something. Discover something about themselves or within themselves that they had never known was there before. And that will convince them to stay the course, and now they are on the course there is no turning back. So they will start to tack a little here, and weave a little there. Just to stay on track. Just to ensure they stay the course.

And then one day they will reach the end of the journey and they will look back. They will look at the distance they have travelled and they will think about everything that has been lost along the way.

They will ask themselves, 'Was it worth it?' And everything these three men have, and everything they have ever had, will rest upon that answer.

Bibliography

At several times during the writing of this book I found myself walking in the footsteps of giants. They include Mehdi Hasan and James Macintyre, *Ed: The Milibands and the making of a Labour leader* (Biteback Publishing Ltd, 2012); Dylan Jones, *Cameron on Cameron* (Fourth Estate, 2010); Chris Bowers, *Nick Clegg: The Biography* (Biteback Publishing Ltd, 2011); Matthew D'Ancona, *In it Together* (Penguin Group, 2014); Tony Benn, *A Blaze of Autumn Sunshine* (Arrow Books, 2014); Andrew Adonis, *5 Days in May* (Biteback Publishing, 2013); Ralph Miliband, *Class War Conservatism and Other Essays* (Verso, 2015); Michael Newman, *Ralph Miliband and the Politics of the New Left* (Merlin Press Ltd, 2002); Charles Moore, *Margaret Thatcher: The Authorized Biography* (Penguin Group, 2013); André Sellier *A History of The Dora Camp: The Untold Story of the Nazi Concentration Camp that Secretly Manufactured V-2 Rockets* (Ivan R Dee Inc, 2003); Janan Ganesh, *George Osborne: The Austerity Chancellor* (Biteback Publishing, 2012).

Acknowledgements

There are so many people who deserve thanks for helping me produce this book I'm bound to have forgotten someone. So if it's you, apologies. Of those I managed to remember: Eugenie Furniss, who took me to lunch and told me to write something, anything. Everyone else at Furniss Lawton who told her to check her answerphone messages and ring me back. Rowland White at Penguin, who waited for me even though I was forty-five minutes late for a different lunch. Nick Lowndes and Fiona Brown who took my ramblings and turned them into English. Or something close. Everyone at the *Telegraph*, especially Luke, Laurence, Sally, Harry, Will and Lucy, who put up with me disappearing mysteriously for 'book days'. Plus Chris, Damian and Rob, who gave me the chance to have 'book days' in the first place. Sion Simon, who started all this. Sanjay Sharma and Ian Taylor, who kept encouraging me with food, beer and laughter. And finally, to those people who spoke to me. Your secret's safe. For now.

He just wanted a decent book to read ...

Not too much to ask, is it? It was in 1935 when Allen Lane, Managing Director of Bodley Head Publishers, stood on a platform at Exeter railway station looking for something good to read on his journey back to London. His choice was limited to popular magazines and poor-quality paperbacks – the same choice faced every day by the vast majority of readers, few of whom could afford hardbacks. Lane's disappointment and subsequent anger at the range of books generally available led him to found a company – and change the world.

'We believed in the existence in this country of a vast reading public for intelligent books at a low price, and staked everything on it'
Sir Allen Lane, 1902–1970, founder of Penguin Books

The quality paperback had arrived – and not just in bookshops. Lane was adamant that his Penguins should appear in chain stores and tobacconists, and should cost no more than a packet of cigarettes.

Reading habits (and cigarette prices) have changed since 1935, but Penguin still believes in publishing the best books for everybody to enjoy. We still believe that good design costs no more than bad design, and we still believe that quality books published passionately and responsibly make the world a better place.

So wherever you see the little bird – whether it's on a piece of prize-winning literary fiction or a celebrity autobiography, political tour de force or historical masterpiece, a serial-killer thriller, reference book, world classic or a piece of pure escapism – you can bet that it represents the very best that the genre has to offer.

Whatever you like to read – trust Penguin.